Rasputin

Rasputin

The Untold Story

Joseph T. Fuhrmann

WILEY

John Wiley & Sons, Inc.

Published by John Wiley & Sons, Inc., Hoboken, New Jersey
Published simultaneously in Canada

Library of Congress Cataloging-in-Publication Data:
Fuhrmann, Joseph T., date.
  Rasputin : the untold story / Joseph T. Fuhrmann.
    p. cm.
  Includes bibliographical references and index.
  ISBN 978-1-118-17276-6 (cloth : acid-free paper); ISBN 978-1-118-22693-3 (ebk);
  ISBN 978-1-118-23985-8 (ebk); ISBN 978-1-118-26458-4 (ebk)
1. Rasputin, Grigori Efimovich, ca. 1870–1916. 2. Russia–Court and courtiers–Biography. 3. Russia–History–Nicholas II, 1894–1917. 4. Rasputin, Grigori Efimovich, ca. 1870–1916–Religion. 5. Mystics–Russia–Biography. 6. Healers–Russia–Biography. 7. Russkaia pravoslavnaia tserkov?–Biography. I. Title.

  DK254.R3F79 2012
  947.08'3092—dc23
  [B]

2012007301

Printed in the United States of America

10 9 8 7 6 5 4 3 2 1

For Mary
and our Scrabble games together
and for the love we share with
Natasha

Contents

Preface

Rasputin's legend has captivated and enthralled people for a century. Restaurants in Siberia, Vancouver, London, and Bangkok bear his name; beers and vodkas display his face on their labels. There have been musicals and operas, cartoons and comic books, as well as documentaries and more than a dozen films about his life.

A mountain of books has chronicled Rasputin's rise and fall with varying degrees of sensationalism and accuracy. Only a few are in English, and even fewer have advanced our understanding of his life. The first was by Iliodor (Sergei Trufanov), an ex-monk who published *The Mad Monk of Russia, Iliodor: Life, Memoirs, and Confessions of Sergei Michailovich Trufanoff (Iliodor)* in 1918. Although Iliodor began as a friend of Rasputin's and ended as his bitter enemy, he conceded that the peasant's religious quest was sincere, at least in the early years. The book remains pivotal as a firsthand account of Rasputin's rise to power, although Iliodor also invented facts and conversations: "I put in a little extra," he later admitted, "especially at the end."

Two important books appeared in 1928 and 1935. In 1928, the popular writer René Fülöp-Miller's *Rasputin, the Holy Devil* provided the first serious English-language biography. Fülöp-Miller drew on memoirs and published primary materials. His work has merit, but the many fictionalized episodes and invented conversations make the book problematic. Yet it was the standard reference on Rasputin's life for most of the twentieth century. Alexander Spiridovich, who headed the security forces guarding the Romanovs, wrote *Raspoutine, 1863–1916: D'après les documents russes et les archives privées de l'auteur* (Rasputin, 1863–1916, based on Russian documents and the author's private archives), in 1935. Although the book contains inaccuracies, Spiridovich was a keen and honest observer who benefited from access to police reports and official records.

Rasputin's older daughter, Maria, was in a position to speak with authority on her father and his life. She published *The Real Rasputin* (1929), *My Father* (1934), and *Rasputin: The Man behind the Myth* (1977), with Patte Barham. The first two books contain valuable information and insights, and they probably reflect much of what Rasputin thought about himself. The third volume is sensationalized and far less reliable, advancing theories and incidents Maria never previously mentioned.

Numerous other works appeared throughout the twentieth century, notably Elizabeth Judas's *Rasputin: Neither Devil nor Saint* (1942), which is based on the author's own interactions with the peasant. Colin Wilson's *Rasputin and the Fall of the Romanovs* (1964) attempted to refute Rasputin's satanic image, while Robert K. Massie's *Nicholas and Alexandra* (1967) offered a magnificent story of the last tsar, although its account of Rasputin was based largely on Fülöp-Miller's book.

A full English-language biography of Rasputin finally appeared in 1982, when Alex de Jonge published *The Life and Times of Grigorii Rasputin*. De Jonge clearly had a good feel for Rasputin. Unfortunately, he was hampered by Soviet policy that tried to control what the world would know about Nicholas II and his circle. This control denied foreign scholars access to archives that would provide vital information and answer even such simple questions as: When was Rasputin born? Did he die rich or poor? A host of errors in the text, the footnotes, and even the bibliography is disappointing.

Brian Moynahan's *Rasputin: The Saint Who Sinned* (1997) focuses on salacious gossip surrounding the peasant and his career. As a serious biography, it failed the test of serious scholarship.

Russia held all of the documents needed to tell Rasputin's story, but for years they remained closed to foreigners. The Soviet government did publish archival documents chronicling the last years of the Romanov dynasty, the most important being *Padenie tsarskogo rezhima* (Fall of the Tsarist Regime), which appeared in seven volumes between 1924 and 1927 and was edited by P. E. Shchegolev. *Padenie* contains interrogations, depositions, and other materials gathered by the Extraordinary Investigatory Commission of the Provisional Government in the spring of 1917. The commission was interested in the public activities and private lives of key figures in the Old Regime. But documents favorable to Nicholas II, Alexandra, and Rasputin were not included in *Padenie*.

--That material was consigned to an enormous secret "file" that was stolen from the archives when the Soviet Union collapsed.

The cellist Mstislav Rostropovich purchased these documents in 1995 and gave them to his friend Edvard Radzinsky, an outstanding figure on the Russian cultural scene. Radzinsky used these documents to write *Rasputin, zhizn' i smert'* (2000), which appeared in English as *The Rasputin File*. Radzinsky's discussion of Rasputin's life is fascinating, and he shows keen insight into the man's sexuality and religious views. Impressive as the book may be, it is not a systematic biography, and its numerous fictional passages undermine its reliability.

Radzinsky is not the only Russian to explore Rasputin's life recently. In the last decade more than a dozen books have appeared in Russia by Alexander Bokhanov, A. P. Kotsiubinskii, Oleg Platonov, Oleg Shishkin, and Vyacheslav Smirnov and Marina Smirnova, each containing useful nuggets of archival information and advancing interesting theories. Some of these recent works are undisguised polemics infused with monarchist and religious sentiments. Even worse, we find a number of writers succumbing to nationalism, anti-Semitism, and a determination to expunge pages from Rasputin's life as inventions of Masonic, Jewish, and Bolshevik conspirators. Even these books are useful to the specialist, but more casual readers need to be cautious.

Two eyewitness accounts of Rasputin's murder are extremely important. Vladimir Purishkevich, the man who fired the shots that actually took Rasputin's life, published *The Murder of Rasputin* in 1918. Prince Felix Yusupov, the architect of the conspiracy, gave his account of the event in 1927. A shorter work, supposedly by another conspirator, Dr. Stanislaus Lazovert, is mere fiction.

Oleg Shishkin was the first to suggest that the British Secret Intelligence Service was behind Rasputin's murder. Andrew Cook developed the idea in *To Kill Rasputin: The Life and Death of Grigori Rasputin* (2006). His book began a revisionist wave that argues that Yusupov was simply the front man in a plot that was concocted and carried out by British agents. Richard Cullen follows this view in *Rasputin: The Role of Britain's Secret Service in His Torture and Murder* (2010). Dr. Cullen, a former Scotland Yard detective, points out discrepancies in the Yusupov and Purishkevich accounts. Cullen seems to expect perfect agreement in the accounts of the main participants, and that reveals the weakness of the revisionist approach. One would think that a policeman, of all people, would recognize that honest eyewitnesses are fallible and disagreement over details does not necessarily indicate deceit. Nevertheless, Cullen is to be admired for his presentation of some very interesting ideas about Rasputin's murder.

Margarita Nelipa's *The Murder of Grigorii Rasputin: A Conspiracy That Brought Down the Russian Empire* (2010) is not a biography of the peasant but an exhaustive discussion of his death. This important book offers information that will interest scholars, particularly biographical details of even minor characters in the story. Nelipa argues that the tsar's cousin, Grand Duke Nicholas Michaelovich, was the driving force behind the murder. This thesis is unconvincing; it is not even supported by circumstantial evidence. A larger problem is the author's reliance on recent books asserting that the tsar was the victim of vast and fantastic conspiracies. Nelipa also insists on viewing Rasputin as a holy man, rejecting abundant evidence about his dark side and selfish motives.

Reviewers greeted my *Rasputin: A Life* (published in 1990) as a serious, well-researched biography of the Siberian mystic and healer that avoided exaggeration or sensationalism. The book was handicapped, however, by a lack of access to Russian and Siberian archives. There was an additional problem: the published English versions of the wartime correspondence between Nicholas and Alexandra were inaccurate and incomplete.

Foreign scholars were suddenly welcomed in Russian archives after the Soviet Union collapsed. In 1994 I made the first of what proved to be seven research trips to Moscow, Tyumen, and Tobolsk to study documents, many of which had not been available even to Soviet historians. My goal was to establish the exact nature of Rasputin's influence with the tsar and his wife. My first step was to publish all of their wartime letters (which were written in English) and telegrams (in Russian). This material is stored in GARF, the State Archive of the Russian Federation, in Moscow. I spent the summers of 1994 and 1995 transcribing these documents, which I published in 1999 as *The Complete Wartime Correspondence of Tsar Nicholas II and Empress Alexandra, April 1914–March 1917*. This large volume offers all of their 1,692 letters and telegrams, many of which had never been published.

Documents in Moscow and Siberia revealed fascinating and previously unknown aspects of Rasputin's life. This material was basic to the second stage of my work—to write a new biography of Rasputin based on archival resources. The present book is the result of these efforts, and to emphasize its originality I have called it *Rasputin: The Untold Story*. My goal has been to synthesize archival sources with published documents, memoirs, and other studies of Rasputin into a single, comprehensive work. This book is directed to the growing audience of general readers who are fascinated by the decline and fall of imperial Russia. My first biography of Rasputin, by contrast, was an academic study.

This is the first study of Rasputin to bring archival information to bear on a series of important problems, beginning with state records for 1639, which show "Izosim, the son of Fedor" and the founder of the family, crossing the Urals into western Siberia. I used baptismal records to fix the exact date of Rasputin's birth—a simple point, one might say, but Rasputin's biographers were not able to do that before the collapse of the Soviet Union threw open the archives. This is the first book to use the records of the church investigation of 1907 to 1908 into charges that Rasputin was a member of the heretical Khlysty, as well as a report from a new bishop that resolved the case in Rasputin's favor in November 1912. These documents yield exciting information on many aspects of Rasputin's life, including his religious teachings and followers.

Rasputin: The Untold Story uses police reports to describe Rasputin's farming activity and daily routine, as well as his religious pursuits. I also used the many large (and impressive) volumes of newspaper clippings the Okhrana, the Russian secret police, maintained on Rasputin. Forgotten police records in the marvelous archive at Tobolsk will give the reader a new and accurate account of a deranged woman's attempt to murder Rasputin in the summer of 1914. I am also the first to publish some of Rasputin's famous notes, as well as letters he received from ordinary citizens. I am grateful to Vyacheslav Smirnov, who created the Rasputin Museum in Pokrovskoye, for giving me access to materials and photographs he has collected for the display. Even the town comes to life, making its decline in the Soviet period all the more striking. The village church was torn down in the 1950s, and Rasputin's house was leveled in February 1980 while Boris Yeltsin was the Communist boss of Siberia.

The research that has gone into this book provides a pioneering account of Rasputin's relations with homosexuals. These men were out of the closet and forging public careers that would have been inconceivable anywhere else in the world at that time. Readers will be surprised to learn how rapidly Russians were coming to accept same-sex relationships at every level of society. Dan Healey has done pioneering work in this important area, and I am grateful to him for helping me in my work. *Rasputin: The Untold Story* is also the first book to make a very interesting point: Nicholas and Alexandra were indifferent to the private lives of a dozen or more gay men who sought their friendship. Unfortunately, these homosexuals were friends of Rasputin's—and they were scoundrels, which does not imply that they were representative of their group. The men who entered into a close relationship with Rasputin were, almost by definition, of low character—and that included heterosexuals who were likewise not typical of their group.

Although I cannot agree that British intelligence agents were deeply involved in Rasputin's assassination, this is the first biography of the Siberian mystic and healer to fully evaluate that argument. *Rasputin: The Untold Story* is also the first to exploit a fascinating document: the inventory of Rasputin's property that the court ordered when he died. This finally yields an answer to the old question: Did the last favorite of the last tsar die rich or poor? All the revelations are here, thanks to the Russian archives.

I hope that this book will give readers a deeper understanding of the peasant's life and role in undermining the Old Regime. Rasputin led a fascinating life that too easily passed into the realm of rumor and legend. If he ended as greedy and corrupt, he was also engaging and human. A crowd of children always greeted "Granddaddy Grisha" when he returned to Pokrovskoye, knowing that he had a bag of gumdrops and other treats waiting for them. Rasputin loved cats and was the proud owner of a stud horse worth a thousand rubles. He was charitable to the poor. He stood for peace and religious toleration; he befriended Jews and prostitutes. The furnishings of his house included an Offenbach piano, a gramophone, and Persian carpets.

An evaluation of Rasputin based on the facts will lay waste to a century of misconception and error.

Acknowledgments

I am glad finally to have the opportunity to thank in print the people who have helped me with this book. Greg King read the entire manuscript more than once and offered countless criticisms and suggestions. Greg also helped me improve my writing skills and encouraged me at times when I sorely needed it. I am greatly indebted to Janet Ashton, researcher at the British Library and the author of books and articles on the Romanovs. (Ashton maintains a website that features important research on Russian history at www.directarticle.org.) She read all of the chapters several times and offered much help. Special thanks go to David Haviland and Sam Jordison, gifted freelance editors, who also gave me valuable lessons in writing for a general audience. I thank Stephen Henley for his computer support and patience in dealing with my problems, ignorance, and frustrations.

Dr. Will Lee has been my adviser on matters pertaining to the Russian Orthodox Church. He also shared information about Dmitry Pavlovich, critiqued several chapters, and gave valuable encouragement. Terry Strieter, chairman of the History Department of Murray State University, read much of the manuscript and offered useful observations. Griffith Henniger II helped in several important ways and has been a good comrade in arms. I am grateful to Dan Healey for sharing information and insights with me on subjects of mutual interest. My agent, Andrew Lownie, knows how indebted I am to him; I thank him for believing in me at times when that must have not been easy. Particular appreciation goes to Levi J. Burkett. I have been a burden sometimes to Levi, but at least I am now able to express my gratitude to him.

All of the people I have named deserve credit for improving my work, but the errors and shortcomings that remain are entirely my responsibility.

I thank IREX (the International Research and Exchanges Board) for short-term travel grants that permitted me to work at GARF, the State Archive of the Russian Federation, in the summers of 1994 and 1995. My research at that time focused on the "Nicky-Sunny Correspondence," that was published in 1999. Murray State University's CISR (the Committee on Institutional Scholarship and Research) provided generous support that permitted me to work with the Rasputin papers in GARF in the summer of 2000 and the winter of 2002 to 2003. Thanks to CISR I was able to work in two wonderful Siberian archives, GATO, the State Archive of Tyumen Oblast' in Tyumen, and TFGATO, the Affiliated State Archive of Tyumen Oblast' in Tobolsk, during the summer of 2005. My warm appreciation goes to three gracious Russian archivists who helped me along the way, Lyubov Tyutyunik of GARF, Olga Tarasova of GATO, and Galina Kushir of TFGATO.

It is surprisingly difficult to be consistent in transliterating Russian words into English. I have rendered Russian titles, words, and phrases in the footnotes and the bibliography according to the Library of Congress system. In the text, I use the more reader-friendly New York Public Library system. Under the NYPL system я, ю, and ский appear as "ya," "yu," and "sky"; under the LOC system they are rendered "ia," "iu," and "skii." Russian names that are familiar in the West are rendered in their Western spellings. Thus the tsar and his wife and their son are referred to as Nicholas, Alexandra, and Alexis, while Rasputin's given name is Gregory. In other instances, a Russian flavor seems appropriate, so Rasputin's youngest daughter appears as Varvara (not Barbara), while his famous crony is Bishop Varnava (not Barnabas). Rasputin's nemesis is Feofan (not Theophanes). The names of Russians with international reputations—for example, Michael Rodzyanko and Paul Milyukov—appear in their familiar forms.

The family names of Russian women usually end in "a" or "ya." For example, Russians would know Rasputin's wife as Praskovaya Rasputina. But Western historians omit the final vowels in such family names, and I follow that practice by referring to Rasputin's spouse as Praskovaya Rasputin. I use the Russian spellings of female patronymics. The tsar's oldest daughter, for example, is Olga Nicholaevna.

Russian titles can be confusing to foreigners. In 1547, Ivan IV, the grand prince (*veliky knyaz'*) of Moscow, assumed the title of tsar, the Russian equivalent of Caesar or the German Kaiser. In taking this title, the man history knows as Ivan the Terrible was asserting that he ruled an empire linked, through his ancestors, to Caesar Augustus. The wife of a tsar was the tsaritsa, often rendered in the west as tsarina (which is actually not a Russian word, although it has established itself in European languages). Peter the Great adopted the Western titles of emperor and empress. Soon after he died, the old and new titles were used interchangeably, and I follow that practice in this book. The tsar's sons held the title of tsarevich; his oldest son—and heir to the throne—was the tsetsarevich. Nicholas II held that title until 1894, when he became tsar. But Russians referred to his only son as the tsarevich, and I follow that practice. Members of the Romanov family had the titles *veliky knyaz'* and *velikaya knyagina*; I refer to them as the grand duke and the grand duchess.

Unfortunately, when Peter the Great introduced the Western calendar into Russia, he chose the Julian calendar, still favored by the Protestant powers that he was cultivating. When the Gregorian calendar became dominant in Western Europe, Russia was left behind in yet another important respect. Dates in this book are "old style" (O.S.) unless identified as "new style" (N.S.). Russian dates are twelve days behind the Gregorian date in the nineteenth century, thirteen days in the twentieth. The difference is especially confusing when a source or secondary account is not consistent in using a single system, and that happens. The "godless communists" resolved these difficulties on February 1, 1918, when they introduced the calendar that Pope Gregory XIII had proclaimed on February 24, 1582.

Cast of Principal Characters, Places, and Terms

PEOPLE OF POKROVSKOYE

Gregory Efimovich Rasputin ("Grisha," "Grishka," "Our Friend"), surname legally changed to Rasputin-Novyi (also Rasputin-Novykh), peasant from Pokrovskoye; married to Praskovaya Dubrovina of the village of Dubrovino; their children were Dmitry, followed by Maria (also Matrëna) and Varvara

Efim and Anna Rasputin, father and mother of Gregory Rasputin

V. I. Kartavtsev, resident of Pokrovskoye, who gave information about Rasputin's early life to the Extraordinary Commission in 1917

Pecherkin sisters, Catherine ("Katya") and **Evdokiya** ("Dunya"), among Rasputin's first followers; later his lovers and servants

Peter Ostroumov, chief priest of Pokrovskoye; Fedor Chemagin was his assistant

THE ROMANOVS

Nicholas II, Russian tsar and emperor, reigned 1894–1917

Alexandra Fedorovna, tsaritsa and empress, wife of Nicholas II; born Princess Alix of Hesse und bei Rhein

Alexis (the tsarevich), son of Nicholas II and Alexandra, heir to the Russian throne; his sisters were Olga, Tatyana, Maria, and Anastasia

Alexander II, Russian tsar and emperor, reigned 1855–1881; grandfather of Nicholas II

Alexander III, Russian tsar and emperor, reigned 1881–1894; father of Nicholas II

Maria Fedorovna, widow of Alexander III and mother of Nicholas II

Xenia Alexandrovna, older sister of Nicholas II and wife of Alexander Michaelovich

Alexander Michaelovich ("Sandro"), grand duke, cousin once removed and brother-in-law to Nicholas II; married to the tsar's older sister, Xenia

Olga Alexandrovna, younger sister of Nicholas II

Michael Alexandrovich ("Misha"), younger brother of Nicholas II

Nicholas Michaelovich, brother of Alexander Michaelovich; historian and man of letters

Montenegrin sisters (the "Black Princesses"), Militsa and Anastasia ("Stana"), daughters of King Nikola Njegos of Montenegro; Militsa was married to the tsar's cousin Peter Nicholaevich while Anastasia was married to his brother, Nicholas Nicholaevich ("Nicholasha"), commander of Russian armies in the west until August 1915

Elisabeth Fedorovna ("Ella"), older sister of the Empress Alexandra

PEOPLE ASSOCIATED WITH NICHOLAS
AND ALEXANDRA

Anna Vyrubova, best friend of the empress and Rasputin

Eugene Botkin, physician to the imperial family

S. P. Fedorov, one of Alexis's physicians

Philippe Nizier-Vachot ("M. Philippe"), French practitioner of occult medicine; lived in Russia, 1901–1904

Vladimir Dedyulin, commandant of the Alexander Palace, 1906–1913, responsible for the imperial family's security; succeeded by Vladimir Voeikov, 1913–1917

Paul Kurlov, assistant-minister of the interior under Peter Stolypin, 1909–1911, and under Alexander Protopopov in 1916

Colonel Alexander Drenteln, major-general of the tsar's suite; commander of the Preobrazhensky Guards Regiment

Sophie Buxhoeveden, baroness, lady-in-waiting, and friend of the Empress Alexandra

Julia von Dehn ("Lili"), friend of the Empress Alexandra and a member of Rasputin's circle

Pierre Gilliard, the imperial children's French tutor and a friend of the family

Charles Sydney Gibbes, the imperial children's English tutor

RASPUTIN'S FRIENDS AND ASSOCIATES

Brother Makary, a starets at the Saint Nicholas Monastery at Verkhoturye

Sister Maria, a staritsa at the Abalak Monastery

Ivan Dobrovolsky, corrupt ex-school inspector; Rasputin's first business manager

Aaron Simanovich, jeweler, gambler, and loan shark; Rasputin's business manager, 1915–1916

Ivan Manasevich-Manuilov, Jewish journalist, police spy, and sometime secretary of Rasputin's

Georgy Sazonov, prominent journalist

Leonid Molchanov, Rasputin's friend; his father was Alexis, bishop of Tobolsk

Dmitry Rubenstein ("Mitya"), Jewish banker

Ignaty Manus, Jewish banker; rival of Dmitry Rubenstein's

Alexis Filippov, Rasputin's publisher and friend

Pitirim, metropolitan of Petrograd and friend of Rasputin's, well known as a homosexual

Ivan Osipenko, secretary of Pitirim's and Rasputin's friend

RASPUTIN'S FOLLOWERS AND ADMIRERS

Barbara Uexkuell, prominent Saint Petersburg socialite and early admirer of Rasputin's

Olga Lokhtina, Rasputin's first follower in Saint Petersburg

Akilina Laptinskaya, former nun and nurse, early follower of Rasputin's; also served as his secretary

Alexandra Pistolkors, sister of Anna Vyrubova; she and her husband, Eric, were followers of Rasputin's

Elena Dzhanumovaya, wife of a wealthy merchant; follower of Rasputin's

Vera Zhukovskaya, **Maria Golovina** ("Munya"), and **Zinaida Manshtedt**, followers of Rasputin's

RASPUTIN'S ENEMIES

Bishop Anthony of Tobolsk, investigated Rasputin as a Khlyst, 1907–1908

Khioniya Berlatskaya, early follower of Rasputin's; turned on him when he made sexual advances to her

Iliodor, born Sergei Trufanov, monk and political figure; initially an ally, ended as Rasputin's bitter antagonist

Alexander Guchkov, leader of Octobrist Party; president of the Third Duma

Michael Rodzyanko, leader of Octobrist Party; president of the Fourth Duma

M. A. Novoselov, taught at Moscow Theological Academy; played a key role in the press campaign against Rasputin in 1910

Archimandrite Feofan, inspector and later rector of the Saint Petersburg Theological Academy; early friend of Rasputin's, although later became a bitter enemy

Bishop Hermogen, bishop of Saratov; friend of Rasputin's, although later became a bitter enemy

Dmitry Kozelsky ("Mitya"), deformed epileptic and religious figure

Khioniya Guseva, follower of Iliodor's; attempted to kill Rasputin on June 29, 1914

Prince Felix Yusupov the Younger, organizer of Rasputin's assassination; married to Nicholas II's niece, Irina

Dmitry Pavlovich, cousin of Nicholas II's, friend of Felix Yusupov's, and member of the conspiracy that took Rasputin's life

V. M. Purishkevich, member of the Duma; fired the shots that actually killed Rasputin

GOVERNMENT FIGURES AND AGENCIES

Okhrana, the secret police; headed ex officio by the assistant minister of the interior

Sergei Witte, prime minister, 1905–1906; admirer of Rasputin's who vainly hoped to return to power with the peasant's support

Peter Arkadievich Stolypin, prime minister and minister of the interior, 1906–1911

Vladimir Kokovtsov, finance minister; prime minister, 1911–1914

Ivan Goremykin, prime minister, 1914–1916

Boris Sturmer, prime minister, January–November 1916

Nicholas Golitsyn, the last tsarist prime minister, January–March 1917

First Troika, alliance organized by Prince Michael Andronikov, shady businessman and flamboyant homosexual, to install Alexis Khvostov and Stephen Beletsky as minister and assistant minister of the interior; they held office September 1915–March 1916

Second Troika, alliance formed in 1916 by Dr. Peter Badmaev, businessman, physician, and ally of Rasputin's; the Troika included Alexander Protopopov (minister of the interior) and Paul Kurlov (assistant minister of the interior and police director)

Alexander Mosolov, director of the Imperial Court

Alexander Protopopov, minister of the interior, 1916

Alexander Khvostov, uncle of Alexis Khvostov; minister of justice, 1915–1916

Vladimir Dzhunkovsky, assistant minister of internal affairs and police director

Alexander Makarov, minister of the interior, 1911–1912; minister of justice, 1916–1917

Nicholas Maklakov, minister of the interior, 1913–1915

Nicholas Shcherbatov, minister of the interior, 1915

Vasily Maklakov, brother of Nicholas Maklakov; member of the Duma and prominent attorney who advised Prince Yusupov in organizing Rasputin's assassination

Vladimir Sukhomlinov, minister of war, 1914–1915

Alexis Polivanov, minister of war, 1915–1916

General Michael Alexeev, replaced Nicholas Nicholaevich as chief of staff in 1915; directed military operations until the March Revolution

Michael Kommisarov, police officer; supervised Rasputin for the First Troika

Dmitry Kosorotov, Petrograd's senior autopsy surgeon; performed the autopsy on Rasputin's body, December 20, 1916

Professor Vladimir Zharov, MD, led the team of medical experts that reassessed the autopsy and its results in 1993

Provisional Government, followed the tsarist regime in March 1917; overthrown by the Bolsheviks in November 1917

Investigatory Commission, "Extraordinary Commission of Inquiry for the Investigation of Illegal Acts by Ministers and Other Responsible Persons of the Tsarist Regime," formed by the Provisional Government in spring 1917

Alexander Kerensky, first minister of justice in the Provisional Government; became prime minister in May 1917

Maurice Paléologue, French ambassador

Vladimir Ilyich Lenin, founder of the Bolsheviks (or Communist Party), which overthrew the Provisional Government in November 1917

PEOPLE AND GROUPS CONNECTED WITH THE RUSSIAN ORTHODOX CHURCH

Sergei Lukyanov, ober-procurator of the Holy Synod, 1911

V. K. Sabler, ober-procurator of the Holy Synod, 1911–1915

Dmitry Samarin, ober-procurator of the Holy Synod, 1915; fought Rasputin's influence in the Church

Nicholas Volzhin, ober-procurator of the Holy Synod, 1915–1916; fought Rasputin's influence in the Church

Nicholas Raev, last tsarist ober-procurator of the Holy Synod, 1916; ally of Rasputin's

Nicholas Zaionchkovsky, assistant ober-procurator of the Holy Synod, 1915–1916; fought Rasputin's influence in the Church

Prince Nicholas Zhevakov, assistant ober-procurator of the Holy Synod, 1916; ally of Rasputin's

Peter Damansky, Holy Synod's financial director and later assistant ober-procurator; a friend and ally of Rasputin's

John of Kronstadt, influential archpriest of the Kronstadt cathedral

Alexis, bishop of Tobolsk, cleared Rasputin of charges of heresy; father of Rasputin's friend, Leonid Molchanov

Isidor, monk and bishop; friend of Rasputin's; well-known homosexual

Varnava ("Suslik"), monk and friend of Rasputin's; archbishop of Tobolsk

Georgy Shavelsky, last head chaplain of the tsar's armed forces; foe of Rasputin's

Bishop Sergei, father superior of the Alexander Nevsky Seminary and one of Rasputin's early admirers; elected patriarch in 1943

Anthony, archbishop of Volhynia; Rasputin's foe at the Holy Synod

Vladimir Vostokov, a priest, publicist, and liberal idealist who pastored a large, working-class church near Moscow

Maria, mother superior of the Balashevskaya Convent near Tsaritsyn; ally of Rasputin's

PRINCIPAL BRITISH FIGURES

British Secret Intelligence Service (BSIS), predecessor of MI6

George Buchanan, British ambassador

Lieutenant Colonel Samuel Hoare, head of the BSIS mission in Petrograd

Oswald Rayner, BSIS agent in Petrograd; Felix Yusupov's friend, helped him write *The End of Rasputin* (1927)

Stephen Alley and **John Scale**, BSIS agents in Petrograd

GEOGRAPHICAL FEATURES AND PLACES

Urals, mountain range separating Russia from Siberia

Pokrovskoye, Rasputin's hometown; located on the Tura River

Tobolsk, city on the Tobol River; capital of the province (*gubernaya*) of western Siberia

Abalak, town near Tobolsk; important as the site of the Znamensky Monastery

Tyumen, economic center of Northwest Siberia; located on the Tura River

Verkhoturye, town overlooking the Tura River; major religious center and site of the Saint Nicholas Monastery

Kazan, city in the upper Volga basin; 760 miles southwest of Tobolsk

Mount Athos, monastic center of the Eastern Orthodox Church; located on the coast of north central Greece

Tsaritsyn, city on the Volga; later Stalingrad, now Volgograd

Saint Petersburg, capital of the Russian Empire; located on the Neva River at the head of the Gulf of Finland on the Baltic Sea

Moscow, known as the Old Capital until 1918, when it became the capital of the USSR

Tsarskoye Selo ("Tsar's Village"); exclusive residential center fifteen miles southeast of Saint Petersburg

Alexander Palace at Tsarskoye Selo, the main residence of the imperial family after 1905

Alexander Nevsky Monastery, founded in Saint Petersburg in 1710; sixteen churches were located there in Rasputin's time, along with Russia's leading theological academy and the headquarters of the metropolitan of Saint Petersburg

Stavka, general headquarters of the Russian army on the Western front; located at Baranovichi until the German advance forced its relocation to Mogilev in August 1915

YAR Restaurant, located in Moscow

TITLES OF CHURCH LEADERS

Patriarch, heads a national Orthodox Church that is autocephalous; that is, independent of any other religious authority; Russia became a patriarchal church in 1589; Peter the Great abolished the office in 1721, but it was restored in 1918 and again in 1943

Most Holy Synod, the state bureau that administered the Russian Orthodox Church after Peter the Great abolished the office of patriarch; headed by the ober-procurator (director general); the governing council was made up of the ober-procurator and six permanent members who sat ex officio, as well as six other members appointed for terms

Metropolitan, title of the bishops who presided over Saint Petersburg, Moscow, and Kiev; the exarch of Georgia was the equivalent of a metropolitan, and his office was fourth in honor and prestige in the Russian Orthodox Church; these four sat ex officio on the governing council of the Holy Synod

Archbishop, title of a senior bishop or a bishop who presides over an important jurisdiction

Bishop, title of the church figure who presides over a diocese, usually a major town

Vicar Bishop, junior figure who assists a presiding bishop or is assigned his own duties

Old Believers, left the Russian Orthodox Church in protest against the reforms of Patriarch Nikon in the 1660s; later split into groups

Sects, had no historic ties to the Russian Orthodox Church and developed in opposition to it

Khlysty ("Flagellants"), a sect that believed that sin ultimately brought its members closer to God; the "Believers in Christ" (as they called themselves) blended sex with worship, and they influenced Rasputin

Starets, a man who was not necessarily a priest or a monk but was recognized by the faithful as a pious man who led a holy life; a woman with this standing is a *staritsa*

Strannik, a pilgrim; a man or a woman whose vocation was to travel on foot to churches, monasteries, shrines, and other places with religious significance; famous for chanting the Jesus Prayer, "Lord Jesus Christ, have mercy upon me, a sinner"

Prologue

O VER HERE!"
 The detectives were too tired to run, too cold. For two long days they had patrolled the banks near the Petrovsky Bridge. They waited and searched, saying little, occasionally jumping up and down for warmth and huddling around their braziers, watching divers searching among the river's ice floes for the body. It had to be in the water: the bloodstains traced a grim path along the bridge, over the railing, and onto the snow below. A day passed in this fashion; curious crowds strained to follow developments. Finally, at a little past two in the afternoon, a river policeman noticed the sleeve of a beaver-skin coat frozen into the ice. It was the body of Gregory Rasputin.

The men hacked away at the frozen crust of the river with spades, picks, and sledgehammers. Then a menacing grappling hook dislodged the body from the ice and dragged it to shore. Strands of hair mercifully covered the distorted facial features. Spectators groaned as they saw the blue silk shirt, the arms free and raised above the head, the legs wrapped together. According to some press reports, a few people armed with pots, buckets, and bottles ran to holes that were in the ice to scoop out the water that would supposedly imbue them with the strange power that had once animated Rasputin.

The story could not be true—the river was entirely frozen that day. It shows, however, that Rasputin was as controversial in death as he was in life. The controversies and questions have continued. Was he a saint or satanic? Did his name really mean "debauched"? Was he a man of God or just a crafty manipulator? Could he heal through prayer? What was the secret of his appeal to women? How much influence did he have over Tsar Nicholas and his wife? Was he Alexandra's lover? Did Rasputin control the Russian government during World War I? Was he a German agent? How much responsibility did he bear for the Russian Revolution?

Then there was his legendary death. It is said that Rasputin was poisoned, shot, and beaten; that he was unconscious but alive when the assassins threw him into a watery grave. Did Rasputin actually drown? Did he free his right arm and make the sign of the cross before he succumbed to the icy river? And for that matter, what about the murder: Was it an aristocratic plot to save the Romanov dynasty? Did it involve British Intelligence?

Legend portrays Rasputin as the "Mad Monk" who rampaged through Saint Petersburg in an alcoholic haze, making love to scores of women, a symbol of excess and religious extremism. Rasputin was not a monk, of course, and he was quite sane, although he did embody the best and worst aspects of human nature—and exemplified the final, troubled years of imperial Russia. Although he began with noble intentions and sincere convictions, he fell victim to greed, lust, and temptation. Some have said that he ended his life as an evil manipulator and debauched charlatan. Perhaps this is a bit harsh. You will decide this question for yourself, based on the facts that follow.

1

The Outsider

GREGORY RASPUTIN WAS BORN IN SIBERIA. This simple fact explained so much about his life: his expansive character, his lack of artifice, his earthy attitudes, his acceptance of fate, his powerful sense of religion, and his almost reckless attitude toward the influence he came to wield. Siberians were different from other Russians: pious and forthright yet deeply suspicious, they remained loyal but independent. These contradictions shaped Rasputin: even at the height of his power, he was proud to be a Siberian peasant.

Mysterious Rasputin came from a land of mystery—a vast realm shrouded in bloody history and intrigue. Three centuries before Rasputin's birth, Ivan the Terrible, grand prince of Moscow and the country's first tsar, launched his troops against Siberia, one of the states that made up the Mongol Empire. The Russian commander known as Yermak was killed even as he conquered; then the settlers arrived, men and women who were ready to create a civilization in the wilderness with stockades, forts, and villages in much the same way as the enterprising people of nineteenth-century America.

Siberia is an enormous territory, and settlers received farmland plus shares of pastures and forests. Churches arose, their crosses scattered across the countryside as tribes were subjugated to Moscow and its Orthodox faith. The Siberians of Rasputin's time farmed and fished, hunted and trapped, just as their ancestors did for centuries. Nature, the passing seasons, the cycle of death and renewal remained sacred to those whose livelihoods and lives were so inter-twined with the land.

Life was harsh, but those who settled Siberia felt superior to peas-ants on the western side of the Ural Mountains, most of whom were serfs under the control of their noble masters. Serfdom was almost unknown in this new land, and people were fiercely independent. If local officials were oppressive, they would awaken one morning to find that an entire village had slipped away during the night. Obedience came on the people's terms—it was never submission. God man-dated divisions in wealth and power, but all men were equal, at least in Siberia.

A barren wasteland of frozen tundra and dark forests stretched from the Urals to the Pacific Ocean. A few substantial cities such as Perm and Yekaterinburg dotted the landscape, but most of Siberia was wild and untamed even in Rasputin's time. Towns and villages were small and spread out, occasionally linked by rail, though more often by boat, horse, and cart. Broad, shallow rivers slashed through groves of white birch trees and clusters of wooden huts before they flowed into featureless grasslands. In the summer, marshes teemed with wildlife and swarms of mosquitoes; in the winter, endless vistas of snow turned the land into a seamless white blanket. The sweep was horizontal, long and low, as if Siberia had no known end but continued to the edge of creation.

Pokrovskoye, Rasputin's birthplace, was one of these isolated vil-lages. It took nearly two days of hard travel to reach Pokrovskoye by road from the Urals; this figure was cut in half by using flat-bottomed river steamers. Winter demanded additional time on sleighs before Pokrovskoye, situated on the western bank of the Tura River, finally emerged against the expansive Siberian sky.

Pokrovskoye began as an outpost when, in 1642, the local arch-bishop sent twenty peasant families to settle on the river's left bank. A wooden church dedicated to the Virgin Mary, the *pokrovitel'nitsa* (the protector), gave the town its name. By the time Rasputin was born, a thousand people lived there in two hundred houses clustered around the church. The postal station came early, for Pokrovskoye was a regular stop on the coach road linking the village with Tyumen to the south and Tobolsk to the north. There were bakeries, timber mills, dairies, stables, markets, inns, taverns, a smithy, and a schoolhouse, although economic factors dictated that few of the village children could attend classes.

Early-eighteenth-century map showing the Pokrovskoye area. The map shows the church and eight buildings as "Sloboda Pokrovskaya" (Pokrovskoye Settlement) on the Tura River. The Tobol' River is indicated in large letters on the right-hand side.

A young officer who visited Pokrovskoye soon after Rasputin was murdered was surprised to hear that Rasputin's ancestors had lived in Pokrovskoye "almost from the time of Catherine the Great." In fact, the family's roots were even deeper. The founder of Rasputin's family is identified in local records as "Izosim, the son of Fedor." He and his wife had no children when they crossed the Ural Mountains in 1639 as part of the great eastern migration. By the time Izosim and his wife (whose name is not recorded) appeared in Pokrovskoye in 1643, they had three sons. Considering that the village was only a year old at that time, we must credit Izosim with being one of its earliest settlers.

It is not surprising that local records do not list Izosim's surname. Settlers were needed on the frontier, and officials asked few questions. Izosim's son, on the other hand, is identified as Nason Rosputin.

The first generations of the family lived unremarkable lives, although in August 1751, the house shared by Igor and Nikifor Rosputin—Nason's great-grandsons—caught fire and threatened to destroy the town. By the beginning of the eighteenth century, 347 people lived in the Pokrovskoye district; Ivan Rosputin and his brother, Miron, were listed among the "better souls" of the village.

The Rasputin Male Lineage

- Izosim, the son of Fedor, arrived in Siberia in 1639 and settled in Pokrovskoye in 1643.
- His son Nason Rosputin is mentioned in state records ca. 1645.
- His son Yakov Rosputin is mentioned in state records in 1666.
- His son Igor Rosputin lived from 1697 to 1761.
- His son Ivan Rosputin lived from 1725 to 1770.
- His son Peter Rosputin lived from 1749 to 1831.
- His son Vasily Rosputin lived from 1776 to 1858.
- His son Yakov Rasputin was born in 1801; his death date was not recorded.
- His son Efim Rasputin lived from 1842 to 1916.
- His son Gregory Rasputin lived from 1869 to 1916.

By the middle of the nineteenth century Rosputin had become Rasputin. Government records list nineteen men in the district with that name from 1869 to 1887. Number 18 was Gregory, the last favorite of the last tsar. (Under the Russian patronymic system, he was known as Gregory Efimovich—"Gregory, the son of Efim.") The Rasputin name was a burden when the Siberian mystic and healer arrived in the Russian capital. According to rumor, his family was so impoverished that it had no surname. Gregory supposedly had a shady past: he drank, chased women, and stole horses, and exasperated neighbors named him "Gregory the Drunk," or Gregory Rasputin. This notion was mistaken—it came from a play on words: *rasputnichat'* means "to be debauched or dissipated." Siberian names are frequently related to nature or topography, and *Rasputin* might have come from *rasputitsa*, the time in spring when snow melts and the roads turn to mud. The large number of Rasputins in Pokrovskoye suggests another derivation: *rasput'e*, a crossroad. The most infamous name in Russian history might well have originated from a mere quirk of geography.

Little is known of Rasputin's parents. Born in Pokrovskoye in 1842, his father, Efim, was described as a "thick, typical Siberian peasant," "chunky, unkempt and stooped." Efim married a village girl in 1863, a blond woman with black eyes named Anna. Villagers told the Investigatory Commission in 1917 that both were "healthy people, with no history of mental illness in their families." Efim farmed and fished. In the summer, he cut hay and worked as a stevedore on steamboats and barges. Money was scarce, and at one point Efim was thrown in jail for not paying his taxes. The state employed him to carry passengers and goods between Tyumen (the main economic center of western Siberia) and Tobolsk (the capital of the province). Efim was proud of his leather arm badge and cap displaying the double-headed eagle, the symbol of imperial Russia. One villager claimed that he was renowned for his "learned conversations and wisdom," and served as an elder in the village church. More talk, though, focused on Efim's penchant for "strong vodka."

Eventually Efim owned a small plot of land and benefited from the fact that the black soil of Pokrovskoye was among the best farmland in the Russian Empire. Maria Rasputin, Gregory's daughter, claims that Efim owned a dozen cows and eighteen horses, which would suggest—if it is true—that by that time he had become comfortable, if not wealthy. A photograph of the couple with some of the other villagers survives: Efim, tall, thin, and bearded, is standing behind and to the right of his celebrated son, who is at the front; Anna is the short, rotund woman with a broad peasant face to her son's right who peers intently at the camera. Most peasants at this time lived and died in obscurity. It is extraordinary that such a photograph exists, and the fact that it was taken is a testament to Gregory's growing reputation.

Legends about Rasputin begin with his birth. Maria claimed he was born on a January midnight in 1873 as a comet ripped across the sky. "A shooting star of such magnitude had always been taken by the God-fearing muzhiks as an omen of some momentous event," she noted. Nervous tongues clucked over such portents. Some were even more dramatic: the ancient chronicles speak of babies born with iron teeth, dogs with six legs, and snakes falling from the sky—clear omens of pestilence and death.

In fact there were no comets or portents when Rasputin was born; Maria even had the year wrong. Official records tell us that "on January 9, 1869, a son was born to Efim Rasputin and his wife Anna, a faithful Orthodox woman." The infant was christened the following day in Pokrovskoye's Church of Our Lady. January 10 on the Orthodox liturgical calendar is the feast day of Saint Gregory of Nyssa, the third-century mystic who defined the Holy Trinity, and the child was named in his honor.

Although Rasputin was not formally educated, he studied theology and read the church fathers, so he probably knew Saint Gregory's teachings about salvation. God, Saint Gregory believed, was beyond human comprehension: people could scarcely know anything about him. Knowledge stood between man and God; learning was more often an obstacle than an asset in the quest for redemption. Not even the greatest sinners were beyond redemption, and only God could assess a person's soul.

Gregory was not his parents' first child. Evdokiya, a daughter, was born in February 1863 and died the same year; a second daughter, also named Evdokiya, was born in August 1864 but perished as an infant. A third daughter, Glikeriya, was born in 1866 but succumbed to childhood illness, as did Andrei, a son, who passed away four months after his birth in August 1867. Gregory was born in 1869 and was murdered on December 17, 1916. Anna Rasputin had another son (also named Andrei), who died shortly after his birth in November 1871; twins Tikhon and Agrippina perished within four days of their births in 1874. It has been suggested that a ninth child, Feodosiya, was born in 1875 and survived to adulthood. Gregory certainly had ties to this woman: he was the witness at her marriage in 1895 and served as godfather to her two children.

It is not likely that any sister of Rasputin's could have escaped the constant probings into Gregory's life by church and state investigators, to say nothing of journalists and the local police who wrote frequent reports on the activities of his entire extended family. This woman might have been related to Rasputin, but the records that have survived do not permit us to say more than that.

Most of the information about Rasputin's childhood comes from the memoirs of his daughter Maria. She minimized her father's faults and recounted some events quite differently from a host of other witnesses. Yet it is impossible to ignore her accounts: she was uniquely positioned to hear tales of her father's childhood from Gregory and his parents and the other villagers. Her versions probably echo what Rasputin believed about himself, especially as he shed his background and embraced a new, mythic persona more in keeping with his status as an imperial favorite.

Maria was told that her father was a restless baby. He tossed and turned, and his mother often could not comfort him. Gregory was unpredictable: one day he might "run about the forest," crying "in a heartrending fashion," while he spent the next day in hiding or clinging to relatives. Shadows terrified him—he seemed to be pursued by unseen phantoms. Gregory did not begin to speak until he was two and a half; as an adult his sentences were long, drawn out, and slurred. When he was a child he wet his bed. This shameful secret got out and made the rounds of the village, turning the boy into an object of ridicule. "It was very hard to bear all this," he later said, "but I had to carry on."

Rasputin's childhood was shaped by Siberia—the land and the struggles that it imposed on its people. He helped his father farm in the spring and the summer; the family huddled around the hearth in winter. Life was hard and filled with work, but people enjoyed life. Until he died, Rasputin returned to Pokrovskoye at least once a year to reinvigorate his spiritual life. "Follow me in the summer to Pokrovskoye, to the great freedom of Siberia," he told his followers. "We will catch fish and work in the fields, and then you will really learn to understand God."

God was constantly present for Rasputin. God was the source of life's great contrasts—especially the conflict between human desires and church teachings. Rasputin sought salvation all his life; the quest challenged his desires and forced him, at times, to bow his head in shame. "A Russian may sin, but he cannot be Godless," Fyodor Dostoyevsky said. This was certainly true of Rasputin. Religion was a force in Russian life; even those who rejected Orthodoxy often honored the church as an institution.

Russians valued faith over reason. Icons, the liturgy, and church feasts were more important than logic, doctrine, and theology. A British journalist concluded that Russian peasants were religious but "profoundly ignorant of religious doctrine. They know little or nothing of Holy Writ. It is said that when a priest asked a peasant to name the Persons of the Trinity, he replied with no hesitation, 'The Savior, the Mother of God, and St. Nicholas the Miracle-Worker!'"

Rasputin believed that God ordained everything: joy and sorrow, suffering and punishment—all were the product of divine wisdom. Life's hardships and the teachings of the church reinforced the peculiarly Russian idea of *sudba*, fate. *Sudba* was God's will; it demanded a passive acceptance of misfortune. Suffering brought redemption and grace, and to complain about misfortune was to question the very order of the universe.

Rasputin never attended school. Education was not considered important for a peasant whose life would be devoted to tilling the soil and hauling goods. Neither Efim nor Anna had an education, and they obviously saw no need for their son to bother himself with schooling. That belief is hardly surprising: while the literacy rate was 20 percent in the Russian Empire in 1900, it was barely 4 percent in Siberia. The census of 1897 noted that Efim, Gregory, and everyone else in their household were illiterate.

Excluded from school and ridiculed by playmates, Gregory became withdrawn. He was quiet and pensive, weak, and sickly. "I was an outsider," he recalled. His peculiar personality caused him endless difficulties. The historian Alexander Bokhanov observed that life in Siberia was "cruel—it offered no comfort for the weak or people who were different. Life favored the strong—those who were by nature direct and brutal, and did not partake of the weaknesses of others."

Gregory knew that brutal reality firsthand. One summer day when he was eight, he and his cousin Dmitry, who was ten, went swimming. Dmitry jumped into the stream, but when he tried to stand, he lost his footing. Gregory reached out his hand, but Dmitry simply pulled him into the water. The current carried them along until some bystanders got them to shore. The boys developed pneumonia. With the nearest doctor in distant Tyumen, a local midwife "did what she could," but it was in vain. Gregory recovered, but Dmitry died.

Dmitry's death sent Gregory spiraling into depression. The tragedy had fallen upon a child who was already isolated and at odds with the world. He found solace only in the company of animals, especially horses. He supposedly communicated with these beasts, and adults came to him for advice about horses. True or not, Rasputin was clearly a strange, mystical boy who trod a lonely path. He was different—and difficult. He claimed that when he was a child he never stole, for, in his mind's eye, he could always see thieves in relation to what they had stolen, and he assumed that everyone had this ability. Whatever powers the young boy possessed, he recalled that they diminished after his cousin's death. They were sufficient, however, for Rasputin to perform what his followers believed was his first miracle.

One evening when he was twelve, Gregory was in bed with a high fever. A horse had just been stolen from one of the poorest men in Pokrovskoye, and Efim was discussing the crime with some friends. Gregory joined the group and, pointing to one man, cried out, "He's the one who stole the horse!" Efim apologized, explaining that his son was sick and delirious. But the outburst made two of the visitors suspicious. They followed the accused man home and caught him moving the stolen animal. According to Maria, the thief was soundly beaten, while her father "obtained a place apart in the village."

There is no point in arguing the story: it remains—like so much of Rasputin's life—an enigma. What is important is that Rasputin and his followers believed it was true. When Rasputin was an adult, he would catalogue the unique moments in his life as a boy in Pokrovskoye, suggesting that, from birth, he was endowed with mystical gifts.

It would be too easy, however, to paint the young man as "just" an extraordinary figure following an exceptional path. In truth, like adolescents the world over, Gregory had no clear path at all. "I spent my first twenty-eight years in the world," he later told his followers, "and I was one with it." "I loved the world and what it offered," he continued, and what it offered was often rebellion. Like his father, he had a taste for "strong vodka," and he drank to excess. After working the farm, hauling goods, fishing, and hunting, he was ready for a night on the town. Gregory harnessed his horses and drove through the area— drunk, of course—shouting obscenities at the respectable citizens who stopped to stare.

Gregory liked the young women of the village even more than alcohol, and he was not subtle in his approach. He often grabbed an attractive young girl and simply began kissing her. Sometimes he reached out and started undoing buttons. Slaps and kicks followed, although some girls gave in. Perhaps they were intrigued: there was an aura of mystery and even danger about the strange young man who was so mystical and moody. Gregory soon had the reputation of a village rake. He later commented that this was, all in all, a "good life for a peasant."

At seventeen Gregory was five feet nine inches tall; his long, thin face suggested malnutrition or an excessive use of alcohol. Dark brown hair parted in the middle fell to his shoulders in oily strands, while a beard and mustache, equally unkempt, covered his lower face. His nose was large and slightly askew, the result of too many barroom brawls. His eyes peered out from beneath his bushy eyebrows, and they became legendary. "His eyes," said a friend, "burned straight through you. They were deep-set in their sockets, and their whites were somehow elevated." Constantly on the move, they "were so brilliant that you couldn't determine their color." The most famous eyes in imperial Russia were variously described as gray, blue, and even alternately blue and brown.

There was power in those eyes and in Gregory's strange way of speaking. He stared at people before addressing them—directing a pointed gaze into their faces. When the words came they seemed disjointed and uncertain. Sentences rolled off his tongue in a peculiar stream of consciousness: he offered fragments of ideas, reflections on life and religion spiced with sexual comments. He seemed nervous;

his limbs jerked, he shuffled his feet, and he reached for nearby objects to keep his hands occupied. Despite these physical tics, he commanded attention.

Gregory's personality embodied divergent and contrasting strains—the religious seeker and the debauched hell-raiser. In one respect he was typical: every village had its troublemakers, and Gregory was known by such derisive nicknames as "Sniveler" and "Snotnose." But young Gregory also went with his parents on pilgrimages to nearby monasteries. He was especially drawn to the Znamensky Monastery at Abalak, near Tobolsk. In the summer of 1886 his parents gave him permission to make the pilgrimage alone.

Something unexpected happened at the monastery: Gregory fell in love. The young lady was Praskovaya Fedorovna Dubrovina. She was from the nearly village of Dubrovino. (It was apparently named for her family.) Respected and religious, Praskovaya had also gone to Abalak to celebrate the Feast of the Assumption. Praskovaya was a short, plump, young peasant woman with dark eyes and luxuriant blond hair. At twenty it was clear that she had been passed over by the most eligible bachelors. But Gregory did not worry about that or anything else. He was smitten; when he and the young woman parted, Gregory told Maria, he left a "fervent kiss upon her willing lips."

Gregory was accustomed to girls who either slapped him or yielded to his roving hands. Praskovaya was interested in her suitor, but she would not yield to his advances until after they were married. The young man spent five months wooing the woman he loved, and Efim and Anna encouraged it. Finally, on February 2, 1887—just three weeks after Gregory's eighteenth birthday—he and Praskovaya were married.

Praskovaya was an excellent choice for a wife—her acceptance and understanding seemed at times almost beyond comprehension. It was something of a union of outsiders: Gregory the conflicted young man and Praskovaya the spinster who was willing to accept the challenge Gregory offered over a lonely life of dependence on relatives. Praskovaya would share Gregory's lot in life, the good and the bad—and that included his adultery, drinking, and lengthy absences. She became convinced that her husband had a religious calling; this equipped her to overlook much and forgive even more. Simple and devout to the end, Praskovaya offered her husband sanctuary when the challenges he faced seemed at the point of overwhelming him.

The young married couple followed custom and moved in with the groom's parents. Their first child, Michael, was born on

September 29, 1888; he died of scarlet fever on May 16, 1893. The twins, Georgy and Anna, were born in May 1894. They succumbed to a whooping cough epidemic that took the lives of six infants in Pokrovskoye in a single day in 1896. The next three children survived to adulthood: Dmitry, born October 25, 1895; Matrëna (also known as Maria), born March 26, 1898; and Varvara, born November 28, 1900. A seventh child, a daughter named Praskovaya, was born in 1903 but died of whooping cough seventy-eight days later. The pattern of high infant mortality was an accepted part of life in Siberia, and Rasputin apparently never spoke of his losses. Such deaths were simply manifestations of God's inexplicable will.

Family life failed to tame Rasputin's restless character. People thought something was wrong with him. He drank and cheated on his wife (quite openly, in fact) even as he gave rambling discourses on religious subjects. A neighbor recalled that Praskovaya "suffered because of him. He would take things from home like bread and sell them to buy drink." Villagers in Pokrovskoye often refused to hire him, and he was the prime suspect whenever a theft or an act of vandalism took place. "People blamed me when things went wrong," he complained, "even if I had nothing to do with it."

A villager named V. I. Kartavtsev once found Rasputin stealing pieces of his fence. "He had just chopped it up and had it in his cart and was about to make off with it," Kartavtsev testified. "But I caught him, and I was going to make him take what he was stealing to the police. He wanted to run and was about to hit me with his axe, but I hit him with a stake so hard that blood started coming from his nose and mouth." Rasputin collapsed, and for a moment Kartavtsev thought he was dead. Rasputin came to but refused to go to the police station. "I hit him several times in the face with my fist," Kartavtsev said; after that Rasputin willingly went to the authorities.

The incident seemed to have marked Rasputin permanently. He let his hair grow long and fall across his broad forehead. The unkempt look, according to Maria, was deliberate; it was meant to hide an "odd little bump reminiscent of a budding horn." It might have been a scar left by Kartavtsev's beating.

Kartavtsev was apparently not given to introspection—he thought that the beatings he dealt Rasputin left him "sorta strange and stupid." For his part Rasputin clung to the conviction that he had spiritual gifts and was called to a higher mission. In later years he spoke of feeling inadequate and worthless as he pondered his future. "I was dissatisfied," he told his followers. "I was sick my whole life and medicine didn't help. I didn't sleep for forty nights each spring."

Forty: a Biblical allusion. Forty days of rain produced the Great Flood; the Israelites wandered forty years in the wilderness; Christ fasted forty days and was tempted by Satan. Rasputin saw this period as his own time of trial as he searched for meaning. He needed to see himself as special, but despite his prayers the answers did not come. He found "much sorrow" in life. Unable to break free of his emotional and spiritual malaise, Rasputin told his followers that he again "turned to drink."

Rasputin might have spent the next forty years lost in uncertainty, fighting his demons, succumbing to temptation, and repenting his transgressions. But an opportunity came from this time in the wilderness, and it was totally unexpected. Two of Kartavtsev's horses vanished in 1897. Suspicion immediately fell on Rasputin and his rowdy friends, Constantine and Trofim. The three were brought up on charges in a town meeting. Constantine and Trofim were found guilty and were permanently exiled from the village. The evidence against Rasputin, though, was not as compelling. The citizens of Pokrovskoye decided that he should be banished for a time.

Rasputin suggested a more constructive alternative: rather than exile, he would go on a pilgrimage. He would walk 325 miles to the great Siberian monastery of Saint Nicholas at Verkhoturye. Once when Efim had run afoul of the law, he had promised—but failed—to make the same journey. The son would now atone for his father's sins as well as his own. The townspeople accepted Rasputin's proposal, hoping that these devotions would reform his wayward character or at least get him out of the way for a while.

And so, on a fine spring morning in the year 1897, Rasputin set out for Verkhoturye. He was twenty-eight and still living under his father's roof with his wife and their infant son. He had not made much of his life at this point—but a new path lay before him. Rasputin was escaping the suffocating, domestic regularity of Pokrovskoye, and he was bound for an unknown destination. As he headed for Saint Nicholas Monastery, Rasputin was leaving the confines of a small Siberian village and stepping onto the pages of history.

2

Seeker and Teacher

RASPUTIN SET OUT FOR VERKHOTURYE as a penitential wanderer, one of a million people who traveled throughout the empire each year in quest of forgiveness and salvation. It probably took him two or three weeks to walk the 325 miles to Verkhoturye. At night he slept in barns or curled up at some roadside. Rasputin demanded much of himself in these early years—it would be difficult to accuse him of insincerity. If he was simply looking for a way to appease his neighbors, accepting a temporary exile from his village would have been an easier option than this. But Rasputin was a seeker, and this was the path he had chosen to follow.

We can imagine that Rasputin communed with nature as he passed from village to village. We know that he had a boyish enthusiasm that found God in birds, animals, and trees, as well as blue skies and the flowers that grew in the fields and forests of western Siberia. "Nature glorifies God and makes us joyful!" he once declared. "Let us thank God for our many blessings."

Rasputin finally reached his goal. He could see the white walls and multicolored domes of Verkhoturye's forty churches, monasteries, and convents in the distance against the green countryside—they beckoned to weary travelers. Most of the pilgrims were headed to the Saint Nicholas Monastery to pray before the relics of Saint Simeon, the renowned nobleman who renounced a life of privilege to care for the poor. Even before this trip, Rasputin had befriended Brother

Verkhoturye in 1910. The monastic complex is on the left. To the right is the Church of the Holy
Trinity at the Saint Nicholas Monastery. Rasputin was converted at the monastery in 1897.

Makary, a young ascetic who wore chains to mortify his flesh. Makary
was illiterate but had memorized the Liturgy, the prayers and lengthy
passages of the Bible. He had a wide following. Makary exemplified an
increasingly powerful strain in Orthodoxy that asserted that the simple, unquestioning faith of the peasants should be imitated by society
as a whole. His speech was disjointed, but his words were penetrating.
Makary spoke the language of the people in drawing parallels between
the challenges of daily life and the search for salvation.

Makary provided powerful inspiration to people who sought the
Christian life, and at this troubled moment, Rasputin turned to him for
guidance. Makary worked unceasingly to understand the will of God,
and he was ready to help others in their quest. He was a mystic—which
meant that he communed directly with God. Makary spoke of discern-
ment and wisdom, of the need to pray and fast, of the temptations
brought about by human nature, and of how even the greatest sinners
might find God.

Although Rasputin was a peasant, he believed that he possessed
extraordinary abilities, even if he had only a vague understanding of
them. Were the powers he demonstrated as a boy an early manifes-
tation of God's plan for his life? Was he meant, like Makary, to lead

others on their religious journeys? Was this the way Rasputin would achieve his own salvation? Makary advised him to pray and ask God for spiritual guidance. It was a time of uncertainty. Rasputin later spoke about an inner voice that was constantly calling him to "take up the cross and follow me."

"I searched my heart to learn how people are saved," Rasputin later wrote. "I worked hard and didn't sleep much." Baptism had made Rasputin a member of the Russian Orthodox Church at birth, but later he lived a wild life and disregarded many of its teachings.

Something unexpected happened on this trip: Rasputin found God. He never shared the details of what he experienced, but he said that he was filled with the living spirit of the Christian faith. He was fired with a determination to lead a Christian life and put himself at God's service. Even at this moment he was searching to find how he might lead others to the Truth.

"I found God at Verkhoturye—with the monks and the brothers," Rasputin said. Makary's influence was particularly important in his conversion, and its results were clear when Gregory returned to Pokrovskoye. Villagers told the Investigatory Commission in 1917 that Rasputin had left the town a loud and lecherous drunk but returned "with disheveled hair and no hat, singing and waving his arms." People were suddenly confronted with a powerful young man who blazed with the fire of a zealous convert and was intent on sharing his experiences with everyone he met.

Rasputin seems to have been sincere in his spiritual strivings, at least in these early years. He also had a sense of theater. He knew how to promote himself by embracing practices that set him apart from ordinary Orthodox Christians and would give him something of a reputation. He gave up alcohol and became a vegetarian, although he did not stop smoking until he arrived in Saint Petersburg in 1903. Rasputin worshipped God in his own flamboyant way. Villagers recalled how, standing in the congregation of the village church, he "cast crazy glances to the side and often sang in an improper voice." But he carefully venerated each icon in the church; he joined in feasts and fasts, sang in the choir, and displayed all the proper signs of piety. He also swung his arms and "made grimaces" throughout the Liturgy.

Rasputin aspired to be a leader and a teacher—that was clear from the outset. He understood that to play that role, he had to be literate. He never commented on when, where, or how he acquired his "education," but it was probably over a period of two or three months

Rasputin's handwriting. Apparently the monks at Verkhoturye gave Rasputin a crash course in reading and writing at the time of his conversion. The first page of this telegram—which is dated July 5, 1910, and is addressed to the Bishop of Tobolsk—shows Rasputin's awkward handwriting; his spelling and grammar were erratic. But his accomplishments were impressive, given the conditions of his schooling. In official documents he identified himself as "semiliterate."

at Verkhoturye, in 1897. This must have been a difficult process, and Rasputin never became what might be called well educated. But he accomplished the most he could in the time available.

"I read a lot," Rasputin said after he returned to Pokrovskoye, and his subsequent ability to quote from the church fathers and the Bible supports that claim. He appreciated education. Years later he met a man and his son on a steamship headed for Pokrovskoye. The lad had a notebook and was writing down the names of the ships he passed. Rasputin urged him to study and stay in school, noting, "It's hard being illiterate!"

Armed with a sense of destiny, Rasputin gathered a small group of people in Pokrovskoye who were open to his views and ready to accept his leadership. His followers included Ilya Arsenov, Nicholas Raspopov, the Korchakov family, and the Pecherkin sisters, Catherine (Katya) and Evdokiya (Dunya). They were ready to join Rasputin in his search for a more intense, personal relationship with God, even if it led beyond the traditional bounds of Orthodoxy. The fact that their meetings were secret slowed the growth of the group, but it kept the authorities from disrupting their activities. Rasputin must also have realized that binding his followers to secrecy cemented his power over them.

The speculation began right away: What was Grishka up to? People whispered that the Pecherkin girls began their services by ceremonially washing Rasputin in the bathhouse while the others gathered in the root cellar of his father's house. They sang as the sisters solemnly conducted Rasputin to a simple altar, decorated with icons. Rasputin read from the Bible and preached; his followers prayed and sang hymns. The music was strange and unearthly; it did not come from the Russian Orthodox Church. The villagers jumped to the conclusion that Rasputin had joined a lurid and infamous sectarian group, the Khlysty.

That was not true, although the Khlysty were important in shaping Rasputin's beliefs. Rasputin remained a member of the Russian Orthodox Church to the end of his life, but his lively, inquisitive mind made him interested in other doctrines. He listened to the Baptists and Evangelical Christians who came to Pokrovskoye after his conversion. He learned much from Yakov Barbarin, a priest imprisoned for heresy at the Abalak Monastery. The sects also shaped his views. Their members were quite different from the Old Believers, who were schismatics; that is, they rejected the reforms that Patriarch Nikon proclaimed in the 1650s. The Old Believers insisted that they maintained the Orthodox faith in its original, pure form and that they worshipped within the Orthodox tradition. The sectarians, by contrast, were never part of the Russian Orthodox Church.

The Khlyst sect began about 1617, when the peasant Daniel Filippovich proclaimed himself to be the "Lord of Hosts." He declared that other ordinary people—women as well as men—had these divine gifts. They called themselves the Believers in Christ, and they were convinced that Filippovich had been sent to lead them from the heresy of the Orthodox Church. Although their members were outlawed, imprisoned, and killed, the sect flourished throughout Siberia and was a perpetual thorn in the side of the authorities.

Enemies called them the Khlysty—*khlyst* being the Russian word for "whip." Their congregations were known as "ships." The faithful met at night, in basements and cellars. Wearing white robes, the Believers in Christ sang hymns and chanted under the direction of a man or a woman known as a "Christ" or a "Mother of God." The Khlysty shouted as they waved their arms, dancing in a frenzy as the leader, armed with a whip, lashed them until their blood flowed. When they reached a certain point of ecstasy, the celebrants cast their robes aside and engaged in sexual intercourse with whoever happened to be at hand.

The Khlysty believed that sex was a sin even in marriage—but sin did not separate the Believers in Christ from God. Sin led them to contrition and a plea for God's grace. They insisted that sin—and only sin—brought salvation. Paradoxically, to be saved, the Believers had to summon what Radzinsky called the "dark courage" to sin.

The charge that Rasputin was a member of the Khlysty dogged him to the end of his life. He did adopt elements of their thought and practice; he rejected alcohol and tobacco, and his followers addressed one another as "Brother" and "Sister." His circle met in cellars; they sang Khlyst hymns. But repeated investigations failed to establish that Rasputin was ever a member of the sect. Indeed, it is interesting to note that Rasputin's worship services did *not* include sex. Rasputin was friendly to the Khlysty, but he was sufficiently shrewd to realize that joining that group would destroy any hope that he might have to become influential in elite circles. Moreover, by his very nature, Rasputin was a leader, not a follower. That meant that he had to forge his own system of ideas and gather his own group of followers.

Rasputin claimed to have had a vision in 1898. One day while working in the fields, he believed that the Virgin Mary appeared before him, hovering in the sky. He fell to his knees, awaiting a command; but the Virgin simply pointed to the horizon. He took her gestures to be a summons for him to embark on another pilgrimage. The experience changed his life—it was something of a second conversion. Rasputin's devotion to Mary increased, and he felt that she constantly guided and instructed him. "I once spent the night with an icon of the Mother of God in the room," he recalled. Once he awoke to find tears streaming down her face as her voice intoned, "I am weeping for the sins of mankind, Gregory. Go, wander, and cleanse the people of their sins."

Rasputin often recounted his vision, as if to impress upon his listeners the sense of mystery that swept over his soul at that moment. It stamped him as a man of destiny, reinforcing his certainty that he had a historic mission. It played on the religious sentiments of the faithful; the Russian Orthodox Church embraces miracles and visions as manifestations of God's grace. About 1900 Rasputin suddenly announced that God was calling him to make a pilgrimage to Mount Athos in Greece, the monastic center of the Eastern Orthodox world.

Efim Rasputin thought that all of this was absurd—he scoffed that his son became a "pilgrim out of laziness." The assessment was not quite fair: Rasputin was proposing to walk hundreds of miles in rain and in sunshine, through villages and the countryside, relying at all times upon odd jobs and charity. Life as a farmer might have been hard, but it must have been easier than the trek Rasputin proposed. In fact, he had been making pilgrimages from the time he was a teenager.

And so Rasputin set out for Greece as a strannik, a pilgrim. One often saw these men and women walking in bast shoes and clad in peasant clothing with their few possessions in knapsacks slung over their shoulders. The "Way of the Pilgrim" was their vocation, and they were intense in pursuing it. The stranniki sought no comforts or joy but led spartan lives as they endlessly repeated the Jesus Prayer: "Lord Jesus Christ, have mercy upon me, a sinner." Rasputin was happy to share their calling.

"I took in life furiously during these years," he said. "Everything interested me: the good, the bad; I accepted everything and questioned nothing. I walked 40–50 *versti* [twenty-seven to thirty-three miles] a day without noticing storms, wind, or rain. I was seldom able to eat: in Tambov, I had only potatoes. I had no money and did not worry about time. God provided, and if I needed lodging for the night, I slept." He went six months without changing his underwear or laying his hands upon himself. He read a few Bible passages every night, prayed, and sought guidance as he walked across Russia. After months on the road, his resolve weakened.

"You're too good for this," a voice whispered—Rasputin knew it was the voice of Satan. "No one even knows what you're doing," the message continued. This was a low point in his life, a time of doubt—but one that he mastered. Although his journey had been difficult, he emerged from the struggle bound with "chains of love." He had also summoned the physical and mental devotion he needed to discover God's purpose for his life.

Crossing Siberia and Ukraine, Rasputin finally reached the Orthodox monastic center at Mount Athos. He claimed that at that time he was entertaining the idea of becoming a monk, but a man who aspired to become a leader was not likely to do that. Rasputin was proud of making the visit but repulsed at finding that some of the monks were openly homosexual. This was Rasputin's first exposure to such practices, and despite his own flexible attitudes toward sin and sex, he left the Holy Mountain profoundly disillusioned. Months passed before he finally reached Siberia. He had to go to Verkhoturye to tell Makary of his experiences. Makary was shocked by Rasputin's description of life at Mount Athos; even so, Makary assured him that great things were in his future. "Remember your mission," Makary concluded. "Since you will not find salvation in a monastery, you must save your soul in the world."

Rasputin was gone from Pokrovskoye for nearly two years when he made that trip to Mount Athos—it was his longest pilgrimage. Since Maria was only a few months old when he left, it must have been in 1898. When he returned, his daughter recalled a "tall man with a long brown beard" and "tired face" moving in obvious fatigue along the road to their house. "Gregory!" Praskovaya cried out. Maria looked on in astonishment as her mother threw herself into her husband's arms. These absences were hard on Praskovaya, but Maria recalled that her mother was proud of her husband, for she was convinced that he was a man of God.

Rasputin met with hostility in Pokrovskoye. He often returned to find the village bristling with suspicion. He certainly gave his enemies ammunition, since he was often accompanied by young women who wore clothing that was similar to nuns' attire. He kissed them good-bye as people looked on in amazement. At least they were willing partners—which was certainly not the case of one young woman who reported that Rasputin took her to his cellar and raped her. He told the sobbing girl at the end that there was no sin in what they had done; they had simply been celebrating the Holy Trinity.

Although Rasputin was married, he pursued other women. Sometimes he would ask a woman to undress and wash him so that they might resist temptation together. Rasputin had an unusually strong sex drive—this was quite striking, and it affected every aspect of his life. He freely admitted that he was a sinner, and he believed that he should resist sin. Sometimes he succeeded in doing that; on other occasions, his defenses collapsed, and he and his partners had sex. Rasputin explained that he took upon himself the sin of such encounters for, as a man of God, he was above judgment. Rasputin was passionate, impulsive, and conflicted. He did his best to manage his urges on a day-to-day basis. Rasputin was constantly embracing his darker side, regarding it as yet another trial sent by God.

Praskovaya was the only person who understood that sex was, for Rasputin, a burden—not a pleasure. Father Peter Ostroumov, the chief priest of Pokrovskoye, was not interested in such subtleties. Maria remembered Ostroumov as a stern, forbidding man "who seemed to feel that the whole purpose of life was to mumble prayers." Ostroumov was outraged at this distinctly non-Orthodox blending of sensual passion with religion.

The scandals were closing in on Rasputin. The sneers and mockery were too much for a man who craved recognition and status so desperately. If people would not take him seriously in his own village, Rasputin had to leave it. And so, in 1902 Rasputin shook the dust of Pokrovskoye from his boots and set out on a journey that would bring him to the great world lying beyond Siberia.

Sprawled along the banks of the Volga River, Kazan was a large population center and the home of a major theological academy. By the time Rasputin arrived in the city, people were calling him a *starets*—a title that the people gave to men and women with mystical qualities who were marked by a powerful prayer life. One might suppose that Rasputin's irregular love life would make such an honor out of the question. But there were conflicting strands in Rasputin's character, and the people outside of Pokrovskoye somehow focused upon Rasputin as a man of God. At any rate, they embraced him as "Starets Gregory." In *The Brothers Karamazov*, Fyodor Dostoyevsky described a starets as one who "takes your soul and will into his soul and will." Combining the roles of a teacher and a spiritual guide, a starets offered prayers and religious guidance, shepherding the faithful through the uncertainties of life to salvation.

Rasputin was thirty-three when he arrived at Kazan. The years he spent trudging the empire's roads and byways worked to his advantage now. The wind and the sun had tanned his skin and toned his narrow, emaciated face. He profited from being a Siberian peasant, for Siberian *muzhiki*—unlike their compatriots in the western provinces who once lived under serfdom—carried themselves proudly and with an independent air. Rasputin radiated self-confidence and authority;

he expected to be in control of every situation. Many people fell under the spell of those bright, brilliant eyes. What Rasputin said was not as important as the fact that his listeners heard exactly what it was that they wanted to hear.

That is not to say that Rasputin always made a favorable impression. His hair hung in greasy strands, and his fingernails were blackened from farm work. His beard revealed, people said, what he had eaten earlier in the day. We sometimes read that Rasputin emitted a powerful, unpleasant aroma. That is something of a puzzle, for as soon as he settled in Kazan, he frequented the bathhouses—and they were a basic feature of Russian life. It is not likely that he was slovenly or smelly; if anything, Rasputin was vain about his appearance. He was constantly combing his hair, and he eagerly accepted gifts of clothing and boots. Ever ready to meet expectations, Rasputin launched into this new, sophisticated world with a determination to conquer it.

Rasputin benefited by appearing at a moment when the Church was in a crisis. Since Orthodoxy was Russia's official faith, it was closely bound to the state. Rising criticism of the government affected the attitudes of people toward the Church. Many were coming to think that Orthodoxy was little more than a collection of corrupt monks and priests who acted as police informers. Glittering vestments and ornate rituals actually separated the hierarchy from some believers, and they took to looking elsewhere for answers. The Slavic revival begun by Tsar Nicholas I in the 1830s turned inward, seeking to reclaim Russia's greatness with appeals to a heroic, uncomplicated past in which subjects stood united with their sovereign under the guidance of the Church. The ultimate symbol of this nostalgia was the peasant, held by myth to be unswervingly loyal and imbued with a deep, unquestioning faith. While some Russians turned to science for the answers to life's deep questions, the Church sought values in the common people. The peasants were said to be closer to God. Their piety was worthy of emulation, and their wisdom was infused with a simple, uncomplicated grace.

The people of Kazan were seeking answers, and Rasputin was ready to supply them. Wandering pilgrims and holy men were common, but Rasputin made a particular impression. He learned to act boldly. Realizing that humility and flattery were unnecessary for a man on a divine mission, he was blunt and insistent on playing a game whose rules he and he alone dictated. He treated church leaders and members of the elite with the same familiarity that he displayed toward his fellow peasants.

Characteristically, he would take a woman by the hand and stare into her face while his eyes probed the depths of her soul. His questions were searching—they got to the bottom of her problems, though they might leave a lady squirming uncomfortably. Rasputin could be belligerent and reassuring by turns. His intuition permitted him to analyze people and respond with just the right word or gesture. This gave him dominance over many of the emotionally fragile souls who came to him for guidance and comfort.

Rasputin was fun—it was a pleasure to be in his company. He gave people nicknames, and they were often cutting and quite appropriate. He might dub a woman "Hot Stuff," "Boss Lady," "Sexy Girl," or "Good Looking," while a man would be called "Fancy Pants," "Big Breeches," "Long Hair," or "Fella." People accepted this as a charming characteristic—the humor of a peasant who meant no real disrespect.

Rasputin quickly established himself in Kazan as a man of great spiritual depth. A young couple who lost two children in a short time came to him during this visit. "My wife's despair grew into insanity," the husband recalled, "and the doctors couldn't do a thing. Someone advised me to send for Rasputin. . . . Imagine this: after speaking with her for a half hour, she became totally serene. Say whatever you like against him, maybe it's even so. But he saved my wife—and that's the truth!"

Rumors abounded at Kazan that Rasputin enjoyed the company of women. He supposedly held their hands and kissed them in a familiar way, but he had his defenders on this matter. One lady told people that Rasputin shared her bed—but his object was to show that, even under those conditions, they could resist temptation. Nothing sexual occurred. Interesting as that might be, Rasputin was not always so proper. Two sisters—one was twenty, the other fifteen—gave themselves willingly to him at a bathhouse in Kazan. When their mother learned what was happening, she rushed to the place, only to encounter the three as they were leaving. "Now you may feel at peace," Rasputin said, smiling maliciously. "The day of salvation has dawned for your daughters."

Despite these scandals, Rasputin cast a powerful spell, and many succumbed to it. He strengthened his reputation enormously by winning the support of Gavril, father superior of the Seven Lakes Monastery, just outside Kazan. Gavril heard of the new arrival and his spiritual gifts, as well as rumors that Rasputin was a heretic and had sex with his female followers. Rasputin was disarmingly frank when Gavril

confronted him with these charges: he admitted that he was a sinner—
what man was not? Yes, he kissed women and treated them in a loving
way, although their relationships were always—he insisted—appropriate. Rasputin denied being a Khlyst. What finally swayed Gavril was
a prediction that Rasputin made concerning a certain Father Philip.
Rasputin warned the father superior to "be careful" about the young
monk. The remark was strange, and Rasputin admitted that he himself could not explain it. Gavril laughed it off—until a few days later,
when Philip attacked him with a knife. Gavril was now convinced that
Rasputin was a true starets, endowed with precognition and mystical
gifts.

Rasputin also made a great impression upon Andrew, the bishop of
Kazan. Rasputin seemed to be exactly the type of person the Russian
Orthodox Church was seeking to forge new links with the faithful.
Andrew insisted that Rasputin visit church leaders in Saint Petersburg.

A member of Andrew's staff accompanied Rasputin on a visit to
Bishop Sergei, the rector of the theological academy located at the
Alexander Nevsky Monastery. Rasputin's days of hard travel were now
in his past. He sped along in a first-class train coach in high comfort.
Rasputin likened himself to "a blind man on the road," but it was a road
he was eager to explore.

Rasputin arrived in Saint Petersburg during Lent in 1903. For the
first time in his life, he faced a real metropolis—a city of over a million
people. Saint Petersburg was spread across nineteen islands and was
laced with canals spanned by delicate bridges and cleaved in half by the
Neva River. It was the antithesis of everything Russian. When Peter
the Great founded this new capital, he was repudiating Moscow's narrow streets and medieval atmosphere. He despised Muscovites, whom
he considered ignorant and opposed to change; the nobles were constantly complaining about the government and plotting against one
another, while the clergy seemed to be interested in little more than
defending their privileges.

The streets of Saint Petersburg, by contrast, were wide and lined
with baroque palaces that were designed by Italian architects. The
people were closer to Europe and more open to its ideas; the nobility
served the state while the Church, now stripped of its independence,
was merely another element of the tsar's oppressive bureaucracy. Saint
Petersburg was hedonistic, artificial, and cynical; here one found
extravagant privilege mingled with grinding despair. Saint Petersburg
would be the stage upon which Rasputin would play his greatest role.

Rasputin's immediate destination was the Alexander Nevsky Monastery, one of the four most important religious centers in the empire. He joined the other visitors in the cathedral in lighting candles and praying; he then changed clothes and got ready to meet Bishop Sergei. Rasputin carried a letter from Bishop Andrew that described Rasputin as a starets, a man of undoubted insight and spiritual wisdom. Andrew advised church leaders in Saint Petersburg to listen to him, for his spiritual gifts equipped him to help the Church strengthen its ties with the common people. Rasputin and Sergei had a long talk. The peasant discoursed on the Bible, the teachings of the Church, and the challenges of everyday living; Sergei recalled the old maxim that God often works through ordinary people. The bishop was so impressed with Rasputin that he invited him to stay at his apartment.

One night soon after this, Sergei presented Rasputin to a group of other bishops. "They were learned and cultured men," an eyewitness recalled. Although they were accustomed to being in authority, their roles were reversed that night: Rasputin was the center of attention, and he relished it. He expounded his views and shared his experiences; he answered questions and presented himself in such a way as to invite his listeners to find in him whatever it was that they were hoping to find. As the pleasant evening was drawing to a close, Rasputin made three predictions—they were bizarre, and one would think that he was taking a horrendous risk in making them. Rasputin said that one bishop would soon suffer a hernia while another would lose his mother and a third would father a child out of wedlock. The lore surrounding Rasputin insists that all these predictions came true. True or not, the episode solidified his reputation among Saint Petersburg's Orthodox elite.

Rasputin also met Father John of Kronstadt, a man who was widely venerated for his oratorical gifts and work with the poor. John was close to Alexander III, who asked him to hear his last confession. According to legend, Rasputin visited Saint Andrew's Cathedral on Kotlin Island in the Gulf of Finland to hear John preach; the enormous congregation and the sincerity of the pastor's words impressed Rasputin. During the service Father John supposedly told the people that he discerned the presence of a man with spiritual gifts, and he asked him to step forward. Rasputin did that. John spoke with the peasant and blessed him and urged him to persevere in his calling. The story cannot be verified, but Rasputin often boasted about it, citing it as evidence that God had chosen him for some extraordinary role in the religious life of his people.

Rasputin with prominent church figures. From right to left: Rasputin, Feofan, and Brother Makary, Rasputin's mentor. Makary, who was important in Rasputin's conversion, was a starets at the Saint Nicholas Monastery at Verkhoturye. Makary also encouraged Rasputin to become a pilgrim and to play the role of a religious leader.

A young student named Iliodor met Rasputin at the Academy in 1903. Born Sergei Trufanov in 1880, the monk blazed with fiery conviction and extravagant ambitions. Iliodor befriended Rasputin and eventually turned against him, denouncing him in the most extreme terms. One senses retrospective judgment when Iliodor describes his first meeting with "Father Gregory from Siberia." We are told that Rasputin "was wearing a plain, cheap, gray colored jacket"; his pants were "tucked under rough men's boots," and he "emitted a disagreeable odor." But Iliodor conceded that Rasputin impressed the faculty and students of the Academy.

Rasputin's most important conquest in Saint Petersburg was Archimandrite Feofan. He was the inspector of the theological academy and the confessor of the tsar and his wife. Feofan was visibly excited when he told his students that "God is raising up a great man from distant Siberia"—he would prove to be the savior of Russia. When Feofan met Rasputin, the inspector was "dazzled" by the peasant's "psychological perspicacity." Rasputin's "face was pale and his eyes were remarkably piercing; he had the look of someone who observed the fasts. And he made a strong impression." According to Iliodor, Feofan asked Rasputin to share his apartment.

Rasputin seized the invitation. Bishop Sergei was popular and influential, but he was also a bit too combative to be of maximum value in advancing Rasputin's career. Feofan, on the other hand, was socially well connected; his circle included people who visited aristocratic salons and imperial palaces. Feofan could open doors for Rasputin in ways that Sergei could not, and Rasputin was soon meeting many of the high and mighty people whose curiosity offered new avenues for him to explore. It was a pivotal moment in Rasputin's life, and he knew it. He later declared that he "finished his universities" during the days he spent with Feofan and his circle at the Saint Petersburg Academy.

Feofan launched Rasputin into those social circles that were interested in religious questions. "The Russian educated classes," declared a British visitor, "though warmly attached to their Church, are in general not at all religious in the sense in which we commonly use the word." The skeptical atmosphere that Rasputin encountered in Kazan was even more pronounced in the capital. Aristocrats were bored, cynical, and seeking new experiences; they saw Orthodoxy as the faith of peasants and priests who were infused with superstition and corrupted by tradition. Séances and Eastern mysticism were popular. Rasputin was broadly welcomed as a man who claimed spiritual communion with God even as he stood in ornate palaces and finely furnished receiving rooms.

Two of those "truth seekers" were sisters, Grand Duchesses Militsa and Anastasia of Montenegro. The ladies were born into an obscure and impoverished kingdom in the Balkans. Alexander III brought them to Saint Petersburg to be educated at the prestigious Smolny Institute, and he acted as their protector. The sisters cemented their places in society through strategic unions in 1889: Militsa married Grand Duke Peter Nicholaevich (a second cousin of Nicholas II) while Anastasia wed Duke George von Leuchtenberg, a member of the Romanov family. Their dark complexions earned them such nicknames as the

"Crows" or the "Black Pearls"; detractors called them the "Black Peril."
Militsa was actually a serious student of the world's great religions, and
she found Rasputin intriguing. "His speech was ungrammatical and
filled with images that made him seem like a prophet," she later said.
"Gregory's exposition of the Gospels and especially the Apocalypse
was penetrating and original."

Rasputin had a keen ability to use and discard people to advance
his career. When Rasputin had exhausted the benefits of living with
Feofan, he moved in with G. P. Sazonov, a journalist who could promote him in the press. A favorable mention here and there in the
newspapers would add to his mystique and increase public curiosity.
Rasputin could also receive women at Sazonov's apartment, which was
not the case at Feofan's.

Rasputin could have continued to reap the advantages of life in Saint
Petersburg, but after just a few months he made a startling decision: he
would return home, to Pokrovskoye. Perhaps the pressure of moving
in those powerful circles was beginning to overwhelm him; perhaps
he felt the need—as he later often did—to reconnect with his Siberian
roots, to find physical and spiritual restoration in the uncomplicated
life of his village. In any event Rasputin knew that he could and would
return to Saint Petersburg when he felt the time was right.

Rasputin returned to Pokrovskoye in the autumn of 1903 a new
and different man. First, he had conquered Kazan; then, he took Saint
Petersburg by storm. His clothing was the most tangible evidence of
the changes in his life. His admirers had bought him several wardrobes
at the capital's finest and most fashionable stores. Rasputin now wore
colorful silk shirts with bright sashes and shining leather boots, as well
as stylish breeches and wide leather belts. The villagers who had once
clucked in disapproval at "Grishka the Prophet" were chastened. They
had to admit that he had accomplished quite a lot. The prodigal son
had returned home again, now in triumph.

3

Nicholas and Alexandra:
Waiting for a Friend

O N A COLD DAY IN 1881, the boy fated to become Russia's
last tsar glimpsed his own destiny. A blanket of snow had fallen
across Saint Petersburg on that first Sunday in March, and it sparkled
beneath the sun as Alexander II's carriage moved quickly down the
frozen street. A man suddenly hurled a bomb into the path of the
horses; the explosion shook the ground and rattled windows as
fire and smoke curled into the sky. Alexander actually escaped injury,
but concern for the wounded caused him to linger at the scene. Another
man flung a charge that exploded at the tsar's feet. With a last gasp
Alexander muttered, "To the palace, to die there!"

Members of the imperial family rushed to the Winter Palace.
Nicholas, twelve, followed the trail of dark red blood to the tsar's
study. He found his grandfather unconscious and horribly disfigured:
Alexander's right leg was missing, the left was shattered; his stomach
was covered in blood while his face was torn by shrapnel. The doctors
could do nothing.

The revolutionaries' hatred of the tsar was ironic because Alexander
II had done so much to reform Russia. He freed the serfs in the 1860s,
modernized the courts, and created a new system of local, elected
government. But the intelligentsia—liberals, students, and fledgling
revolutionaries—saw these as timid, half-hearted concessions that

were designed to head off real change. The rising tide of discontent drove the tsar from further reforms, while his enemies lurched toward violence. The events of that March day were the product of a troubled situation.

The terrible scene in Alexander's bedroom shook Nicholas. The boy who would become the last ruler of Russia later confessed a "presentiment—a secret conviction, even—that I am destined for terrible trials. And my reward will not come on this Earth. How often have I applied Job's words to myself: 'What I fear overtakes me, and what I seek to avoid descends upon my head.'"

Nicholas II's birthday was May 6, 1868, the day the Orthodox Church honors the Old Testament patriarch Job. Deeply religious and inclined to mysticism, Nicholas accepted the trials life visited upon him as the will of God. His gruff, overbearing father intimidated the boy, while his mother, Maria Fedorovna, coddled him, leaving Nicholas emotionally immature and lacking in self-confidence. Alexander III's premature death brought the young man to the throne in 1894. "What am I going to do?" he sobbed to his cousin and brother-in-law, Alexander Michaelovich. "What will happen to me, to you and our family? I'm not prepared to be a Tsar. I never wanted to become one. I know nothing of the business of ruling."

The self-doubt was well founded. Nicholas II was handsome and polite, with polished manners and a gift for foreign languages. His education was haphazard, considering that he was destined to rule Russia. Tutors were not allowed to grade or to question him. The new emperor was intelligent and quick-witted, although he had no flair for critical analysis. Only a year before he came to the throne, Nicholas's father called him an "absolute child," prone to infantile judgments and ruled by instinct and emotion. It is true that Nicholas matured after he ascended to the throne; he was hardworking and nearly fanatical in his devotion to duty. But he was also impulsive and known to make solitary decisions, ignoring sound advice.

Nicholas believed that God had ordained him to rule the Russian Empire. He was convinced that an autocratic system of government had been the basis for Russia's greatness, even if it was a popular assembly that elected Michael the first Romanov tsar in 1613. Nicholas II had "an unshakable faith in the providential nature of his high office," a courtier observed. "His mission emanated from God. He was responsible for his actions only to his conscience and to God." He saw civil liberties and legislatures as alien to Russia. Nicholas swore that he would never "agree to a representative form of government, because I consider it harmful to the people God has entrusted to my care."

Leon Trotsky was a gifted historian, and his evaluation of Nicholas II was quite negative. The Bolshevik leader wrote that the last Romanov inherited an "empire and a revolution" but not a "single quality that would have made him capable of governing a province or even a county." Fair or not, it is true that Russia, the largest country in the world, had massive problems. Eighty percent of Russians were illiterate when Nicholas became tsar, and at least half of his subjects lived in poverty. Some brave souls stood up for reform, and a few even created underground revolutionary parties. Nicholas warned his liberal critics that their hopes for parliamentary government were nothing more than "senseless dreams." The early twentieth century brought strikes, riots, political assassinations, and bloody pogroms. Driven by a reckless sense of mission, Nicholas tried to bring parts of the Far East under Russian influence, a misadventure that triggered a war with Japan in 1904 and led to a string of Russian defeats.

The year 1905 was the turning point. In January troops fired on a peaceful demonstration at the Winter Palace that called for an end to the war and better working conditions. Known as "Bloody Sunday," this event destroyed the myth of the tsar as a benevolent figure. Revolution swept the country: the Black Sea Fleet mutinied, railway and factory workers went on strike, and demonstrators filled the streets. The tsar was forced to act against his conscience: he issued the October Manifesto granting his subjects civil liberties and a legislature, the Duma. The autocracy was over, but Nicholas's mind-set led him to insist that he was still, somehow, an autocrat. He dismissed the First and Second Dumas as too radical. The government changed the electoral formula to secure a more cooperative group of deputies, although the Third Duma often asserted its independence and could be quite critical of the government.

The woman who shared Nicholas II's troubled life and tragic death was Alix, the princess of Hesse. She was born on June 6, 1872, in the beautiful German town of Darmstadt. Louis, her father, was the grand duke; her mother, Alice, was the third of Queen Victoria's nine children and an intelligent, introspective woman of deep religiosity. Alix's mother died when she was six, leaving the young girl melancholy, morbid, and shy. Alix reacted by guarding her emotions and sealing herself off from others. Her grandmother, Queen Victoria, ensured that she became a well-educated and proper young lady. Alix also painted well and excelled at the piano, although she was awkward, stubborn, and deeply devoted to her Lutheran faith.

Nicholas met Alix in 1884 when she came to Russia for the wedding of her older sister, Elizabeth, to his uncle, Sergei Alexandrovich. Five years later, Alix arrived to spend the winter of 1889 with Elizabeth in Saint Petersburg. Nicholas fell madly in love with the beautiful German lady, but his parents were not happy with their son's determination to make Alix his wife. They knew that Alix's cold, aloof demeanor would be a handicap for a future empress. Alix also balked at converting to the Orthodox faith. But Nicholas persisted, and in April 1894 they were engaged.

Alexander III died on October 20, 1894. The next day Alix was received into the Orthodox Church as Alexandra Fedorovna; she married Nicholas a week after his father's funeral. The timing, of course, was terrible: "She came to us behind a coffin," people whispered. The marriage was happy and filled with passion, but the new empress never overcame the early impression that she was ill suited to her role and would bring misfortune to the imperial throne.

Queen Marie of Romania, Alexandra's cousin, recalled that Alexandra "seldom smiled, and when she did it was grudging, as though making a concession." Alexandra was beautiful and could be charming; she also had a profound sense of duty and always tried to do the right thing. But Marie found that she was somehow "not of 'those who win'"; she was "too distrustful, too much on the defensive." Alexandra alienated the Saint Petersburg elite with her aloof manner and disapproval of what she called its hedonistic ways. People compared her unfavorably to Maria Fedorovna, Nicholas II's vibrant and popular mother. Stung by the criticism, Alexandra gradually retreated into private life.

Nicholas and Alexandra lived in Alexander Palace at Tsarskoye Selo. The "Tsar's Village" was an exclusive residential center fifteen miles south of Saint Petersburg, surrounded by iron fences and patrolled by scarlet-coated Cossacks. Nicholas and Alexandra read together, walked in the park, enjoyed cozy teas, and basked in the glow of each other's company. When Alix met Nicholas, she did not know Russian. Their best mutual language was English, and they developed the habit of communicating in that language. Alexandra mastered Russian, but it took years before she felt comfortable using it. In 1916 she wrote proudly to her husband, "I am no longer the slightest bit shy or affraid [*sic*] of the ministers & speak like a waterfall in Russia[n]." Then she added: "They kindly don't laugh at my faults."

Alexandra gave birth to four girls from November 1895 to June 1901: Olga, Tatyana, Maria, and Anastasia. The parents doted over their beautiful, charming, and gifted daughters—but they also presented a problem: Nicholas II needed a son to keep the throne within his family. The emperor Paul hated his mother, Catherine the Great, so much that, when he finally came to the throne in 1796, he changed the succession law to all but eliminate the possibility that a woman would ever again rule Russia. Alexandra—and her detractors—viewed her apparent inability to bear a son as an indication that she had somehow displeased God. Having converted to Orthodoxy, the empress flung herself into her new faith with a fervor that made most Russians uncomfortable. On the point of a male heir, she also seemed to be hoping for a miracle. Nicholas had been raised in the Orthodox Church, and he passively accepted the teaching that God controlled all things. The tsar's outlook was governed by the classic Russian acceptance of fate (*sudba*) as the force that ruled the cosmos. Since everything was a product of God's will, he saw no point in questioning the meaning of events. But his wife's way of looking at all this was quite different.

Alexandra does not seem to have believed in "fate"—or at least she believed that prayer could affect the future. She probably recalled how an angry God initially intended to destroy Sodom, but Abraham had the temerity to bargain on the matter, and he ended with the promise that the city would be spared if it had only ten righteous people. The lesson was clear: God could change his mind. Alexandra also thought that God could put people in her life who would help her bear her burdens. Feofan, a leader of the theological academy and their confessor, influenced the imperial couple on this subject. Feofan told them, "God's men still exist on earth. To this day, Holy Russia abounds in saints. God sends consolation to His people from time to time in the guise of righteous men and they are the mainstays of Holy Russia." This encouraged Nicholas and Alexandra to invite a series of peasants, healers, and holy fools into Alexander Palace. They hoped that these men and women would help the empress through prayer or by drawing on mystical forces that she did not understand. But the most important person in the group before Rasputin was actually a foreigner— "Monsieur Philippe."

Born in Savoy in 1849, Philippe Nazier-Vachot abandoned a butcher's career to develop what he called his spiritual powers. After his expulsion from the medical school at Lyon, he practiced what he called "occult medicine," treating people with "psychic fluids and astral forces." Although Nazier-Vachot faced arrest for practicing medicine without a license, he attracted a number of devoted admirers. Nicholas and Alexandra met Philippe through Anastasia and Militsa, the Montenegrin sisters, when the tsar visited France in 1901. They were impressed with the claim that Nazier-Vachot could select the sex of an embryo through—as he put it—the "most transcendental practices of hermetic medicine, astronomy and psychurgy." Nicholas invited the Frenchman to visit Russia.

Dr. Philippe spent three busy years in Saint Petersburg. His patients addressed the short, jovial Frenchman as "Our Father" and "Lord"; they were pleased when he laid his hands on them and pronounced miraculous cures. Nicholas II awarded him a doctor's diploma, and for a time Nazier-Vachot visited Tsarskoye Selo. Alexandra called him "Our Friend." Many Russian society people took seriously Nazier-Vachot's claim that he had magic hats that would make him and people in his company invisible.

Nazier-Vachot declared that the empress was pregnant with a son in the summer of 1902. Alexandra even put on weight; but it was a hysterical pregnancy. To prevent a scandal, a terse bulletin from the palace announced that Alexandra had suffered a miscarriage. But Alexandra and other members of her family were stunned and angry.

Even though Alexandra actually became pregnant in late 1903, the pressure to send Nazier-Vachot home continued. Nicholas finally decided that the critics were right: it was time for him to take leave of "Our Friend." Alexandra had mixed feelings about this, but when her husband had really made up his mind, she bowed to him—a fact that should be kept in mind as this story progresses. The parting was difficult, but the French mystic eased it by giving the empress a farewell present: an icon with a small bell that would ring, he assured her, when an evil person approached. The empress treasured the gift. Years later, writing to her husband, she referred to the "image with the bell [that will] warn me against those that are not right & will keep them fr. approaching, I shall feel [their evil] & thus guard you fr. them." Nazier-Vachot also left a prophecy: "Someday you will have another friend like me who will speak to you of God." Nazier-Vachot died in 1905, soon after returning to France.

• • •

On July 30, 1904, Alexandra finally gave birth to a son. "An unforgettable, great day for us," Nicholas wrote in his diary—"we were clearly visited by God's grace." Nicholas named the child Alexis, in honor of the second Romanov tsar. Unlike his famous son Peter the Great, Alexis was a traditional ruler who prized religion over modernity and science. Nicholas II was making a political statement: he was expressing his desire to return to an uncomplicated past when autocrats ruled and their subjects showed unswerving loyalty to the throne.

"Alexis was the center of his family, the focus of all its hopes and affections," wrote one of the imperial tutors. "He was the pride and joy of his parents." But joy quickly yielded to despair. "Alix and I have been very much worried," Nicholas wrote six weeks after Alexis's birth. "A hemorrhage began this morning without the slightest cause from the navel of our small Alexis. It lasted with but a few interruptions until evening." The bleeding stopped on the third day. But as the tsarevich crawled and took the normal tumbles of childhood in the following months, his limbs displayed ugly, dark bruises. When he fell from his baby carriage just before his first birthday, the cries were unusually piercing. Then came the diagnosis: Alexis had hemophilia.

"Your Majesty must realize," Dr. Sergei Fedorov warned, "that the Tsarevich will never be completely cured of his disease. The attacks of hemophilia will recur now and then. Strenuous measures of protection will have to be taken to guard the Heir against falls, cuts and scratches, because the slightest bleeding may prove fatal."

Hemophilia is a hereditary disorder. Mothers who are carriers of the defective gene transmit hemophilia to their sons at a statistical ratio of one in two births. This genetic peculiarity made Alexis's blood deficient in the clotting factor needed for normal coagulation; even a minor cut might take hours or days to heal. But the greatest danger came from minor blows that might—or might not—trigger massive internal hemorrhages. If a surgeon operated to repair the damage, his patient would bleed to death. There were certainly painkillers available at this time, not the least of which were morphine, opium, and cocaine. There is some evidence that various members of the Romanov family used them on themselves, but apparently, for some reason, they did not give them to Alexis. They usually let his bouts with hemophilia run their painful course, which meant that he was forced to endure the most profound suffering imaginable.

"This disease is not in our family," Queen Victoria protested in bewilderment when her son, Leopold, displayed the terrible symptoms of hemophilia soon after he was born in 1853. Indeed "Granny" is often blamed for bringing hemophilia into the royal houses of Europe. The disorder either came from a spontaneous mutation in her genetic material or in the X chromosome that she inherited from her father. At any rate, Leopold had the disorder while Alice and Beatrice, his sisters, were carriers. Beatrice introduced hemophilia into the Spanish royal family. Alice, of course, was the mother of Alexandra, the future empress of Russia. Alice also transmitted the disease to her son, Friedrich, who died of a hemorrhage when he was two. Alice's daughter Irene married Kaiser Wilhelm II's brother, Heinrich; two of their sons were hemophiliacs. The first, Prince Waldemar, was born in 1889 and struggled with hemophiliac attacks until he died in 1945. The second, Prince Heinrich, perished at four, only a few days before Alexis was born in 1904. The cause was internal bleeding—the final reward for a lifetime of misery.

Alexandra must have had some understanding of hemophilia. It was beginning to be discussed at this time; surely her family had some notion of its dangers. Alexandra had an uncle, a brother, and two nephews who were hemophiliacs. Did she wonder if she might transmit it to her sons? There is no evidence that Nicholas or Alexandra ever considered that possibility; the news of their son's disease seems to have been a total surprise, and it devastated them. Nicholas accepted his son's illness with the same passivity that marked his entire life, but his wife searched into the meaning of such developments. She realized that she was responsible for Alexis's condition.

"Life lost all meaning for the imperial parents," Alexander Michaelovich recalled. "My wife and I were afraid to smile in their presence. When visiting the palace, we acted as we would in a house of mourning." Alexandra refused to accept "expert medical opinion" as the final word. She rambled endlessly about what she thought was the ignorance of physicians. She was convinced that prayer was the answer to life's problems, but those who prayed had to be worthy—and they had to manifest the proper faith. Perhaps Alexandra needed someone who was closer to God than she seemed to be—a man or a woman who would be her intercessor, someone who could safeguard the health of the tsarevich and defeat those who opposed autocracy and her husband.

And so a young boy's misfortune set the stage for a miracle worker.

4

The New Rasputin

W
E HAD TEA WITH MILITSA AND STANA," the tsar
wrote in his diary under November 1, 1905. "We made
the acquaintance of a man of God—Gregory, from Tobolsk province."
Nicholas and Alexandra had just met Rasputin at Sergeevka, the
Montenegrins' elegant villa at Peterhof. The emperor and his wife
had no idea of the remarkable friendship they would forge with
the man they had just met—or that he would play a major role in
their downfall.

It took two years for the meeting to take place. In 1903, when
Feofan presented Rasputin to the Montenegrin sisters, the peasant was anxious to use these important people to meet the tsar and
his family. The sisters did not think the time was right for that:
Dr. Philippe Nazier-Vachot was still on the scene, so Nicholas and
Alexandra were not likely to shower a new man (such as Rasputin)
with the attention they were giving their French visitor. But when
Rasputin returned to the capital two years later, in 1905, Philippe
was gone. (He died that year in France.) Anastasia and Militsa knew
that Alexandra was depressed over the way her relationship ended
with Nazier-Vachot, so this seemed to be the right time to bring
Rasputin forward. And so, at four o'clock on a gorgeous afternoon
in the autumn of 1905, Nicholas and Alexandra got ready to meet a
"man of God from Tobolsk province."

The Montenegrin sisters. Militsa (left) and her younger sister, Anastasia (right), introduced Rasputin to the tsar and his wife on November 1, 1905. Anastasia was married to the tsar's cousin, Nicholas Nicholaevich (known to the family as "Nicholasha"); Militsa was married to the tsar's cousin, Peter Nicholaevich.

Anastasia and Militsa certainly had worldly motives for advancing Rasputin. They assumed that he would be grateful and subservient—that he would sing their praises to the imperial family and pass along useful information about the ever-shifting political scene at Tsarskoye Selo. The sisters also had an idealistic streak. They were sincere in their religious passions, and that made them anxious to share their new friend with Alexandra. Rasputin reminded them of an Old Testament prophet. They found his exposition of the Gospels and especially the Apocalypse "penetrating and original." Rasputin assured them he could heal sickness, foretell the future, and charm away unhappiness. They were thrilled to finally find—as they put it—the "miracle worker" their hearts had been seeking for so long.

They were also anxious to control Rasputin. They explained to him that he was a simple fellow, and he would crash if he tried to operate on his own. He must *never* try to contact the imperial family on his own. Rasputin must have laughed at this game. One more time, his "betters" were trying to exploit him, and (as usual) they underestimated him; they failed to see that Rasputin was crafty and conniving. As usual, he played along, but he was ready to discard old allies as soon as their usefulness had passed. In the end, he would turn the tables on them.

Rasputin must have experienced a moment of triumph when he actually met the tsar, but Gregory was totally relaxed and self-confident. He addressed the imperial couple as "Batyushka" and "Matushka"—"Little Father" and "Little Mother"—the names peasants used in referring to their sovereign and his consort. In speaking with them, Rasputin used *ty*, the form of "you" that Russians reserve for family members and friends, rather than *vy*, which designates people of superior status. Nicholas and Alexandra hated stuffy, insincere people—they took to this informality right away.

Eight months passed before Nicholas and Alexandra met Rasputin again—he seems to have spent the winter in Pokrovskoye. When he returned to the capital, he sent a telegram, saying, "Father Tsar. Having arrived in this city from Siberia, I would like to bring you an icon of the Holy Righteous Man Simeon of Verkhoturye, the Miracle Worker." The imperial couple invited Rasputin to have tea with them on July 18, 1906.

The meeting must have gone well, for on Friday, October 12, 1906, Rasputin was again invited to the palace. Nicholas and Alexandra were always interested in hearing what they wanted to think was a "voice of the Russian people." Rasputin was sufficiently cunning to satisfy their expectations. Indeed, this visit seems to have been the turning point in his career, for after tea, Rasputin was presented to the tsar's daughters and their two-year-old brother, Alexis. Nicholas II's diary mentions that his son had been unwell at this time and was restless.

Maria Rasputin thought that her father prayed for Alexis's health for the first time in 1906. If so, October 12 might have been the date, since four days later, on October 16, 1906, Nicholas involved Rasputin in a troubled situation that had recently befallen Peter Stolypin. A terrorist bomb had demolished the prime minister's summer villa in August 1906, killing thirty-two people and seriously wounding others, including his fourteen-year-old daughter, Natalya. The tsar wrote Stolypin a note, noting that Rasputin had recently visited his family and "made a remarkably strong impression both on Her Majesty and me, so that our conversation with him lasted for more than an hour instead of five minutes." The emperor explained that the peasant had healing gifts, and it might be useful for him to visit Natalya and pray for her. Stolypin did as requested, although he was not present and no healing took place.

When Rasputin left Alexander Palace on October 12, the tsar asked Prince Putyatin, an aide, for his opinion of the visitor. Putyatin replied that he found the peasant to be insincere and unbalanced. Nicholas dismissed Putyatin with a curt nod and never again mentioned Rasputin to him.

Immediately after this visit Princess Elizabeth Naryshkina-Kurakina, one of the empress's ladies-in-waiting, recalled that from this time the name "Rasputin" came to be heard at Alexander Palace. This adds weight to the argument that the meeting of October 12 was the first time Rasputin was asked to pray for the health of the tsarevich. Rasputin was crossing the line that separated just another wandering pilgrim from a miracle worker. "Militsa and Stana dined with us," the tsar noted on December 9, 1906. "We talked about Gregory the whole evening."

Six days later, on December 15, it was Rasputin's turn to ask Nicholas for a favor: he petitioned the tsar to legally modify his name. The peasant explained that six families in Pokrovskoye bore the surname Rasputin, and this was producing "every sort of confusion." Rasputin asked Nicholas "to end this confusion by permitting me and my descendents to take the name Rasputin-Novyi," which means "Rasputin-New" or even the "New Rasputin." Nicholas not only approved the request; he also wrote on the petition that "His Majesty has deigned to express his *particular* desire that this request be granted." Indeed, it was expedited; the edict proclaiming the change was dated December 22, 1906. Russia was known for its fumbling bureaucracy, but seven days was speedy service by any reasonable standard. The tsar's attention to the matter suggests that he had come to look upon Rasputin in a special way by December 1906.

Rasputin's request was probably provoked by the rumors that his family was so poor that it had no surname. His fellow villagers supposedly named him Rasputin because of his wasted ways. The notion that the name *Rasputin* came from "to be drunken or debauched" has become legendary—and it bothered his supporters. Nicholas and Alexandra referred to the peasant as "Gregory" or "Our Friend," but never "Rasputin." Alexandra once complained in a letter to her husband that a mutual acquaintance was using the old surname. In making her point, the empress wrote "Rasput."—it might seem that she found the name to be so disagreeable that she could not bring herself to complete it. "I don't like it," she wrote of her friend's practice, "& I will try & get him out of this habit."

Although it was Rasputin who asked that he be permitted to adopt the name "Novyi" or "Novykh," he would not admit that it was his idea. Rasputin claimed that the first time he entered the imperial nursery, Alexis jumped up and down in his crib, crying out, "New! New!" This was not true, and it was typical of Rasputin to tell other lies that contradicted one another. Sometimes he boasted that Nicholas named him Novyi without even asking permission. As if this would prove the point, Rasputin would whisk out his internal passport to show that it did indeed identify the bearer as "Rasputin-Novyi." Novyi is not a Russian name, and a man who would be taking it would seem to have been breaking with his past and tradition. In 1906, Rasputin was a new man in a new environment, meeting new people and savoring new experiences. He was anxious to forge a new identity based on the present, not the past.

Rasputin returned to the palace again on April 6, 1907, and June 19. On one of these occasions—probably the latter—he found Alexis in terrible agony. Olga, the tsar's younger sister, recalled that her nephew had fallen and was suffering an internal hemorrhage. "Within a few hours the child was racked with excruciating pain." The doctors were powerless. Late that night, Alexandra sent for Rasputin. The next morning, Olga found her nephew well. Alexandra told her that Rasputin had come in the night and prayed for her son.

Alexandra believed that God had sent Rasputin to her. She was convinced of the power of prayer. A lady-in-waiting once expressed anger at a news report that certain children had died because their parents treated their illnesses with prayer, not medicine. "They did not pray hard enough!" Alexandra replied. "Had their prayers been fervent, the children would have recovered!"

This was a sad opinion, actually, considering that Alexandra constantly prayed for her son without producing the results she sought so desperately. It also seems that she wondered if her son's tragedy was a punishment for her sins. Princess Elizabeth Naryshkina-Kurakina thought that Rasputin practiced emotional blackmail in this touchy area. She claims that he "influenced the Empress mainly through his insistence on her guilt." Rasputin was probably too clever to do that directly. If the subject came up, he probably assured the empress that her son's misfortune was *not* a judgment from God, knowing that whatever concerns remained would work to his advantage. It would be more prudent for him to encourage Nicholas and Alexandra to think that their son's life would be secure as long as he was on hand. And what if he were gone? Let them ponder that possibility.

• • •

Rasputin was an exotic figure—a "simple, semi-literate fellow" whose very strangeness garnered interest and respect, and it would have taken a strong man to resist the attention and flattery that came his way. Life in the capital increasingly overwhelmed the unsophisticated peasant. The accolades confirmed what Rasputin already believed: that he was meant to do great things. Money did not motivate him so much as the conviction that God had brought him to the capital to serve the tsar and safeguard the tsarevich. Some have dismissed Rasputin as a mere adventurer, a charlatan who abused people's trust; but the true story was far more complicated than that. "At a first glance, he appeared to be a typical peasant from the frozen North," one lady recalled, "but his eyes held mine, those shining steel-like eyes which seemed to read one's inmost thoughts."

Ever an actor, Rasputin played his roles quite well. Knowing that the worldly-wise aristocrats he encountered would not be impressed with humility or flattery, he seized control of every situation. Entering the house of Baroness Uexkuell, Rasputin glanced about and chastised her, saying, "What's this, little mother, pictures on your walls like a museum? You could feed five villages of starving people with what's on a single wall. Just imagine how the peasants go without food!"

Guilt was a powerful weapon. Ignoring the rules that dictated how peasants should behave with rich and powerful people, he addressed them as *ty*, rather than *vy*. He jumped from topic to topic, offering bits of biblical wisdom punctuated with observations about society, spiritual exhortations, and personal questions. "The way you live isn't right!" he repeatedly intoned. "You must have love—that's it! So, what's going on with you?" If that kind of discourse alienated most people, some found it compelling: "Father Gregory has the key to life," they said, "he speaks the truth and discerns everything."

Rasputin liked to shock people. He loved to describe the sex life of horses and to pull a distinguished lady toward him, whispering (almost menacingly), "Come, my lovely mare!" He insisted that his village was the best place in the world to commune with God. Guilt again—showing his hands, he barked, "They're rough, hard work made 'em like that!" His listeners, by contrast, had soft lives. "You must be simpler, far simpler," he intoned. "Come with me in the summer to Pokrovskoye, to the open spaces of Siberia. We will catch fish and work in the fields. And then you will really learn to understand God."

Rasputin was not handsome, but he had an electric spark that simultaneously captivated and repelled women. He made no distinction between a princess and a peasant. When Nicholas II presented his sister, Olga, to the starets at Alexander Palace one evening, Rasputin immediately launched into his litany of prying questions. "Are you happy? Do you love your husband? Why isn't he here? Why don't you have children?" Olga was embarrassed, but Rasputin did not back off. Joining her on the sofa a bit later, he put his arm around her shoulder and began stroking it—how could he have been so brazen! Olga jumped up and joined her brother and his wife, who "looked rather uncomfortable." This was a remarkable episode—and it certainly dispels the notion that Nicholas and Alexandra were ignorant of the "real Rasputin."

The drawing rooms of Saint Petersburg were full of ladies whose husbands cheated on them. They sought meaning in social life and charitable activities—sad alternatives to family happiness. Rasputin understood their needs. He listened to their stories and nodded in consolation, providing validation and sympathy. He asked questions and gave advice, but in these early years (at least) he did not take advantage of their emotional fragility. He gave many a measure of hope that they had long abandoned.

Several women were totally committed to Rasputin: they tended to his needs, showered him with gifts, arranged his schedule, and listened eagerly to each word he spoke. They even tried to emulate his mannerisms. He called them his "little ladies."

Olga Lokhtina was the first of this group. When this aristocratic lady met Rasputin in November 1905, she was forty and, in her own words, "disenchanted with the secular world." She was also nearly incapacitated by a severe and chronic intestinal flu. Rasputin came to her bed and prayed. "I felt well," she recalled, "and from that time I was free of my illness." Lokhtina and her husband invited Rasputin to stay at their fashionable apartment. Acting as his secretary, Lokhtina arranged his appointments and answered letters that Rasputin signed with a large, awkward "G." Lokhtina also visited the empress at Tsarskoye Selo, regaling her with tales of the peasant's wise sayings and amazing character.

Akilina Laptinskaya was another member of Rasputin's inner circle. Thirty-one and single when they met, Laptinskaya was a Ukrainian peasant and a trained nurse who saw Rasputin through illnesses and hangovers. She told the commission that investigated Rasputin for heresy in 1907 that he had "pure love" in his heart; she saw nothing wrong in the "affectionate way" he treated the women who gathered around him.

Khioniya Berlatskaya was another devotee. Her husband, an army lieutenant, was shattered by her adultery and committed suicide. When Berlatskaya came to Rasputin, she was thirty and brimming with guilt; he did not try to take advantage of her. He advised her to seek God's mercy and pray for the strength to resist future temptation. All the "little ladies" denied having sex with Rasputin, and they were probably telling the truth, at least in these early years. They insisted that he "taught his followers how to love with a totally clear conscience," whatever *that* meant. Yes—they called him "Father Gregory," but only in jest—so they claimed. The kisses, caresses, and even the trips to the bathhouse "did not seem improper or strange to any of us," said Lokhtina. "Bad and dirty thoughts," she added, "occur only to bad people."

Rasputin's most important convert was Anna Vyrubova, a woman of vast contradictions and childish character. She was born in 1884. Her father, Alexander Taneyev, was an official in Nicholas II's Chancery and an amateur composer whose works are still performed in Russia. Her mother was a Tolstoy and a direct descendant of Field Marshal Kutuzov. Prince Felix Yusupov described Vyrubova as "tall and stout with a puffy, shiny face, and no charm whatsoever." He dismissed her as "not at all intelligent, though she was extremely crafty and rather sly." In 1903 she was presented at court and became a maid of honor with the title of Fräulein.

The lonely empress recognized a kindred spirit in the young woman. They became friends, and Vyrubova even joined the imperial family on their annual Baltic cruises. Alexandra prized Anna's uncomplicated manner, while Anna was excited over her sudden and unexpected entry to the private world of the tsar. The empress demanded—and got—her complete devotion. No one could quite understand why the empress preferred Anna's company to that of the sophisticated ladies of Saint Petersburg, and jealousy burst forth in spiteful comments as well as rumors that she and Alexandra were lesbian lovers.

An unfortunate marriage cemented Anna's relationship with the empress and brought her into Rasputin's growing circle. Anna attracted the attentions of Lieutenant Alexander Vyrubov in the fall of 1906. He pursued her with a zeal that suggested he foresaw career benefits in marrying a woman so close to the imperial family. Although Anna was not in love, everyone—her parents, friends, and even the empress—urged her to accept his proposal. She shared her doubts with Grand Duchess Militsa, who urged her to seek Rasputin's guidance. The meeting took place at Militsa's palace on the English Embankment, one of the most fashionable streets in Saint Petersburg.

Anna found Rasputin to be an "elderly peasant, thin, with a pale face, long hair and an unkempt beard." He was wearing a "long peasant coat [that was] black and rather shabby from hard wear and much travel." He had the "most extraordinary eyes, large, light, brilliant, set deep within their sockets, and apparently capable of seeing into the very mind and soul of a person." "I asked for his advice about my marriage," she testified. "He told me that I should marry," although he also predicted that the union would be unhappy.

Anna and Alexander were married on April 30, 1907. Neither was ready for marriage, at least not to each other. The bride claimed that Vyrubov was a deranged alcoholic who beat her—and was impotent. The truth is murkier. Anna presented herself as she wished to be seen: the innocent victim of an unstable, brutish husband. She apparently refused to have sex with him, for a medical exam in 1917 established her virginity while he eventually fathered children. Alexander Vyrubov was probably willing to endure the situation to advance his career, but that did not happen. Anna ignored her husband in favor of the empress, and when he complained, she locked him out of their house. Divorce in 1908 finally brought this sad marital misadventure to an end.

Free of a burdensome union, Anna Vyrubova now devoted herself entirely to the empress, though Alexandra refused to give her a position at court. In her memoirs Anna claimed that she was poor—her sole asset was supposedly a small villa two hundred yards from Alexander Palace, at 2 Church Street. As Anna's influence grew, office seekers and shady people of every description made their way to this little yellow house. Alexander Protopopov, the last imperial minister of the interior, called it the "portico to power." Anna was obsessive about her close relationship with Alexandra; if the empress could not see her for a day, Anna pouted. Even Alexandra found the endless devotion wearying, and at times she handled her friend in "much the same way that one treats a helpless child."

Anna came to believe wholeheartedly in Rasputin, calling him a "saint who uttered Heaven-inspired words." He seemed infallible—he was "an intelligent person, a person with natural gifts, and I loved to listen to him." One wonders how much of Anna's faith in Rasputin was shaped by Alexandra's attitude; Vyrubova realized that Rasputin occupied a unique place in the empress's life. Yet Anna had her own devotion to Rasputin. She was impressed by his knowledge: Rasputin "knew all holy writing, the Bible, everything," she said, even though he lacked a formal education.

No one understood Rasputin and the empress better than Anna Vyrubova, and immature though she might have been, she offered an authoritative explanation for their relationship. "Let any American mother," she said, "imagine that she had an only son who had come into the world a weakling, one whose life had always hung on a thread, and that that child had suddenly and miraculously been restored to health. Let her suppose that the person who did this wonderful thing was not a doctor but a monk of her own church. Wouldn't it be natural for that mother to regard the man with almost superstitious gratitude for the rest of her life? Wouldn't she . . . want to keep the monk near her, at least until the child grew up, to have the benefit of his advice and help in case of return of the illness? Well, that is the whole truth about the Empress and Rasputin."

5

The Church Strikes Back

RASPUTIN RETURNED TO POKROVSKOYE a conquering hero in September 1907. Ridicule and doubt were in the past. "I came home joyful!" he declared, bragging about his money, followers, and friendship with the imperial family. Four admirers accompanied him: Olga Lokhtina, Khioniya Berlatskaya, Akilina Laptinskaya, and Zinaida Manshtedt, the wife of a high official. The old town had never seen anything like it.

Lokhtina was amazed to see that Praskovaya fell at Rasputin's feet when she welcomed him home. Praskovaya always gave in when differences surfaced with her husband, even when it was clear that she was in the right. Pressed on the matter, she replied philosophically, "A husband and wife have to live with one heart. Sometimes you yield, and sometimes they do."

"I used to live in a peasant hut, but now I have a really big house," Rasputin told Feofan when he visited Pokrovskoye. Militsa the Montenegrin princess gave Rasputin money to buy this home from a pilot on the Tura River. It was a traditional, wooden, two-story house with flower boxes at the carved wood windows and a tin roof. A gated fence surrounded the property, which extended to the house of Gregory's father and its scrappy garden. Efim could have lived with his son after his wife, Anna, died in 1904, but the old man preferred to remain independent. Rasputin used the money that remained after the purchase to decorate and improve his new home.

Rasputin and his family lived on the ground floor while the upper rooms were furnished for the guests that he knew would soon be arriving. A piano graced its drawing room, along with a plush sofa, a gramophone, an expensive desk, and a large floor clock encased in a beautiful ebony cabinet. The walls were covered with icons and prints, including portraits of Nicholas and Alexandra. An expensive chandelier swung above the enormous carpet—"It cost 600 rubles!" Rasputin boasted. Feofan told the Investigatory Commission in 1917 that the whole scene revealed a "semi-indigent peasant's notion of how rich people lived in the cities."

Rasputin's major assets consisted of his house with the farm and its livestock. Contrary to popular belief, Rasputin got little financial benefit from his friendship with the imperial family—he relied on gifts from his followers for everyday needs. He was close to the Montenegrin sisters from 1906 to 1908; they joined other wealthy people in giving him lavish support that permitted him to impress people with his generosity. The people of Pokrovskoye referred to him as "Gospodin"—a "Noble Lord"—in recognition of his new and exalted status.

"All the kids had a holiday when Granddaddy Grisha returned home," one villager recalled. "He gave us fruit drops and spice cakes. He didn't put the money in our hands, but he wrote notes to the storekeeper to give the kids whatever it was they needed—a coat or boots—and he paid for all of it." Another woman added that "Rasputin helped his fellow villagers as soon as he came back to town." He gave people the money to buy horses and cows; he built houses for poor families and paid for funerals. The drunken scoundrel who had so often stolen his wife's grocery money to buy alcohol was now being hailed as "righteous," "perspicacious," and "wise."

The plight of one villager particularly touched Rasputin's heart. She was a poor woman who could not buy the clothes her daughters needed to attend school, so they were forced to stay at home. She asked Rasputin to buy the leather for a single pair of shoes so that at least one of the girls could get an education. Rasputin's own lack of formal instruction made him value learning, and so he agreed. But he planned a surprise: he ordered the leather needed for all the girls to have shoes. When Rasputin learned that the merchant gave the mother the material for just one pair, he was livid—and loud. The merchant promptly delivered everything that Rasputin had bought.

Rasputin was proud of his position at court, but it brought the surveillance of the police in the capital and his hometown. The tsar's police routinely monitored the mail and activities of important people, including members of the Romanov family. The police were automatically interested in an obscure peasant who popped up in Saint Petersburg and was suddenly such a hit with powerful people. They followed Rasputin's movements, read his correspondence, and wrote reports that yield valuable information today.

A police report dated January 7, 1910, for example, notes that Rasputin still "farms regularly and conducts his life in the manner of his fellow villagers." But good fortune was affecting the peasant. "Perhaps success did not affect Rasputin immediately, but as it grew he has become arrogant and characterized by satanic pride and 'demonic charm.'" Rasputin had never been a humble man, and the embrace of high society along with Nicholas II's friendship inflated his ego. He bragged about his house and its furnishings, and he constantly reminded villagers of his standing with the imperial family. "See the gold cross?" he asked a visitor. "It's got 'N' stamped on it. The Tsar gave it—did it to honor me." He showed icons that Nicholas and Alexandra gave him along with little jeweled Easter eggs and elegant lanterns hanging in his house. "Her Majesty sewed this shirt for me!" Rasputin added. "I got other shirts she sewed."

The police report quoted above expressed the opinion that Rasputin's "devotion and Godly life clashed with many of his actions and statements." He disdained his fellow villagers: "I'm leaving Pokrovskoye once and for all," he wrote in one letter. "No one understands a thing in this village, you see." A church official noted that Rasputin was a "poorly educated man from the common people." He was eager to tell everyone about his "visits to the courts of the Grand Dukes and other important figures."

Many people in Pokrovskoye embraced Rasputin as the Bountiful Father, but others did not share that attitude, and they displayed open animosity. "I offered to help the priests but they tried to ruin me," he declared. "They accused me of heresy and things so strange I couldn't even tell you about 'em because they don't make any sense. The enemy's powerful, and he dug a pit to catch people, not to do anything good. They accused me of being the champion of the lowest and most vile sect, and the church leaders rose up against me in every sort of way."

The issue began when Rasputin donated 5,000 rubles to beautify the Church of Our Lady of Pokrovskoye. Nicholas II actually provided the money, probably because he wanted to shore up Rasputin's authority in his hometown. Rasputin had the privilege of deciding how it would be spent. He ordered a gilded silver cross for the altar, as well as four gilded silver lamps to illuminate the iconostasis, and a large gold cross "like people wear on their necks" for the sanctuary. Rasputin had the miracle-working icon in the church decorated and made more secure. Many grumbled that if Rasputin really wanted to help the town, he might have donated the money to improve the school instead of trying to impress—and perhaps influence—local church officials into leaving him alone.

The clergy disliked Rasputin before his conversion, and they doubted his sincerity after it. They were unimpressed by the claim that God had selected him for some great purpose. They were bothered by the fact that Rasputin formed his own group, and it was so secretive. Then there was the familiarity with women—as well as the strange hymns that came from his root cellar and such Khlyst salutations as "Brother" and "Sister." It was time to put Rasputin in his place.

Fathers Peter Ostroumov and Feodor Chemagin of Pokrovskoye formally denounced Rasputin as a heretic to Bishop Anthony of Tobolsk in early September 1907. They charged that "Gregory Novyi has taken on the role of special mentor, spiritual leader, prayer guide, counselor and comforter. He is known for spiritually uplifting conversations, saying there is 'much love in me' and 'I love everybody.' He has been invited to give advice on the spiritual life." This last sentence might indicate the real problem: Rasputin was upstaging the priests.

The theory that Militsa and Anastasia secretly initiated the investigation is not convincing. Supposedly the sisters resented Rasputin's increasing influence over the empress and tried to use the old rumors against him to decrease his influence with Alexandra. Although Anna Vyrubova diminished the importance of the sisters in Alexandra's life, the Montenegrins still frequented the palace. Rasputin supported Anastasia in divorcing her first husband and taking as a new spouse the brother of her sister's husband, Grand Duke Nicholas Nicholaevich, known in society as "Nicholasha." Militsa and Anastasia were still among Rasputin's most vocal supporters in 1907, when the investigation took place. They had just paid for Rasputin's new house and its furnishings. All in all, it seems unlikely that the Montenegrin sisters were behind the investigation.

Bishop Anthony of Tobolsk was so ready to act that one wonders if *he* was not the instigator. He certainly had good reason to be angry: Anthony was one of the bishops who did not think that Seraphim, a holy man of Sarov who died in 1833, deserved to be recognized as a saint. Nicholas ignored these objections and forced the canonization through the Holy Synod in 1903. He then punished Anthony by transferring him from Tambov (a pleasant place in southern Russia) to the frozen wilds of western Siberia. Perhaps Anthony saw striking out at Rasputin as a way to even the score against Nicholas II.

At any rate, Anthony announced on September 6, 1907, that he was launching an investigation against Rasputin for "spreading false, *Khlyst*-like doctrines and forming a society of followers of this false doctrine." It was not against the law to belong to the Khlysty after Russians gained civil liberties in the Revolution of 1905; but if it could be established that Rasputin was a member of a heretical sect, he could have been excommunicated. Investigators immediately swooped down on Pokrovskoye to search the homes of Gregory and his father. Agents spent six months interrogating everyone from family members to neighbors and associates. Some claimed that Rasputin converted to the Khlysty while working at a factory in Perm, although there is no evidence that Rasputin had ever lived in the city for a long period.

Gossips reported that people "dressed in black coats" and "white head scarves" gathered for services at Rasputin's house, and that he wore a "monastic-type black cassock with a gold pectoral cross." They testified that the music coming from their late-night meetings was "strange"—its melodies and harmonies came from the sect's "obscure manuscripts and publications," not the Orthodox Church. Their songs included "Zion Sleeps" and "The Mountains of Mt. Athos"—famous Khlyst hymns. Everyone agreed that Rasputin, a basso profundo, sang well.

Since the inquisitors were not finding much evidence that Rasputin was a Khlyst, their investigation took a new direction: Rasputin supposedly used religion to gratify his passions. He and his female followers were known to "walk hand in hand" in Pokrovskoye; he "kisses, pets, strokes and embraces them" and gave them such pet names as "Khonei," "Elya," and "Zinochka." Father Chemagin testified that one day he *just happened* to see Rasputin "returning wet from the bathhouse, followed by several women who were staying with him and were also wet and steamy." Rasputin made light of all this, admitting that he liked to "hug and kiss" the "little ladies" and "often accompanied them to the bathhouse." Then there were those young, unmarried women who lived in Rasputin's house. Praskovaya claimed that they worked for her, but Chemagin sensed that something improper was taking place.

Rasputin's detractors charged that he led a "disorderly life," and that his mannerisms during the Liturgy were distracting. They suspected that his beliefs departed from Orthodoxy, although they could not explain how. A tale surfaced about a woman from Praskovaya's hometown of Dubrovino who died of consumption because Rasputin (supposedly) forced her to walk barefoot on a pilgrimage in winter. But no one knew her name or anything more about her.

Rasputin's enemies must have been astounded when Bishop Anthony's report (dated May 15, 1908) announced that the investigation had failed to establish that Rasputin was—or was not—a Khlyst. The bishop obviously hoped to reach that conclusion, but the facts as presented to him did not permit it. Anthony complained about the sloppy work of his agents. They did not find a whip or any of the "symbols and icons" that would suggest that Rasputin might be a Khlyst. They did not know that the sect's celebrations were held in "bath houses, barns, cellars, threshing floors, and even underground, but never in the leader's house." The inquisitors ignored the outbuildings and did not search for the "holy books" used in Khlyst services. "They did not find a notebook or a single verse that might have been sung at the gatherings held by Gregory Novyi."

The bishop admitted that under these circumstances, he could only reach obvious (and bland) conclusions: Rasputin had a religious society that gathered at night; he read from the Bible and taught them; they sang and prayed. "But the evidence does not disclose what happens at these meetings or what he teaches at them. Isolated phrases from his teachings might seem to be close to Khlyst teaching. But the proceedings do not offer a case that is sufficiently solid for us to conclude that it represents the Khlyst heresy."

The bishop's report actually praised Rasputin. He was "no stranger to the Orthodox Church but goes to God's temple regularly and sings in the choir of his parish church. . . . He pays devotions to each icon in the Church; he strictly observes the fasts; he unfailingly fulfills the Christian duty to go to confession and to receive Holy Communion; he contributes to the Church. And his entire family does the same."

The report endorses religious pluralism; this was perhaps the greatest surprise. Although it would seem that Anthony was not compelled to do it, he recognized Rasputin's right to form "his own group apart from Orthodoxy. . . . It is a particular society with its own religious-moral views and way of life. Gregory Novyi is their special mentor, spiritual leader, prayer guide, counselor and comforter"; he "gives advice on the spiritual life" and is known for his "spiritually uplifting conversations." The report noted that he often said, "I love everybody." "He teaches his followers to love each other and do good."

Although the evidence suggested that Rasputin was sincere, Anthony wondered if he was truly a "special, elected man of God, a teacher and prayer guide." "His display of piety and devotion to the Orthodox Church" might have been "simply external, designed to hide the fact that he is a false teacher, a propagator . . . of the dangerous and evil *Khlysty* teaching." The report suggests that the "question of Rasputin's ties to the Khlysty should be the subject of a new inquest led by an experienced and informed man, such as a missionary against the sectarians."

An uneasy détente settled over Rasputin's relations with local church leaders after the church inquest. Just four months before the investigation, Father Ostroumov at a parish meeting had formally thanked Rasputin for his generosity to the church. Anthony must have hated to do it, but on June 1, 1908, the *Tobolsk Diocese News* finally published an article—and it was on the front page—in which the authorities of Tobolsk diocese likewise expressed gratitude "to Gregory Novyi (he is also known as Rasputin) for his goodness to the peasants of the Pokrovskoye [and his] sacrifices to the parish church." The effort of the local priests to discipline their most troublesome parishioner had failed.

Rasputin avoided Ostroumov and Chemagin in the months following the report. Anthony still hoped to link Rasputin to the Khlysty, and he had three local priests send monthly bulletins on Rasputin's activities. The reports are amazingly objective—this might also be surprising: Rasputin received mild criticism and frequent praise. Ostroumov mentions a pilgrimage Rasputin made to the Abalak Monastery in 1911, as well as trips to Tobolsk and Saint Petersburg. Father Ostroumov noted that Rasputin had just toured the area, passing out a recently published "brochure" (with his picture) to his fellow peasants. "As for service to God," the priest wrote, "he goes to church as strictly as before, and he farms." He also described Rasputin as a "religious man; he goes to church regularly, though lately he has been saying that going to church is only a formality."

Rasputin was indeed disillusioned with organized religion—he complained that the Church was full of false, spiritually corrupt leaders. He thought that most priests "sing and read in a crude, loud way, like a peasant chopping wood with an axe." Although Rasputin still went to "God's temple," he was irritated by the members of the clergy who used guilt and fear to control people. Rasputin believed that love should be the cornerstone of religion. He complained that all too many priests displayed external piety and inner hypocrisy, leaving no room for the joy of salvation.

Rasputin's experiences shaped those sentiments. The quest for meaning was more important to him than gratifying his desires, at least in the period from 1906 to 1911. Rasputin was bold in his sins and in his spirituality. He tried to recapture the past—to reconnect with the love he had felt in moments of religious ecstasy. At first the search came through prayer and contemplation; from 1912 on he used sex and alcohol.

Rasputin turned to the writings of the saints and church fathers as he sought his own way. His education was minimal, but his keen mind sought an understanding of how others handled the missions to which they were called. His studies included Saint Augustine and especially his namesake, Saint Gregory of Nyssa. Rasputin hoped that uncovering their secrets and emulating their lives would aid his own search.

Praskovaya was always at Rasputin's side—keeping house, tending the children, and comforting her restless, ambitious husband. Aaron Simanovich wrote that his old boss "was quite considerate of his wife. They lived in sincere friendship and never quarreled." When Praskovaya was showing a couple around Pokrovskoye one day, they came upon her husband "exorcising a demon"—that is, having sex with a female devotee. The visitors were appalled, but Praskovaya was not surprised or even displeased. "Each man must bear his cross," she said, "and this is his."

Rasputin carried a cross—what a remarkable observation. Most people then and now have supposed that Rasputin enjoyed his sexual escapades, but Praskovaya understood that it was a burden. What superficial observers assumed was pleasure was actually an ordeal. Praskovaya agreed that her husband was on a mission from God and that sex with other women was part of it. She knew that Rasputin battled temptation—and was downcast when he failed. But Praskovaya was always there. In the words of a friend, she was a "charming, sensible woman."

6

The Romanovs' Holy Fool

IT WAS TOO EARLY FOR RASPUTIN to celebrate victory over his enemies in the Church. Even as he lingered in Pokrovskoye another campaign against him was being hatched in Saint Petersburg. This time the stakes were even higher, and there would be no presumption of innocence. Peter Stolypin, the prime minister, had decided to bring Rasputin's political career to a sudden end.

Rasputin's trips to Tsarskoye Selo drew the attention of the police. His visits were certainly not secret. People could see Rasputin at the Tsarskoye Selo railroad station; his car passed through public streets and was detained at various barriers and gates. Although Rasputin used a side entrance of Alexander Palace, he waited at checkpoints while the officer on duty telephoned for permission to admit him. Rasputin's movements were open and closely observed.

People in government were on edge in those years. The regime had barely survived war and revolution; members of the imperial family faced assassination when they left their estates. One agent of the Okhrana—the tsar's secret police—recalled that "every newcomer was viewed negatively" in 1908. A holy man might be a terrorist, and foreign agents were thought to be everywhere. Vladimir Dedyulin, the palace commandant and the man charged with the imperial family's security, was immediately suspicious of Rasputin. He thought that Rasputin was being "sponsored by Anna Vyrubova"—hardly a recommendation, given that the police were equally skeptical of her and her motives. Dedyulin ordered the police to check into Rasputin's background.

Dedyulin apparently took his findings to Stolypin, who launched his own investigation. The prime minister was a colossal force: a member of an aristocratic family, he shot to the top of the bureaucracy thanks to intellect, ability, and considerable wealth. Stolypin was intensely loyal to the tsar and hoped to strengthen the throne through a combination of far-sighted reforms and brutal repression. He understood that certain sweeping changes in Russian society would strengthen the imperial system. Stolypin saw Rasputin and the rumors that swirled around him as obstacles to his goals.

Stolypin expanded the scope of Dedyulin's inquiry. The report has disappeared, but we may assume that it presented Rasputin in a negative light. The imperial police were not subtle—even the clothes that the detectives wore made them amusingly visible. Rasputin complained to Nicholas, who took the matter up with Stolypin at his next scheduled report. Unfortunately the prime minister did not know that Alexis suffered from hemophilia. Had the boy's parents disclosed this information, the world would have understood why Rasputin was a frequent guest at the Alexander Palace. As it was, people could only speculate. For his part, Nicholas II could not grasp why people were so obsessed with this humble peasant. Nicholas saw Rasputin as a man of God and a voice of the people—he could never see why anyone would make more of it than that. It was naive, but the tsar supposed that Stolypin would come to the same understanding if he met Rasputin.

Stolypin could not refuse the tsar's request, although he agreed reluctantly and had Paul Kurlov, assistant minister of the interior and ex officio police director, sit in on their meeting. It was a strange encounter. Kurlov recalled Rasputin as a "lean ordinary fellow with a dark, wedge-shaped beard and piercing, intelligent eyes." Rasputin assured them that he was a peaceful man with no political agenda— there was no need for the police to worry about him. If this were true, the prime minister replied, Rasputin did not need to fear the police. This obviously unsettled Rasputin, for at this point, he tried to put Stolypin under a spell. "He ran his pale eyes over me," the prime minister told his daughter. "He mumbled mysterious and inarticulate words from the Scriptures and made strange movements with his hands." Rasputin's hypnotic power amazed Stolypin. He also felt an enormous "loathing" and "repulsion" for this "vermin"—and that probably explains his poor handling of the conflict that followed.

Pulling himself together, Stolypin declared that he had enough evidence to prosecute Rasputin as a sectarian. Rasputin could leave the capital or face the charges—it was his choice. Rasputin stormed out, and Stolypin ordered Kurlov to assemble a dossier with all of the information at his disposal for the tsar. "I advised Stolypin against doing this," Kurlov wrote, "for Nicholas would conclude that people were simply out to discredit someone he liked." Events did indeed show that the tsar was not happy to hear that Rasputin was being attacked. At his next report to the emperor, Stolypin unexpectedly launched into a discussion of Rasputin and his malevolent influence. Nicholas was surprised, and his face showed displeasure, although he was silent. Since it was obvious that this issue *really* bothered Stolypin and he would pursue it relentlessly, Nicholas made a concession: he promised that *he* would not see Rasputin again.

Stolypin's hatred for Rasputin was affecting his judgment: he read the tsar's promise to avoid contact with the peasant as permission to take action against him. Stolypin issued a decree banning the peasant from the capital for five years. Rasputin was in Pokrovskoye as Stolypin was preparing this action. The police were waiting at the train station to serve the papers the moment Rasputin returned to Saint Petersburg. Rasputin had been alerted, and as soon as the train pulled into the station, he tumbled into a waiting car that sped to the home of Nicholasha and Anastasia. The police could not enter an imperial residence without an order from the tsar, so the Okhrana could only place agents outside the palace, waiting to arrest the peasant when he appeared. But Rasputin slipped through their net; he boarded a train and returned to Pokrovskoye. Stolypin had been a gigantic force in Russian history—he defeated the revolution and crushed the violence that lingered from 1906 and 1908. But a peasant had gotten the best of him. When an officer asked Stolypin if he wanted the order served in Siberia, he made a gesture indicating, "It's no use! Let it go!" The decree banishing Rasputin from the capital was destroyed. Despite this, Rasputin was not entirely secure.

The charges clearly bothered Alexandra, and she conducted her own investigations into Rasputin's life. She asked Archimandrite Feofan to visit Siberia and examine the evidence in 1908. The evidence he gathered was both reassuring and disturbing. No one accused Rasputin of sectarian activity, and Father Peter, still stung by the unexpected results of the church inquiry, agreed that Rasputin appeared to be a devout member of the Russian Orthodox Church. But Feofan found the awkward elegance of his host's home disturbing. When he asked the mother superior of the Diveev Convent near Sarov about the peasant, she angrily replied, "This is what should be done to your Rasputin!" as she hurled her fork into the floor.

Feofan's report failed to resolve Alexandra's doubts, so she asked Anna Vyrubova and two other ladies to go to Pokrovskoye in 1909 to investigate the rumors. "I don't have the slightest skills as a detective!" Vyrubova protested, but she did as asked. Rasputin met their train at Perm. He shared the ladies' compartment and agreed to spend the night in an upper berth with the maid. This was simply too much temptation: the young woman began screaming that Gregory was fondling her—and she ended up in the corridor for the rest of the evening. Rasputin claimed to be innocent, and the ladies had to admit that they did not actually *see* him do anything improper.

Everything in Pokrovskoye enchanted Anna Vyrubova. She praised the Rasputins' living area as "almost Biblical in its stark simplicity." They were simple folk; their meals largely consisted of "raisins, bread, nuts, and perhaps a bit of pastry." Rasputin's friends came in the evening to sing hymns and pray with "rustic faith and fervor."

The other ladies were less impressed, although their reports were contradictory and inconclusive. The lady whose maid Rasputin had tried to seduce warned the empress that Rasputin was a dangerous lecher. Annoyed, Alexandra pressed the issue. Did she witness Rasputin molesting her maid? No. It was night and she had actually been asleep. Vyrubova insisted that nothing had happened—that Rasputin was again falling victim to his "naiveté and saintliness," although she had to admit that she had not been on the scene. Alexandra heard what she wanted to hear and ignored the rest; she dismissed the incident as a misunderstanding.

Alexandra had a rare ability to evaluate events and people in ways that reinforced her opinions. The visit to Pokrovskoye that she requested showed that she was capable of ignoring unpleasant facts and following her instincts, and it foretold much that would follow in the future. Alexandra's view of Rasputin was shaped by her faith and reliance on him as a healer and counselor. Nicholas was never that committed to the peasant; but as a father who loved his son, he was equally dependent on the Siberian mystic and healer. The tsar hinted at this on one occasion, when Stolypin was arguing that Rasputin was undermining the prestige of the throne. "Everything you say may be true," the tsar finally said. "But I must ask that you never speak with me again about Rasputin. In any event, I can do nothing at all about it." The remark was cryptic, and Stolypin almost certainly misinterpreted it. He thought that Nicholas was admitting that he lacked the strength or courage to stand up to his wife—which happened to be true, of course. But the emperor might have also been thinking of the weightier fact that Alexis had hemophilia and Rasputin was his healer.

The situation made it unlikely that Rasputin could be expelled from the court, although his enemies, not knowing that, kept trying to bring it about. Their cause was strengthened in 1909 when Rasputin raped Khioniya Berlatskaya, one of his earliest and most ardent followers. Berlatskaya was shaken, and she took the matter to Feofan, hoping that the Church would punish the scoundrel. This was the first time that Feofan heard this sort of accusation from Rasputin's inner circle. Feofan was a devout monarchist, and he finally decided that Rasputin was a false starets who had to be stopped before he destroyed the throne.

The storm was building. Evidence against Rasputin mounted throughout 1910 as rumors of his licentious behavior rippled throughout society. Feofan took the scandalous information about Berlatskaya to the Montenegrin sisters, and this time they were ready to listen. Their relationship with Alexandra had steadily deteriorated after 1908. At first it was a matter of Anna Vyrubova: her increasing importance destroyed the Montenegrins' previous friendship with the empress. Then lurid rumors swept the capital, and the sisters came to view their former protégé with a suspicion that ripened into hostility. Militsa and Anastasia joined Feofan in the conviction that Rasputin was just a crafty charlatan who posed a danger to the Romanov dynasty.

New and still more troubling accusations against Rasputin came from within Alexander Palace in the spring of 1910. Sophie Tyutcheva, governess of the four grand duchesses, complained that Rasputin visited the girls when they were in their nightclothes at bedtime. This might have been acceptable when they were children, but Olga was nearly fifteen and Tatyana was thirteen—they were budding ladies. Tyutcheva noted that the imperial court thrived on scandal: why give the gossips ammunition? Nicholas finally realized that Tyutcheva was going to be a problem, and he confronted her. "You do not know the man," he scolded. "And if you had criticisms of anyone known to this Household you should have made them to us, not to the public." Since Tyutcheva was defiant, Alexandra dismissed her.

Rasputin had wronged or offended many women in the capital by this point, and several stepped forward to tell their stories. The first was Berlatskaya; Tyutcheva was next, and now a third woman raised her voice. Maria Vyshnekova, the tsarevich's nursemaid, claimed that Rasputin sexually assaulted her at the palace. The empress refused to believe it, but Vyshnekova insisted, and Alexandra fired her. While Vyshnekova was recovering at a sanitarium at Kislovodsk in the Caucasus, she happened to meet Anthony, who, as the metropolitan of Saint Petersburg, was the most powerful bishop in the Russian Orthodox Church. Vyshnekova persuaded Anthony that she was telling the truth and that he must save Alexis from the "clutches of Satan." Anthony took the matter up with Nicholas and was shocked when the tsar insisted the palace's affairs were entirely his concern. Anthony was upset, and he reprimanded the tsar, insisting that the ruler of Russia had to lead a life free of scandal.

Militsa and Anastasia joined Feofan in warning Alexandra of the situation, but she rejected everything. The empress told the Montenegrins to never mention Rasputin again—and she did her best in the future to ignore their existence within the family. Feofan was transferred to the Crimea.

Newspaper journalists throughout the empire leaped into action, launching what must have been an orchestrated effort to discredit Rasputin in the early summer of 1910. The church observer, Michael Novoselov, wrote a major article in the *Moscow News* labeling Rasputin "A Spiritual Fake." The liberal *Speech* called for an investigation into the starets's connections with "leading figures in the state." The censor would not permit a journalist to attach Rasputin's name to a member of the Romanov family, but everyone grasped the message. The *New Times* often reflected government views; it dismissed the stories as exaggerations and lies, arguing that the only "news" was that some people were showing how far they would go to discredit Rasputin.

Why did Rasputin engage in such reckless behavior? He controlled himself during his first two years in the capital. But something changed in the next three years. Perhaps success beguiled him into thinking that he no longer needed to control his impulses. Rasputin's conviction that he had spiritual gifts and was called to a divine mission allowed him to excuse quite a lot about himself. The exalted and base elements of his personality were always at war with each other; the balance started to shift around 1908.

It was one thing for Rasputin to adopt such attitudes; it was quite another for Nicholas and Alexandra to ignore his faults, dismiss reports, and punish people who challenged their views. People concluded that

Rasputin around 1910. The caption in the original work rather neatly written by Rasputin's standards, proclaims that "Our Life is in Christ."

the tsar and his wife were gullible or naive—and to some extent, they were. But they understood more than many supposed. Olga insisted that her brother and his wife were "fully aware" of Rasputin's character. "It is completely false to suggest that they regarded him as a saint incapable of evil," she declared years later. Neither "was duped by Rasputin or had the least illusion about him."

We might dismiss this as a loving sister's devotion to her brother—but there was the time Rasputin joined Olga on the sofa and forced her to move suddenly as Nicholas and Alexandra looked on uncomfortably. Still, they never saw Rasputin's worst behavior. If Rasputin was drunk and suddenly forced to appear at Tsarskoye Selo, he always managed to pull himself together and conduct himself in a normal fashion. On one occasion in 1916 Alexandra reported to her husband that their friend had been "very gay after the dinner in the vestry—but not tipsy." Even if Nicholas and Alexandra rejected the most lurid tales, they had some sense of the darker aspects of Rasputin's character.

What were they to do with that knowledge? Should they part with the only man who could safeguard their son's life? They needed Rasputin—and that forced Nicholas and Alexandra to rationalize his misbehavior and vent their anger on those who raised troublesome issues. The tsar was known to deal with a report outlining the familiar charges by seizing on minor errors to dismiss all the accusations, even if the thrust of the evidence was perfectly clear. Nicholas ignored what he did not wish to accept: the facts that called Rasputin's status as a holy man into question. Nicholas once told a critic that Rasputin calmed his doubts and gave him peace. Rasputin was a man of "pure faith."

Lili Dehn was one of the empress's few confidantes, and she made some insightful observations about Alexandra's relationship with the peasant. Dehn thought that the empress defended Rasputin because "she and the Emperor had extended the hand of friendship to him" and could not admit that this might have been a mistake. Dehn likened the empress's faith in Rasputin to Queen Victoria's relationship with John Brown. Both women "refused to be dictated to" in their choice of confidants; protests against these friends simply produced intransigent attitudes that shut out all contrary opinions.

Beyond this Alexandra struggled with Rasputin's darker side, although she never admitted it. She actually commissioned a study called *Russian Saints Who Were Holy Fools in Christ* to justify Rasputin. The author was Father Alexis Kuznetsov, and his work was initially rejected as a master's thesis at the Saint Petersburg Theological Academy. Alexandra had it published. Kuznetsov was also promoted to vicar bishop in Moscow, apparently through Rasputin's influence. Kuznetsov himself was alarmingly forthright: "I don't care about Rasputin, how he lives, or what he does. The fact is that thanks to him I'm now a Moscow prelate making 18,000 rubles a year, with all the fringe benefits!"

Russian Saints Who Were Holy Fools explored the tradition of the "Holy Fool in Christ"—men and women who were regarded as eccentric or even insane in their own time but were still embraced by the Church. Alexandra lent a copy to Countess Karlova, a friend who had been critical of Rasputin. Karlova noticed that someone had underlined the passages in the book that detailed "sexual dissoluteness" on the part of some Holy Fools. Perhaps Alexandra hoped this would put Rasputin's behavior "in perspective." It also shows that she was not oblivious to her friend's disreputable side, although she hoped to redeem his reputation. Alexandra ignored the fact that these Holy

Fools had sinned when they were young but lived blameless lives after they found God. This was not true of Rasputin. To the end he alternated between sin and repentance, lamenting his failings only to repeat them. This made Rasputin human, but it also separated him from the men and women whose lives Alexandra found so similar to Rasputin's.

Rasputin was important to Alexandra, but her admiration had to be constantly reinforced. This typically required praise from those who were willing to provide it plus another healing of her son and several meetings with the master himself. It took all of this for her to overlook the harsher realities of her friend's life. "Our Lord," she once told Lili Dehn, "did not choose well-born members of Jewish society for His followers." She likened Rasputin to the Old Testament prophets—sent by God to bear witness to truth and holiness.

7

The Captain's Mysterious Report

I T WAS THE MORNING OF SHROVE TUESDAY in 1911. A blast of cold air greeted Alexander Mandryka as he stepped from his warm railway compartment onto the railway platform at Tsarskoye Selo. A car carried the young Guards captain to Alexander Palace, where sentries waved him through the iron gates. Mandryka had come to deliver a report on Gregory Rasputin—and it was devastating.

Mandryka's meeting with Nicholas and Alexandra on February 10, 1911, was another chapter in a saga that involved religious zealotry, anti-Semitism, and the ambitions of obscure men for power. The central figure was Iliodor; his bizarre behavior shook the Russian Empire and threw the tsarist regime into a major crisis. At the end, Iliodor created a situation that even threatened Rasputin's position at the Imperial Court.

Rasputin met Iliodor in 1903 when he was a student at the Saint Petersburg Theological Academy. The revolution of 1905 gave Russia a new political system that permitted men with his oratorical gifts to build mass movements and gain influence that would have been inconceivable in the past. Iliodor grasped the opportunity. Like Rasputin, he was convinced that he had been sent by God to save the empire, although he saw different enemies. His list included Jews and intellectuals as well as liberals, Marxists, and especially aristocrats who "speak in every accent except Russian."

Iliodor blended religion with politics. Like many clergymen, he aligned himself with such anti-Semitic organizations as the Black

Hundreds, the Union of the Russian People, and the League of Saint Michael the Archangel. These right-wing groups enjoyed imperial favor because they matched leftist terror with their own brand of violence: pogroms and attacks on students and trade unionists. They also engaged in shrill propaganda about the conspiracies against Russia carried on by Jews, Freemasons, and leftist agitators.

Iliodor became extremely popular, and his followers built an armed compound at Tsaritsyn, on the banks of the Volga. Conflict with the authorities seemed inevitable, given his constant attacks on all officials except for the tsar. The Church chastised Iliodor, but he refused to tone down his rhetoric. He even accused the Orthodox hierarchy of conspiring against the throne. Peasants and lower-class people packed the halls to hear his lengthy speeches that brought them to the brink of violence. "Don't hand Russia over to the cruel enemy!" he shouted. "Down with the Yid kingdom! Down with the Red banners! Down with the Red freedom! Down with the Red Yid equality and brotherhood! Long live our one Father Tsar, our Orthodox Tsar and autocrat!"

The local authorities seemed powerless against Iliodor, and people were soon comparing him to Yemelyan Pugachev, leader of the great peasant uprising that shook Russia under Catherine the Great. In March 1909 Iliodor's superiors reassigned him to a post far from Tsaritsyn, but he refused to leave. He understood, however, that the authorities would defeat him if they struck him with full force. What the rabble-rousing monk really needed was a way to save face. When Rasputin offered to intercede on his behalf, Iliodor—aware of the peasant's influence at court—seized at the lifeline.

It was an odd alliance between men of humble origins who claimed to be on missions to save Russia. Iliodor hoped to use Rasputin to advance his career, while Rasputin knew that he would strengthen his position with the tsar by bringing the crisis to a peaceful resolution. It was actually Nicholas II who asked Rasputin to tame Iliodor, and Rasputin promised to do it.

At first Rasputin was successful: he persuaded Iliodor to leave his compound and meet him in Saint Petersburg in April 1909. Rasputin assured Iliodor that he could remain at Tsaritsyn if he ended his attacks on the authorities. Now Rasputin turned to Nicholas II, asking him to rescind the order that banished the monk from Tsaritsyn. Rasputin stressed that Iliodor was truly repentant. Nicholas wondered if he could set aside his earlier decree—it was so categorical. "It won't be hard to do," Rasputin insisted: "You wrote your first order from left to right. You can write a new one from right to left."

The next stage of Rasputin's plan called for Iliodor to meet the empress at Anna Vyrubova's house. Alexandra was in an angry mood. She scolded Iliodor—calling him a pain and warning him that his actions were unacceptable to her husband. She told Iliodor that he had to agree to stop attacking the authorities. Iliodor signed the paper she suddenly produced, although he later claimed that it violated his conscience. There was no time for reflection or argument, though, since Alexandra forged ahead with her lecture. "Listen to Father Gregory," she urged. He was a "saint," a "great prophet," "He will lead you to the light." Ironically this was precisely how Iliodor saw himself, but he was silent. The monk was simply grateful to return to his flock at Tsaritsyn.

Rasputin's apparent success with Iliodor led Nicholas II to ask him to intervene with a second difficult cleric. He was Georgy Dalganov, the son of a wealthy Crimean merchant. Dalganov abandoned legal studies to become a priest and a monk. He took the name Hermogen and became the bishop of Saratov in 1903. Hermogen was a brilliant, imposing figure. Tall and muscular, he had an enormous, thick beard and a high-pitched voice that led many to think that he had castrated himself in a burst of religious fervor. Hermogen and Iliodor were friends and political allies. Hermogen also attacked the Duma as the "enemy of the Orthodox Russian people, thieves and robbers who will stop at nothing" to destroy the nation. Hermogen's rhetoric was so outrageous that local officials—and they were certainly not leftists—suppressed the newspaper of his diocese until its editor brought the unruly bishop under control.

Rasputin seemed to have a calming effect on Hermogen when they met at Saratov in September 1909. Flushed with success, Rasputin proceeded to Tsaritsyn to join Iliodor and gauge the mood at his compound. Still grateful to be reunited with his followers, Iliodor introduced Rasputin as a "worthy, pious man." Everything went smoothly, and adoring crowds surrounded Rasputin; he even made several shaky attempts to address large gatherings. Although his listeners were friendly and receptive, the peasant was uncomfortable in this role and quickly reverted to the strategy that brought him greater success: intrigue at the Alexander Palace.

Gratitude turned to irritation when Iliodor caught Rasputin kissing young women. Iliodor was also unhappy to see that Rasputin was not interested in the older, less attractive females. He pushed one

Rasputin (left) with church associates at Saratov in 1910. Initially close to Bishop Hermogen (center) and the monk Iliodor (right), Rasputin tried—but failed—to persuade them to moderate their rightist agitations against the Russian state. Rasputin stood for peace and religious toleration; he courageously opposed nationalism, anti-Semitism, and war.

elderly woman away, commenting, "Your love pleases me, Mother, but God ain't with it!" Iliodor's followers were likewise becoming uncomfortable with their guest. "Why's the Master associating with such a scoundrel?" they grumbled.

Rasputin imagined that he could increase his hold over Iliodor by inviting him to spend Christmas in Pokrovskoye. Rasputin botched his own mission. This time it was his mouth that caused difficulties, not alcohol or women. Rasputin boasted of his sexual exploits while tweaking Iliodor's monkish innocence. Rasputin boasted of his standing with the imperial family. Full of himself and not knowing when to stop, Rasputin claimed that the emperor called him "Christ incarnate," while the empress knelt at his feet and promised never to abandon him.

Rasputin boasted of his gifts from "Mama," including five silk shirts that Alexandra embroidered for him. Iliodor asked why one had a missing collar: "Papa had a sore throat and asked for my help. I told him to smoke less and wear the collar on his throat at night. He got well and thought it was a miracle."

Iliodor was livid at the mere suggestion that Rasputin had influence over Nicholas and Alexandra—it was the main reason for the collapse of the monk's friendship with Rasputin. Convinced that Rasputin had far too much power in the government, Iliodor returned to Tsaritsyn to unleash new and blistering attacks on the authorities—and now he included the tsar. Nicholas II was at the point of ordering the army to expel Iliodor from Tsaritsyn. At this delicate moment, Rasputin proposed a peaceful solution: since Rasputin's efforts had failed, Nicholas should send another emissary to Tsaritsyn to persuade Iliodor to leave.

Rasputin even suggested the man who could solve the crisis: Captain Alexander Mandryka. Why Mandryka? Was it that the handsome young officer was charming and persuasive, or was it that Mandryka had a cousin, Sister Maria, who was the mother superior of the Balashevskaya Convent near Tsaritsyn? Since Maria owed her position to Rasputin—she is the one woman we can identify as attaining a leadership position in the Church with his help—she could be expected to cooperate with his plans, which were to convince her cousin that Iliodor posed no threat. Mandryka would then persuade Nicholas to let Iliodor remain with his followers. Rasputin was playing another double game—he loved to do that! While he was leading Nicholas to think he could induce Iliodor to leave Tsaritsyn, Rasputin was assuring Iliodor that he would find a way for him to remain at Tsaritsyn.

At this point, Rasputin sent Maria a fateful telegram: "One of your relatives is on the way to Tsaritsyn on a matter that concerns us. Use your influence on him." Maria was actually in the capital on business when Mandryka arrived to visit her. The nuns told the captain of Rasputin's frequent visits and how he bathed with the younger sisters while they prayed and sang hymns. Rasputin loved to tell the nuns of his influence with Nicholas and Alexandra; he seduced some of the sisters, and they engaged in "orgies"—all under the observation of a mother superior who was obviously under his thumb. The nuns had taken this for a long time, and they were angry. They finally showed Mandryka Rasputin's fateful telegram. The idealistic young officer was stunned and outraged.

Mandryka returned to the capital to report to the tsar. Nicholas was delighted to see the captain, and Mandryka was invited to deliver his report after lunch, over coffee. Mandryka gave his impressions of Iliodor and the situation at Tsaritsyn. He then turned to the Balashevskaya Convent, describing Rasputin's influence there and the scandalous stories the sisters had to tell. "It is even said," Mandryka whispered, "that he enjoys the favor of Your Majesty!" The captain collapsed in tears; Nicholas rushed for a glass of water while Alexandra tried to comfort their guest. Mandryka submitted his written report and departed, leaving a troubled tsar and his wife to come to terms with what they had just heard.

The captain was loyal and honest—he had not even heard of Rasputin before this episode. Rasputin's telegram showed that he, by contrast, was a two-faced, double-dealing scoundrel. Nicholas and Alexandra realized that Rasputin had abused their trust, and for the first time in his career, they were truly angry with him.

Rasputin must have heard that he faced "trouble" at the palace, since he avoided contact with the family until a new development forced him to renew contact with them. Incredibly, his shaky position was about to become even worse. Rasputin's enemies launched a new attack, using the Finnish ballerina Lisa Tansin to draw Rasputin into a compromising situation. She invited him to a party at her house and got him drunk. The conspirators stripped off his clothing, and a photographer took several snapshots of the starets with prostitutes. Maria Rasputin writes that the photographs were "taken by magnesium light at night debaucheries," and perhaps on several occasions.

Rasputin was blissfully ignorant of the plot that was in motion until a man knocked at the door of his apartment with an envelope. Rasputin glanced at its contents, and the messenger departed after a spirited exchange. Rasputin's servant and former lover Dunya Pecherkin found him in a panic: the envoy had delivered photographs of an "obscene nature." Maria writes that they showed her father "surrounded by a bevy of nude women—a fallen saint shown in the act of falling." Rasputin faced an ultimatum: leave Saint Petersburg immediately or the pictures would be sent to the tsar.

What should I do? he wondered. Normally Rasputin would have insisted upon his innocence, but this time there was evidence at hand that he could not simply ignore. The shrewd and faithful Dunya suggested that Rasputin take the photographs to the tsar. This might elicit sympathy and a measure of goodwill, especially if Rasputin brought the right attitude to the situation—and he could certainly be counted upon to do that.

"I believe the Little Father will be sympathetic," Rasputin said, after thinking it over. "If not, well, that will be God's will." Rasputin requested an audience knowing that it might be his last. He handed over the photographs and explained the situation as best he could. Nicholas silently looked at each print, shaking his head from time to time, frowning and fixing Rasputin with an occasional questioning stare. He then thanked Rasputin for bringing the matter to him. Nicholas pointed out that if Rasputin remained in the capital, the people behind the photographs would find another way to discredit him. "You have mentioned your desire to make a pilgrimage to the Holy Land," Nicholas said. "I think this would be a good time for it. I will, of course, give you the journey as a token of our esteem. The Lord knows you have earned it through your many services to the Crown."

This direct approach was effective—it allowed Rasputin to control how the tsar received the information, and it showed from the outset that he was contrite. Nicholas probably did not tell his wife about the photographs—he generally shielded her from unpleasant matters. As for Rasputin, he might have ended up in Pokrovskoye, banished from the court with his reputation in ruins. But he believed that God forgave sinners if they repented of their sins. Christ offered his grace to murderers, thieves, and adulterers—and this told Rasputin that even when he fell short, hope remained. Rasputin actually got a reward: he would observe Lent 1911 with a pilgrimage to the Holy Land. There his soul would be filled with new and fervent religious fires.

A pilgrimage to the Holy Land was the greatest gift Orthodox Christians could make to their faith. Some two thousand Russian pilgrims made the journey each year, thanks to the Imperial Orthodox Palestine Society, which arranged their trips. They usually set out on foot, but Rasputin was no ordinary pilgrim. Since the tsar paid for his journey, he probably traveled in a first-class train car.

Rasputin left an account of his experiences in a thin volume titled *My Thoughts and Meditations: A Short Description of a Visit to the Holy Places and Meditations on Religious Questions Aroused Thereby*. It was probably based on his letters and descriptions of the trip. Alexis Filippov, his publisher and friend, released the book in 1915. Alexandra probably covered the expenses, hoping the book would strengthen Rasputin's credentials as a man of God. It was not marketed. The peasant presented copies as gifts to friends and admirers, inscribing them with awkward dedications and a large, scrawled *G* for "Gregory."

The book is a travelogue—it describes the places Rasputin visited, with the spiritual reflections that each place produced. This is a familiar genre in Orthodox literature, but the book is as enigmatic as its author. Since Rasputin described himself as "semiliterate," it seems obvious that he did not "write" the book in the normal sense of the term. Filippov tells us that Alexandra corrected the page proofs; this suggests that she and the person Rasputin refers to as his "inseparable friend" (Anna Vyrubova?) did the actual writing. But Rasputin was clearly the creative force behind the book. Many of its turns of phrase are consistent with his two other published volumes and the manuscripts bearing his name that are now in the Central Archive of the Russian Federation. *My Thoughts and Meditations* definitely reflects Rasputin's mind and personality.

Rasputin begins by reflecting on his joy at escaping Saint Petersburg, the center of "vain and worldly things." His first stop was Kiev, the "Mother of Russian Towns" and home of the Monastery of the Caves. Rasputin prayed in the cathedral and at the tombs of the saints who still rest in the region's massive catacombs. Rasputin was impressed with the "light of silence that shines here"—he joined the other "true worshippers" in gathering "jewels of truth" for their journey. Rasputin had a special reverence for the Virgin Mary from the time that she appeared to him in 1898. He felt her presence when "fear and a great trembling swept over" him in prayer.

Rasputin boarded a ship at Odessa to cross the Black Sea. "My soul became one with the sea," he wrote, "and I slept peacefully." He meditated upon the "boundless power of the soul" and the beauty of the bright crimson sunsets; one could hear the waves splashing gently against the steamer during the moonlit nights. In Constantinople he visited the "great and wonderful Cathedral of St. Sophia." Although it had been converted into a museum, Rasputin felt that he was in God's house as he prayed for guidance from the Virgin Mary. "We receive everything She asks of our Lord," he wrote. "Her whole concern is to forgive and console us."

Rasputin traveled to Mitylene, "where the Apostle Paul preached"; then on to Smyrna and the ruins of Ephesus. Although he traveled at the tsar's expense and was probably quite comfortable, Rasputin associated with his fellow peasants; their lack of pretensions put him at ease, and he liked the fact that they were in a constant "state of fear and trembling." It is difficult to reconcile Rasputin the Sinner with Rasputin the Seeker, but he obviously struggled in those days to recapture the spiritual intensity of earlier times.

"My journey was finished," Rasputin declared upon reaching Jerusalem, the "earthly realm of tranquility." The Turks allowed the Russians to build a large compound in the city—pilgrims found hostels, hospitals, and monasteries grouped around the Holy Trinity Cathedral. As a friend of the imperial family, Rasputin probably took a room at a lavish villa that catered to upper-class pilgrims.

Rasputin proceeded to the Mount of Olives, where Tsar Alexander III had erected the Church of St. Mary Magdalene. He was overwhelmed to realize that he was standing in the garden of Gethsemane, the very place where Jesus prayed. Tears filled his eyes, and he was filled with shame to reflect on how far he had fallen from God's grace. "We slumber and fall into evil ways," he wrote. He prayed for redemption as he walked the streets of Jerusalem. As he stood at Golgotha and prayed before Christ's tomb, Rasputin joined the others in vowing that he would never sin again.

Rasputin celebrated Easter in Jerusalem. Thanks to the difference in their calendars, he was able to view the Catholic ceremonies a week before the Orthodox celebrations. "I do not want to be critical," he wrote, and "do not pretend to plumb the depths of wisdom." But it seemed to him that there was no joy in their Easter, "not even within the church itself." The Orthodox Easter, on the other hand, was radiant. Rasputin watched as the patriarch of Jerusalem reenacted the blessing of the Great Sabbath at Christ's tomb; Rasputin joined in the midnight service marking the arrival of Easter. He held his lighted taper beneath the great blue dome of the Holy Trinity Cathedral. "I do not wish for our faith to be under-valued," he wrote. Our faith "shines upon Faithful people [such] as our Father, John of Kronstadt, and the many other bright stars of our Orthodox Church—thousands of God's people!"

Easter was over, and Rasputin's pilgrimage had come to an end. He had recaptured some of the spiritual intensity that once filled his life. We are bound to be skeptical in viewing a man like Rasputin, but *My Thoughts and Meditations* has the ring of truth. His days of devotion had now ended, though. It was time to return to the capital and to renew his engagement in politics at the highest level.

8

Black Boars Become Bishops

RASPUTIN RETURNED TO RUSSIA to find another storm brewing. While he was gone, Nicholas made Vladimir Sabler ober-procurator of the Holy Synod, the state bureau that administered the Russian Orthodox Church after Peter the Great abolished the office of patriarch. Gossips attributed the appointment to Rasputin's influence, but actually he had nothing to do with it. Sabler was intelligent and hardworking; he was a logical choice to lead the Holy Synod. Sabler had recently collaborated with Alexandra in raising funds for her charities, and several leading bishops supported his promotion.

Even so, gossip held that Sabler had kneeled before Rasputin and begged for the appointment. As a reward Rasputin supposedly lived in Sabler's home. A member of the Duma received a letter that claimed to speak for "1,000 citizens of Tsaritsyn" grumbling that Sabler was under Rasputin's thumb. Sabler claimed that he had never even met Rasputin, and that was probably true. But Rasputin's determination to control the Church made him anxious to bring the new ober-procurator under his influence.

A scandal just after Sabler's promotion involved Vasily Nakropin, an ambitious fellow of lower-class origins who was destined to play an important role in Rasputin's life. Nakropin was a devout young man, and the local clergy of Archangel encouraged him to plan a career in the church. Nakropin was short, slender, and handsome; he could pass for a woman with his high-pitched voice. Clad in an expensive gown, he became famous for attracting the amorous attentions of the local governor at a costume ball. The other guests were shocked when the attractive lady was exposed as a man. The governor was mortified, and Nakropin delighted in his sudden notoriety.

Nakropin was tonsured as the monk Varnava (Barnabas), and he rapidly advanced, being blessed with a sharp mind and an eloquent tongue. Varnava was a novice at thirty-five; he became a monk two years later and at thirty-eight was serving as the father superior of a small monastery. His bishop looked to him to bring order to cloisters that needed reform. He also established new monastic houses, infusing them with what one observer called the "spirit of the living God."

Varnava's dark side was striking. He relished being photographed in strange poses and settings. One snapshot shows him in a coffin, dressed in his clerical robes, while another catches him with a group of effeminate friends. An unfriendly commentator tells us that his face "displayed the features of a satyr or the god Pan." Reports of wild parties at his monastery were so persistent that the local metropolitan decided to drop in for a surprise investigation. His "young friends"—perhaps a euphemism for "gay lovers"—warned the father superior, and he greeted his visitor "with a modest face and polite bows."

Since Varnava did not have a higher education, tradition dictated that he could never become a bishop. But Rasputin was determined to see "new men" of his type advanced to leadership positions in the Church. Nicholas and his wife absolutely agreed with that view—they disdained the stuffy, unimaginative men who led the Church. Nicholas and Alexandra prized unpretentious, lower-class candidates who spoke the language of ordinary believers. The tsar was absolutely indifferent to their private lives—historians have failed to notice this surprising fact. Rasputin, of course, was partial to libertines—so much for their vows of poverty, chastity, and obedience. To be fair, one could argue that these traditions were outmoded, although few people at that time would have agreed with that view. At the very least the stage was set for conflict.

Rasputin and Varnava had much in common: they were both of humble origins and followed religious devotions that were at once sincere and at odds with tradition. They had inflated egos and delusions of grandeur; both generated scandal as naturally as holy people did good works. Rasputin probably saw Varnava as a kindred spirit with his own spiritual gifts; a detached observer thought that Varnava's short-comings "were absorbed by his very many good qualities."

Rasputin presented Varnava to the empress. Alexandra was not favorably impressed: she found Varnava dishonest and sycophantic. She called him "Suslik," a squirrel-like rodent with a fat body and bushy tail—not exactly a compliment. But Rasputin kept to his mission and finally persuaded the imperial couple to support Varnava.

Sabler was stunned when Nicholas II told him that he wanted Varnava made a vicar bishop, which meant he would assist a bishop and in time would be promoted to full rank. Rasputin anticipated such negative reactions—he was eager to bring discomfort to the bureau-cratic mind-set that dominated the Holy Synod. "The archbishops will feel insulted if a peasant is thrust into their midst," he growled. "The academics! So what? They'll get used to it. The *suslik* should become a bishop. He stands up for me." This was the issue for Rasputin: Varnava was an ally, and his promotion would give Rasputin a voice among church leaders.

Rasputin had become friends with Peter Damansky, the Synod's financial director—this alone shows the peasant's growing influence. Damansky was entirely open in showing respect for "Starets Gregory," and he pressured members of the governing council to make Varnava a vicar bishop. Sabler lacked the strength to fight for the rules that traditionalists claimed assured high standards in such appointments. His own promotion was a reward for faithful bureaucratic service, so he bowed to pressure and asked the council to make Varnava a vicar bishop at Kargopol, in Olonets province. Leaders of the Holy Synod were astounded. Anthony, the acerbic archbishop of Volhynia, asked Sabler to explain Varnava's qualifications for the post or drop his pro-posal because "we would not want to be responsible for consecrating rascals!" Stung by this reception, Sabler set the issue aside, hoping that it would die of its own accord. But Nicholas was persistent. "Why has Varnava not been elevated yet to the rank of bishop?" he asked at his next meeting with Sabler. When the ober-procurator explained that the Holy Synod did not support it, Nicholas insisted that God placed all power over the Church and the state in the emperor's hands. Sabler was a monarchist, and it would have been difficult for him to object to that argument.

When the governing council continued to oppose the promo-tion, Sabler could see that his position was untenable. He was caught in the middle of a clash between his sovereign and the Church.

Sabler threatened to resign. But the members of the council realized that would lead to other problems: it would throw the spotlight on Rasputin's influence over Nicholas II. That would inflame the Duma, which had to approve ecclesiastical budgets and reforms that were pending in the Church. A collision course always produces damage. "We would make a black boar bishop to keep you in your position," Anthony grumbled, speaking for his colleagues. The Holy Synod gave in and agreed to Varnava's promotion.

"It is now clear that Rasputin installed Varnava in the episcopate," Anthony wrote a friend. Although the archbishop went along with the promotion, he seethed at Rasputin's ability to get his way, even if it shamed the Church. "Rasputin is to blame for the Holy Synod's rascalish behavior," Anthony concluded. "He is a *Khlyst* and takes part in their rituals."

Rasputin loved controversy, and he was about to throw himself into another one. A bishop by the name of Alexis had just been transferred from the warm, beautiful Crimea to the frozen climes of Siberia. Alexis was being punished for living openly with a young lady and protecting a band of heretics who worshipped the late John of Kronstadt as the earthly incarnation of Christ. Alexis's son, Leonid Molchanov, was on his way to visit his father, and he just happened to meet Rasputin on the way. Molchanov explained that Alexis was in bad health and the cold weather at Tobolsk threatened his health. The bishop was living in sin, and he defended heretics from persecution! Rasputin was entirely sympathetic. He promised to speak to "Papa" and "Mama" about the situation. Anna Vyrubova soon invited Alexis to visit her at Tsarskoye Selo. Anna instantly liked the old gentleman, and she sent a wire to Alexandra, who was on holiday with her family on the imperial yacht *Standart*.

Alexis was suddenly aware that Rasputin was important to his future, and he decided to resolve the charges of heresy that were still pending against Rasputin. Alexis reviewed the written record and traveled to Pokrovskoye, interviewing people involved in the case, including Rasputin. The evidence that the peasant was a member of the Khlysty had never been strong, and nothing new emerged in the next four years to change that. The very priests who spied on Rasputin praised him as a faithful son of the Orthodox Church. The report Alexis issued on November 29, 1912, exonerating Rasputin was probably justified. It also pleased Nicholas and Alexandra.

It did not take long for Alexis's favor to be rewarded. The exarch of Georgia—the fourth highest bishop in the Russian Orthodox

Church—died in August 1913. Sabler followed protocol by preparing a list of suitable candidates for the post, and he presented it to the tsar. "Your candidates have gone by the board," Nicholas declared. "The choice of Exarch has fallen upon Alexis, the Bishop of Tobolsk." Sabler was stunned. If Varnava had caused scandals, Alexis promised something even worse. Sabler also reminded Nicholas how Alexis had once offended him with a crude joke in a welcoming address. "I forgave him for that," Nicholas replied curtly, ending the discussion. The tsar insisted that the Synod again promote Alexis—and again Nicholas had his way. This led to a further interesting—and shocking—development.

With Alexis off to Georgia, someone had to fill his post—and who deserved that honor more than Varnava? As the bishop of Tobolsk, Varnava would block any future investigations of Rasputin. Still, Rasputin was taking a risk. Varnava and Rasputin were friends, but tensions sometimes surfaced. Varnava considered himself to be a strict monk, and he looked down on Rasputin as a libertine. Varnava was also ambitious—he probably imagined replacing Rasputin in the affections of the imperial family.

Rasputin seemed to read Varnava's mind—and he tried to keep Suslik in check. "Ain't you satisfied?" he once snarled when he suddenly realized that Varnava had been going rather often to Tsarskoye Selo. "You got here by car—but you can get home on your own two legs. This ain't the place where you get to take it easy!"

Despite their possible rivalry, Varnava tended to Rasputin's interests. As soon as he arrived at Tobolsk, Varnava launched a campaign to intimidate Rasputin's critics. He divided the clergy into two camps: those who favored Rasputin and those who opposed him. The first group was rewarded, the second was punished. Varnava transferred the priests he disliked to distant corners of Siberia. One man with a large family was sent to three increasingly difficult assignments. When the priest begged Varnava not to do it again, the bishop did precisely that. Now the priest complained to Vladimir Vostokov, a suburban Moscow clergyman with a large following and—not coincidentally, the editor of the journal *Responses to Life* that regularly attacked Rasputin. Vostokov was soon criticizing Varnava and his ties to the Siberian mystic and healer.

Rasputin had skillfully planned for such an attack. As the exarch of Georgia, Alexis had a permanent seat on the governing council of the Holy Synod. This gave Rasputin an ally to defend his interests at the highest level. Vostokov's exposés did not lead the council to criticize Rasputin or Varnava. It attacked the fiery idealist—demanding that *Vostokov* explain himself and publicly apologize to Varnava. What a remarkable turn of events!

Vostokov refused to back down. He found a worthy—and powerful—ally in Vladimir, the metropolitan of Saint Petersburg. Vladimir was also a member of the governing council of the Holy Synod, and he denounced Varnava as "absolutely unprepared" to hold the rank of bishop. During a stormy session of the council, he demanded that Varnava be stripped of his position and exiled to a monastery. Vladimir even moved that the tsar be informed of the brewing scandal, and that threw Sabler into consternation. "Excuse me from that task," Sabler told the Council. "I am unable to struggle against the most august will." Sabler was making clear that he did not have the courage to stand up for what he knew was right even if most of his colleagues supported him. The Synod's acceptance of the tsar's repeated interference in its affairs determined the outcome of this particular crisis. The members of the governing council fell silent: only Vladimir had been willing to risk his career by denouncing Varnava. Vladimir withdrew his motion, and the Council moved to the next item on its agenda. A moment of high drama was ending in a whimper.

Each scandal was followed by another scandal—and they all advanced Rasputin's power. Rasputin was dividing the Church. After 1912, few clergymen dared to oppose the peasant, but Gregory was not acting alone. Nicholas and Alexandra were his accomplices; his opinions echoed their own views. They were unable to grasp the fact that their reckless actions were confusing the Church and undermining the tsarist regime itself.

It was against this background that Iliodor finally turned on Rasputin. Rasputin naively supposed that he could win Iliodor's support by protecting him. To this end, Rasputin even resorted to emotional blackmail. He warned Nicholas II in a telegram to order the authorities to quit harassing Iliodor. If that did not happen, God would take revenge on the tsarevich. Even more amazingly, Nicholas yielded to this intimidation.

Rasputin set off for Tsaritsyn in June 1911 to deliver the good news in person, but Iliodor was not impressed. Although Iliodor had benefited greatly from his friendship with Rasputin, he was now convinced that Rasputin was a false starets. The monk's refusal to even meet with the peasant infuriated him; Gregory threatened to destroy Iliodor unless he showed proper respect for the tsar and his favorite.

Rasputin by now had also alienated Hermogen—and that was a bold step since he was probably the most widely respected figure in the Russian Orthodox Church. Hermogen had a seat on the governing council of the Holy Synod, and he commanded a large following among the clergy and laity. Church reformers were demanding that the office of patriarch be restored, arguing that it would strengthen the Church by making it more independent of the state. If that happened—and Nicholas opposed it—most people took for granted that the honor would go to Hermogen.

Hermogen set a trap for Rasputin in the summer of 1911 when both men were sharing a guest room at the Balashevskaya Convent. Hermogen pretended to be asleep. At one in the morning Rasputin slipped out of their room and headed for the apartment of a priest who was absent on a trip. The bishop followed and caught him trying to seduce the priest's wife. Exploding in anger, Hermogen pointed out that it was only a matter of time until such indiscretions would reach the tsar and cause a scandal. Rasputin was unrepentant, and Hermogen was forced to conclude that the peasant was nothing more than an adventurer.

Iliodor now unleashed a stream of facts and falsehoods about Rasputin. Hermogen finally agreed that Russia had to be protected from Rasputin's godless behavior. Hermogen went to Ivan Shcheglovitov, the minister of justice, proposing that Rasputin be kidnapped while agents searched his home for evidence that would force Nicholas to see the "truth"—that Gregory was not truly a man of God. When the minister refused, Hermogen suggested that the conspirators deliver Rasputin to Shcheglovitov and let him punish the peasant. Shcheglovitov pointed out that, thanks to the liberal reforms that followed the revolution of 1905, the government could no longer arbitrarily detain the tsar's subjects or seize their property. The minister made clear that he would have nothing to do with Hermogen's harebrained schemes.

Hermogen now opted for the direct approach, using Iliodor to bait the trap. On the morning of December 16, 1911, Rasputin returned to the capital and telephoned Iliodor, who was in town, appealing the orders to remove him from Tsaritsyn. When Rasputin asked if they could get together, Iliodor suggested that they visit Hermogen.

Rasputin was favorable to the idea, not realizing that he was walk-ing into a trap. The peasant chattered on as their car approached the bishop's residence on Vasilievsky Island.

When Rasputin walked into the reception room, he was amazed to find Hermogen dressed in his finest vestments, holding a large gold cross. Colonel Ivan Rodionov (a journalist and member of the Duma) and Dmitry Kolyaba (the epileptic half-wit who once enjoyed the favor of Nicholas and Alexandra) were at the bishop's side. Hermogen launched into a litany of accusations: Rasputin seduced and raped women; he was a drunk who boasted of his influence over the imperial couple; he meddled in Church affairs; he preached heresy while mingling sex and salvation; he was a member of the Khlysty; and he had been caught in compromising situations that undermined the prestige of the throne.

Rasputin proclaimed his innocence. If he thought he could lie his way out of the situation or threaten his enemies with the tsar's wrath, those strategies collapsed when Kolyaba began shrieking and screaming. He hurled himself at Rasputin and grabbed him by the penis. Rasputin fought free of that attack, but he was trapped. Hermogen demanded that he confess his sins. "It's true, it's true—it's all true!" Rasputin cried, hoping to escape. But the group dragged him to the chapel and made him swear that he would never again see the imperial family. Rasputin must go to the Monastery of the Caves at Kiev to pray for forgiveness. He would also make pilgrim-ages to Mount Athos and Jerusalem to atone for his sins. "You won't return to Russia for three years," Hermogen thundered. "If you disobey me, I'll pronounce an anathema against you."

Rasputin crawled away from the confrontation seething. He rushed to Tsarskoye Selo the next morning for an emergency meeting with Nicholas. His experience with the staged and misleading photographs of 1911 taught Rasputin that the direct approach was the best approach. This allowed him to present his version of the events; he could express whatever guilt and remorse was needed to turn disaster to his advantage. Rasputin learned that he could safely place his fate in the tsar's hands.

The outcome should have surprised no one. Hermogen was stripped of his seat on the Holy Synod and ordered into exile. As a bishop, Hermogen was entitled to a formal hearing before twelve fellow clerics, but Nicholas was in no mood for legal niceties. Hermogen was thrown into a car that took him directly to the railway station. There he was placed on a train that took him away from Saint Petersburg. The most powerful bishop in the Church was suddenly a criminal.

Iliodor proved to be more difficult. He went into hiding with the police in hot pursuit—all to Rasputin's delight. In a telegram addressed to "Papa and my Darling Mama," he warned, "you are above everyone else—and you must be that." They must subdue Iliodor. "He's a malicious dog," Rasputin insisted. "He doesn't care. It's necessary to break his teeth. Treat him more firmly. More guards. Yes."

Eluding the authorities, Iliodor went on the attack. He denounced the Orthodox Church as an "abomination and desolation," claiming that "Christ is not in it." The Holy Synod was a "house of pigs." As for Nicholas and Alexandra: "A dog lies on the throne, the *Sovereign Emperor* is a little man, a drunk, a weed puffer and a fool; the *Empress* is a *rasputnaya* [debauched] woman; the *Heir* was fathered by Grishka Rasputin. Sabler and Grishka Rasputin rule the state, not the Tsar."

The hysteria reached a crescendo in 1912. Iliodor petitioned the Holy Synod to revoke his clerical rank while he renounced his faith, signing the statement in his own blood. Orthodoxy was "only magic and superstition," he declared; its priests were "stupid people." Denying the divinity of Christ, the Resurrection, and eternal salvation, he promised to establish a new faith free of "superfluous" elements like marriage and the sacraments. "I was a sorcerer and fooled the people," Iliodor proclaimed defiantly. "I am a deist. Paganism is a fine religion." Rasputin himself could not have done a better job of discrediting his enemy or getting him out of the way.

9

"You Are Our All"

Rasputin had good reason to be cheerful in the summer of 1911: Peter Stolypin's time in office was obviously drawing to a close. Alexandra had long disliked the man, but Nicholas valued his ability and loyalty. Stolypin had just handled a political crisis involving the Polish provinces so clumsily as to alienate Nicholas, however. Stolypin was never an easy man to work with, and Nicholas decided that it was finally time for him to go. Rumors were flying about the capital by the summer that Stolypin would soon be made governor-general of the Caucasus. That would have been quite a demotion.

Stolypin was both prime minister and minister of the interior, the bureau that oversaw the police. In combining the two positions, Nicholas was placing the entire power of the Russian state in the hands of a single man with the assignment of crushing the revolution of 1905. Ironically, since Stolypin had succeeded in this, he was no longer indispensable. Like many heads of state, Nicholas had limited faith in his own bureaucracy, so he turned to a private citizen, the conservative journalist Georgy Sazonov, to help him find Stolypin's successor. The emperor also sought Rasputin's advice. Nicholas had made a fateful decision: for the first time he was involving Rasputin in the affairs of the state at the very highest level.

Nicholas II was considering Sergei Witte or Vladimir Kokovtsov as prime minister. Witte had held the post in 1905 and was widely admired, although Nicholas disliked him personally. Kokovtsov was competent if not gifted, and he was attracting universal praise as the minister of finance. Nicholas was interested in Alexis Khvostov as the minister of the interior. At thirty-nine, Khvostov had risen in the provincial bureaucracy through ability, hard work, and a flair for ingratiating himself with his superiors. Indeed, it was a bold move that brought Khvostov to the tsar's attention in 1911. Hearing rumors that Stolypin was on the way out, he submitted a memorandum outlining the policies he would follow if he became minister of the interior. Nicholas was impressed, but he also knew that the young man had liabilities.

Khvostov was "repulsively fat" and was generally regarded as a scoundrel. He was once described as a "bright young man, energetic and enterprising, except on matters of state." His own uncle Alexander Khvostov—an official who eventually became minister of justice—voiced a common opinion when he told the tsar that "my nephew is no stranger to intrigue and his entire state service will be devoted not to [public] business but to considerations that are alien to it. He is an unsuitable character, quite bright but unable to criticize his own motives and thoughts." The chatter about Khvostov was quite negative, and yet he fascinated the emperor. Nicholas seemed to be searching for something in the young man that others had missed.

Nicholas II asked Sazonov and Rasputin to visit Khvostov in Nizhnyi-Novgorod, where he was serving as governor. Sazonov was to discuss political issues while Rasputin "gazed into his soul." Khvostov had no notion of who Rasputin was or why he was important. "I spoke with him in a jesting manner," he later admitted. "After a while, I sent for a policeman to conduct him to the railway station."

Soon after this Rasputin traveled to Kiev for the grand celebration of the fiftieth anniversary of the abolition of serfdom. Stolypin accompanied the tsar—this would be their last undertaking together. Rasputin stood on the sidewalk, watching the parade that was held in honor of these dignitaries. He suddenly had the premonition that a tragedy was about to occur and a terrible pogrom would follow it. Rasputin became highly agitated when Stolypin's carriage passed. "Death is following him!" Rasputin shouted. "Death is riding behind him! Behind Peter! Don't you believe me?" Rasputin tossed and turned that night, mumbling repeatedly, "Death is coming! Don't you believe me?" In fact, no one took him seriously.

There was a gala performance of Rimsky-Korsakov's *Tale of Tsar Saltan* the following evening, September 1, 1911. Nicholas II was in the imperial box with his daughters, Olga and Tatyana, while Stolypin was seated on the ground floor, at the front. During the intermission a student shot the prime minister. The doctors expected Stolypin to recover, and Nicholas proceeded on his scheduled tour of Ukraine. When Stolypin died five days later, the tsar rushed to the hospital, fell to his knees at the bedside of his fallen servant, and whispered repeatedly, "Forgive me!"

Nicholas and his family did not attend Stolypin's funeral—some took this as a sign of their hostility to the great statesman. The truth was actually more complicated, and, as usual, a full review of the evidence that has only recently come to light shows that Alexandra was judged unfairly by contemporaries and historians. Although she disliked Stolypin because he had been Rasputin's passionate foe, the empress was shaken by the attempt on his life. In a letter to her sister-in-law Eleonore dated September 2, 1911, the tsaritsa echoed the general opinion that the prime minister would recover. She was thankful that Stolypin "slept for five hours and is not in great pain"; he never lost consciousness and was speaking "very lucidly." "They think he is out of danger," Alexandra continued. "His liver seems to be only slightly affected. . . . Fortunately, N., O. and T. were in the foyer when it happened; Tatiana came home very tearful and is still a little shaken whereas Olga put on a brave face throughout. . . . Pray God he will make a full recovery. It is such a sorrowful event, and I was not there with the others!"

An eyewitness found Alexandra to be in "nervous shock" at the news that Stolypin had breathed his last. She later expressed the opinion that "those who have offended God in the person of Our Friend may no longer count on divine protection." Rasputin's behavior had certainly been to his credit—he sounded the alarm that Stolypin was in danger, and he did everything possible to comfort the empress while Stolypin was struggling for his life. When Nicholas visited Kiev five years later, he described the emotion he felt when he "went through our old rooms—they reminded me so of bygone days & of poor Stolypin's death."

Nicholas chose Vladimir Kokovtsov to succeed Stolypin as the head of his government. The new prime minister opposed appointing Alexis Khvostov minister of the interior, noting his lack of experience and extreme anti-Semitic views. Stolypin's assassination had thrown

Russia into a crisis, and Kokovtsov did not think that Khvostov had a "single quality" that a minister of the interior needed at that critical moment. Nicholas honored Kokovtsov's preference for Alexander Makarov, a solid and experienced official.

The crisis ended on something of a humorous note. Having learned that it was a mistake to have alienated Rasputin, Khvostov rushed to Saint Petersburg to apologize. Rasputin was unimpressed. He told Khvostov that he had already wired Anna Vyrubova, asking her to "tell Mama that God is with him, but he lacks something." Khvostov continued to intrigue Nicholas—the tsar was drawn to him like a moth to a deadly flame. Khvostov became minister of the interior four years later, in 1915.

Kokovtsov was just settling into his new duties when he received a letter from Rasputin: "'I am planning to leave for good, and would like to see you to exchange thoughts," Rasputin wrote. "Say when." When Rasputin entered the prime minister's office, he sat down without saying a word. "His eyes were fixed on me," Kokovtsov recalled—his "eyes set deep in their sockets, close to each other, small, and steel-gray in color. Rasputin did not take them off me for a long time, as if he imagined that he was casting some sort of hypnotic spell. Or was he merely studying me?"

Rasputin finally asked, "So, should I leave or not? I don't have a life any more, and they're telling tales about me!"

"Yes, it would be good if you departed," Kokovtsov replied. "Your place is not here, and you are threatening the Sovereign by appearing at the palace and feeding the most outlandish notions and conclusions."

"Okay, I'm bad," Rasputin mumbled. "I'll go. Next time they call to tell me somethin' or other, let 'em do without me." Rasputin stared at the prime minister for a while, as if to give him the opportunity to say something conciliatory. Rasputin finally jumped from his chair and said, "So long!" as he left.

The meeting was a test: Would Kokovtsov continue the government's campaign against Rasputin, or would he be "reasonable?"— Alexandra wanted to know. The new prime minister showed that he saw Rasputin as a problem and wanted him out of the way. Rasputin apparently told Alexandra that Kokovtsov threatened to expel him from Saint Petersburg, because a few days later Nicholas questioned him on the subject. The tsar was glad to hear his servant deny saying anything of the sort, conceding that it would be unfortunate "if *anyone* became uncomfortable because of us." The tsar then asked his opinion of Rasputin—this was another test. Kokovtsov told the emperor that Rasputin reminded him of a "typical Siberian tramp," much like the convicts he had encountered working in the Central Prison Administration. "People like that would grab you by the throat and strangle you, while they made the sign of the cross with a smile on their lips."

A new crisis over Rasputin erupted in 1912. Michael Novoselov had published a pamphlet in 1910 titled *Gregory Rasputin and Mystical Debauchery* that recycled the old stories about Rasputin, some true and others false. Novoselov claimed that, although the Siberian mystic and healer was a Khlyst, he was supported by people in "high places." The police seemed to confirm this when they confiscated the pamphlet, raiding the publisher's offices and destroying the plates. Certain powerful forces really were protecting Rasputin.

Alexander Guchkov deplored the situation. He was a leader of the Octobrist Party, the president of the Third Duma, and a shrewd tactician. As a moderate conservative he had once hoped to work with the tsar to build a constitutional monarchy in Russia. But Nicholas had a different vision: he believed that he was still *rightfully* an autocratic ruler. He thought that the creation of the Duma was a mistake. Nicholas might have been well advised to form a partnership with Guchkov and the Octobrists. But Guchkov's response to the tsar's rejection was nearly as problematic.

Guchkov's allies, even, conceded that he was an "ambitious man who had become embittered and restless." Rasputin was constantly providing new evidence for his argument, which was that Nicholas and Alexandra were imbeciles who were blocking the development of constitutional government in Russia. As the president of the Third Duma, Guchkov scheduled a debate on the starets. He also had the support of Russia's major daily newspaper, the *Voice of Moscow*. The censor gave journalists the right to discuss Rasputin's activities, although they could not link him to a member of the Romanov family by name. "Letters to the Editor," however, enjoyed more leeway, so Guchkov published Novoselov's pamphlet in that format. If dozens of people read the pamphlet, thousands now saw Rasputin castigated as a "sly conspirator" who "corrupts people's souls [and] impudently uses the Church as a cover."

Other newspapers picked up Novoselov's story and expanded it. The police seized copies of newspapers with articles that offended the authorities, while stray issues sold for enormous sums. Rasputin was accomplishing something that no one else had been able to do. He was uniting Nicholas's critics on a common objective: to expose the "infamous starets and his ties to the government."

The Fourth Duma elected a new president when it convened in 1912. The deputies chose Michael Rodzyanko, another Octobrist leader—and he was quite different from his predecessor. While Guchkov hoped to discredit Nicholas II, Rodzyanko loved the tsar and set out on a mission to persuade Nicholas to restore faith in the government by sending Rasputin home.

Nicholas assumed that an honest survey of the evidence would show any open-minded person that Rasputin was not guilty of the charges so often leveled against him. He asked Rodzyanko to investigate the situation and report his findings. Rodzyanko was flattered. He was also determined to review every file and document on Rasputin, although such an ambitious undertaking was clearly *not* what Nicholas had in mind.

It was difficult to get the Synod's dossier on Rasputin, but Rodzyanko managed to do it. The following day, Peter Damansky, the assistant ober-procurator and Rasputin's ally, appeared at Rodzyanko's office to demand that the file be returned. Damansky often bullied his opponents into submission, but he could not intimidate the bulky president of the Duma. (Rodzyanko had once fetched a hearty laugh from Alexis, the tsarevich, when he introduced himself as the "fattest man in Russia.") Damansky finally admitted that it was the empress who had sent him to retrieve the dossier.

Rodzyanko insisted that Alexandra had the same obligation as other Russians to obey the tsar's commands. He ordered Damansky to tell her that he would not "comply with her wishes." Rodzyanko was *so* dense. Kokovtsov and other high officials immediately grasped Nicholas's objective, but the fattest man in Russia never got it. The tsar assumed that Rodzyanko would find Rasputin innocent of the familiar charges. But the president of the Duma concluded that they were true. This made for a very tense meeting with Nicholas on February 26, 1912.

Rodzyanko began by criticizing Rasputin, offering to be silent if this offended the tsar, but loyalty to the throne demanded honesty. Nicholas permitted him to continue, silently bowing his head and smoking one cigarette after another. When Rodzyanko showed him a photograph of Rasputin dressed as a priest, an irritated tsar replied, "Yes, this is really going too far. He has no right to wear a pectoral cross." But Nicholas rejected the request that Rasputin be expelled from the capital.

By now these scandals were affecting Alexander Palace. The courtiers—the men and women who served at the Imperial Court—despised Rasputin, and they finally decided that they had to take a stand against him. They launched a coordinated (and secret) campaign to speak to the tsar and his wife. Their efforts failed, of course. Nicholas listened politely to each person, concluding the interview with a request that the subject not be raised again. Alexandra, on the other hand, was furious. "Saints are always calumniated!" she complained to Dr. Botkin, the family physician. Although the empress knew that some of the accusations against Rasputin were true, she insisted that the entire scandal stemmed from jealousy. "He is hated because we love him," she told Anna Vyrubova.

Nicholas expected the storm to run its course, but it was actually building to a new crisis. The Holy Synod's budget was to be discussed in the Duma, and Rasputin's enemies used the occasion to strike out against him. The applause was thunderous when Guchkov attacked Vladimir Sabler for letting the peasant dictate church policy. The ober-procurator looked about nervously, hoping that someone would defend him. Bishop Evlogii rose to speak. He had great prestige—he was an elected deputy and held a seat on the Synod's governing council. He knew that Sabler was an honorable man. Unfortunately, he was also a weakling who would not stand up to the tsar, and he permitted Rasputin to meddle in church affairs.

Evlogii mumbled that he "hoped the ober-procurator would defend his good name." Sabler did so, and with striking dignity. But everyone knew that the attacks were justified. "The Church fell into disrepute" under Sabler's leadership. "Rasputin threw it into the mud and created ill will against everything that concerned it."

This was the first time that Rasputin was the subject of a Duma debate. Deputies had been getting complaints from their constituents. Some claimed firsthand knowledge of Rasputin's misdeeds; others asserted that he was a Khlyst. A few simply requested information. Paul Milyukov, a leader of the liberal Kadet Party, heard from a man who had met Rasputin in 1910. He noted that Rasputin "gave people spiritual comfort. He helped them with difficult problems and sickness. He gave advice, presented himself as someone devoted to the spiritual life, a holy man." But Milyukov's correspondent wondered, "Who was the real Rasputin, the heretic or the righteous man?"

That was, in fact, an excellent question. Rasputin was constantly bragging about his relationship with Nicholas and Alexandra. He showed people the imperial portraits on his walls, the lamps that hung throughout his house, and the silk shirts the empress had embroidered for him. It was only a matter of time until such arrogance would backfire. As we saw in chapter 7, it happened when Iliodor spent Christmas with Rasputin in Pokrovskoye in 1909. Rasputin showed the visitor a packet of letters from the empress and her children. Iliodor claimed that Rasputin gave him seven letters. Or did Iliodor steal them?

Iliodor obviously gave the letters to Rasputin's enemies, for they began to appear in hectographed form in Saint Petersburg in late 1911. Who released them? Although Nicholas suspected Guchkov, as did Kokovtsov and Milyukov, we still do not know who, exactly, was behind their publication.

Today those letters would not make the back pages of a scandal magazine, but they do show how deeply Rasputin had entered into the lives of the imperial family. Olga, the oldest child, had confessed her feelings for a certain young officer, and Rasputin advised her not to see him "too much." We find hints of Alexandra's increasingly fragile health. "God grant that dear Mama will not be sick any more this winter," Olga wrote; she also referred to the uneasy relationship she had with her mother. Olga hoped that Alexandra would "not be so totally terribly melancholy and difficult." Tatyana was the second and most obedient daughter—and the one most like Alexandra in temperament. She asked Rasputin to "forgive all the sins I have committed against you," and to "ask God to forgive and save us sinners." Maria, the third daughter, slept with the Bible that was a gift from Rasputin. She hoped that her mother might "let me see you alone about God. It would be wonderful if I prayed to God with you." The cynics probably did not notice that this refuted the notion that Rasputin had an inappropriate relationship with the girls.

The most damaging letter was from Alexandra, and it is dated February 7, 1909:

> It is an unspeakable joy that You, our beloved, were here with us. How [can we] thank You enough for everything? . . . I wish only one thing: to fall asleep on Your shoulder. . . . You are our all.

Forgive me, my teacher—I know I have sinned much and still do—forgive and be patient. I try to do better, but I don't succeed—I know that much of what I do and think is not good—I want to be a good Christian, a good person—but it is so hard. So often I have to fight bad habits. But help me, don't abandon me. I am weak and not good. . . . I love You and I believe in You. . . . God grant us the joy of meeting soon. I kiss You warmly. Bless and forgive me—I am Your child.

Kokovtsov and Nicholas confirmed that the documents were genuine when they were finally retrieved. Given the rumors that had been swirling about for several months, people felt that Alexandra's letter proved that she and Rasputin were lovers. This was certainly not true, although it was an enduring myth. No one realized at the time that the letters were appearing because they had slipped out of Rasputin's hands. The police finally located the originals—and that raised a new and unexpected problem. "Makarov and I did not know what to do with the letters," Kokovtsov recalled. He suggested they be returned to the empress, but the minister of the interior gave them to Nicholas. "The Tsar turned pale," Makarov told Kokovtsov. "He nervously took the letters from the envelope." Looking at the letter from Alexandra, Nicholas growled, "Yes, this is not a counterfeit letter" as he tossed the packet into his desk drawer. "Now your dismissal is certain!" Kokovtsov warned, and within a few weeks his prophecy was fulfilled.

Alexandra fired off an angry telegram to Pokrovskoye chastising Rasputin for his carelessness. Rasputin's excuse was that Iliodor must have stolen the letters. But the empress was in no mood for excuses, and she refused to receive Rasputin when he rushed back to the capital. Anna Vyrubova hoped that the man who had once been an imperial favorite would join the family when they traveled to the Crimea for Easter, knowing this was a time of forgiveness and reconciliation. Nicholas rejected the idea. When he learned that Vyrubova had stashed the peasant on the train, the stowaway and his luggage were dumped at the next station.

Rasputin still proceeded to Yalta, and his arrival set tongues wagging. "Now I can rest easy," Prince Vladimir Orlov, a courtier, declared sarcastically. "Rasputin's here—everything will go well!"

In fact, things did not "go well" for Rasputin. For years people had been trying to persuade Nicholas and Alexandra to end their friendship with Rasputin, but without success. Apparently no rumor or scandal could separate them. If Rasputin's career was now coming to a sudden end, his own lousy judgment was to blame. But Rasputin was still convinced that God had sent him to save the Romanovs. He was forced to wait, hoping to reclaim his mission. And then, on October 2, 1912, something happened that threw events in a totally different direction.

10

"God Has Heard Your Prayers!"

OR HALF A CENTURY THE TSARS HAD HUNTED in Poland, escaping the pressures and scrutiny of court life. In September 1912 the family arrived at Bialowieza, a sprawling estate near Brest-Litovsk where Nicholas could commune with nature while his family relaxed. Alexis, who was now eight years old, fell one day while he was jumping into a boat. An internal hemorrhage soon developed in his lower left abdomen, and the tsarevich took to bed. His fever rose, and for a few days it seemed as if Alexis faced another crisis. But the swelling inexplicably disappeared, and by September 16 the boy was sufficiently well for the Romanovs to move on to the imperial hunting preserve at Spala.

The lodge at Spala was a rambling, overgrown chalet at the edge of a forest; its rooms were so dark and gloomy that the lights had to be left on even during the brightest days. Nicholas hunted while the grand duchesses played tennis and Alexandra enjoyed the sunshine. There were picnics in the forest, and the Romanovs entertained visiting Polish nobles. Only Alexis's health disturbed this bucolic world. Anna Vyrubova described him at this moment as "pale and decidedly out of condition." In fact, he was still recovering from his fall at Bialowieza and was restless at having to stay home. One day Alexandra took him for a drive. The carriage jostled along the uneven roads: the constant motion shook Alexis, and he was soon complaining of pain. The boy screamed during the return trip and was almost unconscious by the time they reached Spala. The date was October 2, 1912—the beginning of a nightmare.

Dr. Eugene Botkin found a severe hemorrhage in the upper left thigh near the groin. A purple swelling formed as the boy's temperature rose dramatically. The internal pressure was so intense that the tsarevich would not let the doctor examine the swelling. The hemorrhage was worse by the time Dr. Sergei Fedorov arrived on the overnight train from Saint Petersburg. As blood seeped from the groin into his abdomen, Alexis drew up his left leg to alleviate the pain, but the internal bleeding pressed against nerves with increasing force, making that position unbearable. Delirious and in agony, the tsarevich drifted in and out of consciousness. His screams filled the lodge, alternating with rasping, desperate moans. He slept little, ate nothing, and kept repeating, "Oh Lord, have mercy upon me!"

Alexandra sat by her son's bedside hour after hour as he cried "Mama, help me!"—but there was nothing she could do. Nicholas often relieved his wife, but he admitted that she "bore the ordeal better than I." Once he was so overwhelmed at his son's agony that he ran from the bedroom, weeping bitterly. Princess Irene of Prussia, Alexandra's sister, was at Spala that autumn; the tsar wrote that she was "a godsend to both of us." Irene noted that Nicholas was "so kindhearted, so level-headed and shows such composure in all circumstances."

Irene had a unique understanding of the situation: after losing one child to hemophilia in 1904, she constantly worried over Waldemar, her other hemophiliac son. The sisters shared an overwhelming sense of guilt at transmitting the illness to their sons, but at least they gave each other emotional support. Alexandra and Alexis both realized that his fragile life was slipping away. He was reflective at times. "When I'm dead," he asked his mother, "it won't hurt any more, will it?" He told his parents to build "a little monument of stones in the wood" after he was gone.

Servants and members of the household staff stuffed their ears with cotton to carry on their work. Since Alexis's hemophilia was a carefully guarded secret, they could only speculate as to why he was suffering. It was an extraordinary situation: the heir to the Russian throne lay dying, but everyone carried on as normal. Nicholas hunted, the grand duchesses played tennis, while Alexandra presided over teas and dinners for the Polish nobles. It was an exercise in deceptive banality—all to maintain the secret of Alexis's illness.

After ten years at court, the children's French tutor, Pierre Gilliard, accidentally learned of the family's terrible secret. One evening a group of local aristocrats arrived to enjoy Maria and Anastasia performing scenes from Molière's *Le Bourgeois Gentilhomme*. Their parents sat in front, chatting with guests, as Gilliard looked on from the side. He saw the empress slowly rise from her seat and excuse herself; as soon as she was out of the sight of her guests, she rushed to her son's bedside with a "distracted and terror-stricken look on her face." She soon returned to her company, smiling and carrying on the tragic game that dominated her life.

Alexis's fever rose dramatically on October 6. He was exhausted and weak, and his heartbeat was irregular; blood poisoning and peritonitis were probably setting in. That night Fedorov told the parents that their son's stomach was hemorrhaging. Nicholas finally agreed to issue regular medical bulletins informing the world that the tsarevich was ill. No mention was made of hemophilia—even now the deception continued. Prayers for the boy's recovery were offered throughout the empire; crowds in the capital flooded into the Cathedral of Our Lady of Kazan to light candles. At least the pretense of normalcy at Spala stopped. Since there was no church on the grounds of the estate, a tent was erected on the lawn. Father Alexander Vasiliev, religious instructor to the imperial children, led the prayers. "The servants, the Cossacks, the soldiers, and all the rest of the people were wonderfully sympathetic," Nicholas later wrote to his mother. "Polish peasants came in crowds and wept."

Millions prayed during the next two days, but Alexis got worse. Nicholas was having lunch with guests on October 8 when Alexandra sent him a hastily scrawled note, warning that the end was near. The tsar rushed to his son's bedside, sitting with his exhausted wife and watching helplessly. Father Vasiliev administered the Last Rites; the medical bulletin was already prepared for the next day announcing the tsarevich's death. The situation was dire, but Alexandra had not quite abandoned hope: there was still Rasputin.

The appeal to Rasputin was a last, desperate move, and it obviously came in the wake of a struggle. The faith of Nicholas and Alexandra in Rasputin had waned, but the situation gave them no choice. Although Rasputin was thousands of miles away, Alexandra wanted his prayers, and she asked Anna to send a telegram to Pokrovskoye on her behalf.

The answer arrived early the next morning. The exhausted, terrified mother was gone when Alexandra greeted her well wishers in the drawing room; she was now smiling and serene. She announced that the doctors "notice no improvement yet, but I am not the least bit anxious *myself.* During the night I received a telegram from Father

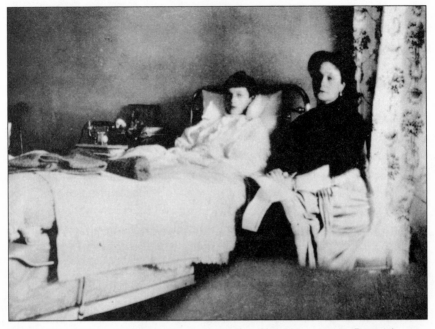

The tsarevich and Alexandra at Spala. The empress attributed her son's recovery to Rasputin's prayers and a telegram that she received on the morning of October 9, 1912. Anna Vyrubova recalled that it read, "The Little One will not die. Do not allow the doctors to bother him too much."

Gregory and he has reassured me completely." The cable was short and direct: "The Little One will not die. Do not allow the doctors to bother him too much."

Alexander Spiridovich writes that Rasputin actually sent two telegrams. The first said "Fear nothing—the illness is not as dangerous as they are saying. See that the doctors do not bother him." Spiridovich does not quote the second, but it supposedly assured Alexandra that God had heard her prayers and answered them. Mythmaking insisted on heightening the drama and poetry of the moment. We often read that Rasputin's single telegram read, "God has seen your tears and heard your prayers. Do not grieve. The Little One will not die. Do not allow the doctors to bother him too much." This parallels Isaiah 38:5, where King Hezekiah is told, "I have heard your prayer and seen your tears, I will . . . add fifteen years to your life." It also conflates Spiridovich's two cables into one text.

What happened next was apparently inexplicable. Nicholas noted in his diary that Alexis grew calm at two o'clock that afternoon, October 9, 1912; he slept, and his temperature fell. His improvement over the next twenty-four hours was so striking that the doctors issued a bulletin suggesting that the crisis had passed. The hemorrhage stopped two days later, and the swelling receded. Prayers for recovery gave way to thanksgiving in the tent church at Spala. Nicholas returned to the hunt while Alexandra joined her guests at increasingly festive dinners.

"Alexis's recovery will be very slow," Nicholas wrote to his mother. He "still has pain in his left knee . . . and has to be propped up on a pillow. But that does not worry the doctors, for the chief thing is that the process of internal absorption continues, and for this complete immobility is necessary. His complexion is quite good now though at one time he looked like wax: his hands and feet, his face, everything. He has grown terribly thin, but the doctors are now stuffing him for all they are worth." It would take months before Alexis could straighten his left leg, and even then he had to wear a cumbersome iron brace and undergo mud baths and massages to revive his atrophied muscles. But he was alive.

It is impossible to unravel precisely what happened at Spala. Dates and details remain unclear. When did Anna Vyrubova send Rasputin the telegram? Did his reply reach Spala early in the morning, or was it later in the day, when the tsarevich was already beginning to improve? Did Rasputin send the single cable described by Anna or the two shorter messages referred to by Spiridovich?

Alexis's recovery was the biggest mystery. Since this was not a fatal attack, it would seem that the crisis reached a high point and healing began of its own accord. Yet at some point the doctors had apparently abandoned hope. Fedorov suggested that "only a miracle" could save the boy's life and thought that the chance of such a miracle was less than one in a hundred. The doctors at that point were uncertain.

Or were they? Fedorov initially rejected an operation to relieve the pressure. As the situation continued to deteriorate, he told Alexander Mosolov, the director of the imperial court, that it was "most urgently necessary to apply far more drastic measures; but they involve a risk. What do you think: ought I say this to the Empress? Or would it be better to prescribe without letting her know?" Mosolov did not describe the "drastic measures" that Fedorov might have been consider-ing. Perhaps it was surgery to stop the internal bleeding. Later, when Alexis had recovered, Mosolov asked the surgeon if he had resorted to the measures that he had been considering. "If I had done so," Fedorov replied, "I should not have admitted it. You can see how things are around here!" That was not exactly a denial. Fedorov later conceded that the tsarevich's recovery was "wholly inexplicable from a medical point of view."

Spala leads to a larger issue: how did Rasputin deal with his young patient's hemophilia? We often read that Rasputin "cured" or "healed" Alexis, but obviously those are figures of speech. Alexis had hemophilia the day he was born and the day he died. It was Rasputin's ability to alleviate the symptoms of each attack that fixed his place in history. What was the secret of his success? Did Rasputin drug Alexis? Did he use hypnosis? Was it auto-suggestion? Did he possess some other strange ability that would not even occur to us now?

Hemophilia baffled the medical experts of the day—they could not even alleviate the pain of its attacks. An authoritative source for laypeople from 1885 noted that the men who were afflicted with this disease had a "remarkable disposition to bleed with or without the provocation of an injury." On one occasion a bump or a bruise might pass without incident, while on another it could produce an "incredibly painful" crisis. Spontaneous bleeding—from the nose, the mouth, and the throat—was common and unavoidable. In all of these instances, physicians were absolutely helpless.

Rasputin, however, was highly successful. One official at court reported that "people whose honesty I cannot doubt" told him that Alexis's doctors were "unable to stop a hemorrhage"—but when Rasputin appeared and prayed, the bleeding stopped. Alexander Mosolov admitted that "Rasputin had incontestable success in the art of healing. I have no idea how he managed it." The doctors at court despised Rasputin, but they reluctantly conceded his ability to relieve the suffering. "When Alexis was bleeding, I was unable to stop it with any method," Fedorov testified. But Rasputin "casually went up to the sick fellow and after the briefest time the bleeding stopped." Dr. Sergei Ostrogorsky loathed Rasputin, but this eminent pediatric specialist admitted that he "personally observed" Rasputin "bring relief to the Heir" on several occasions.

Some of Rasputin's enemies fancied that he "secretly drugged Alexis with the help of a lady-in-waiting to the Court," presumably Anna Vyrubova. The "drugs were discontinued" just before Rasputin appeared, the tsarevich improved, and Alexandra "put this down to the healing magnetism" of Rasputin. Another person who was suspected of being Rasputin's accomplice was Peter Badmaev, a member of the Buryat tribe of eastern Siberia. Badmaev rose to prominence in Saint Petersburg on the eve of the war by treating his upper-class patients with what he called "Tibetan medicine." Supposedly Badmaev applied and discontinued his potions in such a way as to convince Alexis's gullible parents that Rasputin was a miracle worker.

These ideas flourished thanks to the fact that the imperial family was so isolated. Few people would have understood at the time that Anna's primary loyalty was to the empress, not Rasputin. It is also true that Badmaev and Rasputin were enemies—not allies—during the peasant's early years at court. More important, no one could identify a potion that would cause a bogus attack of hemophilia.

Many have supposed that Rasputin used hypnosis. Charles Sydney Gibbes, the imperial children's English tutor, believed that hypnosis was the secret of Rasputin's success. The historian George Katkov thought that hypnosis could "affect the vaso-motor system and cause a contraction of the vessels comparable to the effect of adrenalin and similar drugs." He attributed Rasputin's "cures" to an ability to calm the boy at times of crisis.

Maria Rasputin insisted that her father had nothing to do with hypnosis, viewing it as "Satanic." She was wrong—and this is a prime example of how she idealized her father. The fact is that at one point, Rasputin was extremely interested in studying hypnosis. In 1913 the Okhrana intercepted a letter from a leading mesmerist telling his mistress that Rasputin had just approached him for lessons. Before the instruction could materialize, the police expelled the would-be tutor from the capital. But Rasputin persisted in his quest, and in 1914 his guards reported that he was studying hypnotism with a certain Gerasim Papandato. But Rasputin began healing Alexis through prayer in 1906.

It is interesting to note that no one ever claimed to have witnessed Rasputin hypnotizing Alexis. Nicholas and Alexandra were obtuse in certain ways, but surely they (or someone) would have noticed a man doing that to their son—and they would have been grateful for it. Sometimes Rasputin cured his young patient without being present. Perhaps that was the product of auto-suggestion? On one occasion when Alexis was suffering an attack, a call summoned Rasputin to the palace. He was drunk, and it would not have been wise for him to appear in that condition. Rasputin took the telephone call and predicted that the bleeding would stop within an hour, promising to come if it did not. Recovery occurred just as Rasputin had predicted.

Alexis was undoubtedly under the sway of Rasputin's powerful personality. Nicholas's sister, Olga, saw that one evening at Alexander Palace. The tsarevich was pretending to be a rabbit, "jumping up and down in the room. And then, quite suddenly, Rasputin caught the child's hand and led him to his bedroom. . . . There was something like a hush as though we found ourselves in church. . . . The children stood very still by the side of the giant, whose head was bowed. I knew he was praying. It was all most impressive. I also knew that my little nephew had joined him in prayer. I really cannot describe it, but I was then conscious of the man's sincerity."

Rasputin's presence, his methodical speech, and his aura of religious intensity—all this would have calmed troubled situations. Alexandra's attitude was important. She was convinced from the outset that Rasputin could heal her son; she associated his presence and prayers with recovery. Belief in those abilities eased her mind, and she undoubtedly conveyed that assurance to Alexis. A reduction of his stress might have slowed the bleeding and aided the natural healing process. None of this, though, would explain Rasputin's early successes. They came at a time when Nicholas and Alexandra had no reason to expect miracles. As for Alexis, he was two and unconscious when Rasputin first came to his bedside in 1906. It is difficult to imagine that hypnosis would have been useful under those conditions.

Some have suggested that Rasputin's good fortune was due to coincidence. Pierre Gilliard believed that Alexandra took "certain perfectly casual coincidences" as Rasputin's miracles. Baroness Sophie Buxhoeveden, one of the empress's ladies-in-waiting, likewise attributed Rasputin's successes to fortunate timing. She thought that Rasputin had "sources of information" that permitted him to appear at just the right moment for the tsarevich's recoveries "to be attributed to him." Buxhoeveden probably had Anna Vyrubova in mind as the accomplice. Another of Alexandra's friends, Lili Dehn, insisted that "coincidence and coincidence alone" was responsible for Rasputin's cures. This conviction was echoed by Nicholas's mother, Maria Fedorovna, and his cousin Alexander Michaelovich.

Coincidence might explain some of Rasputin's successes. There were surely times when Alexis was recovering just at the moment Rasputin appeared, but this could not have been true in many cases. Nor is the suggestion that Rasputin had a confederate in the palace convincing. Anna would not have agreed to deceive Alexandra in this way; a suggestion of that sort would have killed their friendship. Rasputin also could not have relied on coincidence early in his career.

An incident from Sophie Buxhoeveden's childhood opens up another line of thought. The countess noted that certain people possessed a gift called *zagovarivat' krov'*—literally "parleying with the blood." This power was not confined to Russia; English-speaking people refer to the people who have this skill as "horse whisperers" or "blood-stillers." They generally helped animals, although occasionally they treated people. Buxhoeveden recalled how "Alexander the Horse Leech" was summoned when a horse on her estate suffered a severe cut to its fetlock. The peasant removed the bandages and massaged the wound as he mumbled words that no one could decipher. The bleeding stopped, and the horse was restored to health. Another aristocrat recorded a case involving a woodsman who was cutting down a tree when his ax slipped, nearly severing his foot. Someone fetched a peasant who was a blood-stiller. He arrived and prayed, and the bleeding suddenly stopped.

Given the claim that Rasputin possessed a special understanding of horses when he was young, Buxhoeveden wondered if he might not have drawn on some power similar to "parleying with the blood." That is possible—but it is also true that some aspects of the human experience cannot be explained by reason alone. The Russian Orthodox Church teaches that miracles occur in modern times; it was (and is) open to the possibility that certain icons have the power to heal the sick. Rasputin's enemies, of course, adamantly rejected the notion that Rasputin possessed spiritual gifts or that he could have used anything of that sort to treat the tsarevich.

Rasputin did not claim to work miracles. He insisted that his healings were manifestations of God's will—expressions of divine grace. "There is no saint on earth," he often said. "As long as a person lives, he sins." This was how Nicholas and Alexandra perceived him: Rasputin was not a saint; he was a man with spiritual gifts who safeguarded their son's life. Rasputin was the intermediary God used to safeguard all of the members of their family. It was God who had the power.

Alexandra embraced the more mystical features of the Orthodox faith with such enthusiasm as to make more casual believers uneasy. They regarded the empress as extreme and narrow-minded. They also sensed that her attitudes were related to her faith in Rasputin. Nicholas was more rational—he was something of the proverbial husband who accepted his wife's passions to keep peace under his own roof. But he was equally convinced that Rasputin was a man of God, especially after Spala. The facts would have been clear to Alexandra and her husband: Alexis was at the brink of death, and Rasputin appeared and prayed, and their son recovered. The emperor and his wife were convinced that a miracle took place at Spala in that autumn of 1912. The experience drew them even closer to Rasputin. It must have seemed that they had no choice. Which was more important—the carping of skeptics or the life of their son? Given that events had cast the problem in those terms, it was not difficult for them to reach a decision.

11

Spiritual Crisis

A TWENTY-ONE-GUN SALUTE RANG OUT from the Peter and
Paul Fortress on the morning of February 21, 1913, beginning
the celebration of three hundred years of Romanov rule over Russia.
In a manifesto, Nicholas II prayed that "our Lord's benediction upon
us and our dear subjects will not grow scantier than it is now"—an odd
turn of phrase, actually, and one that seemed to complain that God
had not been so favorable to Russia in recent years. Rasputin's notoriety had certainly lowered the prestige of the throne. Yet Nicholas
was hopeful: "May our Omnipotent God strengthen and glorify the
Russian land and grant Us the strength to hold high and steady the
glorious banner of our Fatherland."

Nicholas led his family that morning in a procession from the
Winter Palace to the Cathedral of Our Lady of Kazan. A Te Deum
was scheduled for noon. Michael Rodzyanko created a scene at the
last moment when he learned that members of the Duma had been
assigned a block of seats toward the rear of the church. No sooner
had Rodzyanko secured a more prominent place for his colleagues
than he learned that an "unknown man in peasant dress and wearing
a pectoral cross" was sitting in that area and refused to move. "Sure
enough, it was Rasputin," Rodzyanko recalled. He ordered the peasant to leave, but Rasputin would not budge; instead he gazed intensely
into the face of the fat president, as if he was trying to hypnotize him.
Rodzyanko felt a "tremendous force" washing over him, but he finally

regained control over himself and commanded Rasputin to leave. "I was invited here at the wish of people more highly placed than you!" Rasputin snarled as he showed his invitation. As Rodzyanko hovered over Rasputin menacingly, he fell to his knees and cried out, "Oh Lord, forgive him such sin!" Rodzyanko called for the guards. Seeing that he was defeated, Rasputin rose from the marble floor, gave the president a last, angry stare, and proudly exited the cathedral.

The aftershocks of the confrontation were still rippling through the church as the imperial family arrived. Their procession through the streets leading to the cathedral had not generated much enthusiasm. The aristocrats and officials in the church turned censorious eyes toward Nicholas and Alexandra as they walked down the long aisle to the front. The tsar seemed preoccupied, while his wife was nervous and aloof. Events that followed throughout the empire as the spring unfolded confirmed the Tercentenary's shaky start. Curiosity and indifference were more evident than loyalty or goodwill.

Prime Minister Vladimir Kokovtsov noted the "rather colorless" celebrations in Vladimir, Suzdal, and Nizhnyi-Novgorod. The "lack of enthusiasm and the smallness of the crowds" suggested "shallow curiosity" at best. The city of Kostroma on the Volga offered the first sign of "anything approaching enthusiasm." Kostroma had a rich association with Michael, the first Romanov to rule Russia. The sixteen-year-old boy took refuge at the Ipatiev Monastery near the city in 1613, trying to hide from the delegation that was coming to tell him that he had been elected tsar. The crowds that greeted Nicholas and Alexandra three hundred years later were similarly enthusiastic. Then Rasputin appeared and everything changed.

Rasputin must have come to Kostroma at Alexandra's request, for he held an invitation to the grand service scheduled at the cathedral. He boldly assumed a prominent place at the front, just across the aisle from the spot where the imperial family would stand. This set the entire congregation abuzz. People strained to see the most infamous man in Russia, whispering and pointing as he obliviously stared ahead. Police Director Stephen Beletsky finally asked Rasputin to take a less conspicuous spot. Rasputin only shifted a few steps; indeed he remained the focus of attention. Rasputin smiled at the ladies and exchanged meaningful glances as he finally left.

Rasputin also attracted attention when the imperial family reached Moscow in May. He was spotted in the Kremlin, watching as the tsar and his party passed through the citadel. Nicholas II's sister, Xenia, complained that the peasant was "again in evidence all over the place." Officials and members of the clergy had protested, but to no avail. "How unfortunate it all is!" she concluded helplessly.

Rasputin's frequent appearances undermined the regime's efforts to elicit popular support, for they reminded everyone of the fact that he enjoyed imperial favor. Nicholas and Alexandra seized on a few positive moments as proof of what they wanted to believe. "Now you can see for yourself what cowards the ministers are," the empress insisted to a lady-in-waiting at one event. "They are constantly frightening the Emperor with threats and forebodings of a revolution, and here—as you can see for yourself—we only need show ourselves and at once their hearts are ours."

Rasputin's finances had been precarious during his early years in the capital. He moved from apartment to apartment as better opportunities appeared. In 1913, with the support of his friends, he rented a single room with a "simple bed and painted wooden table" at No. 3 English Prospekt. Rasputin was proud of this flat—he finally had a place in the city that he could call his own. He was also glad to trade it for a more spacious apartment at No. 70 Nicholaevsky Street.

Rasputin's favor at court did not make him rich. Rumor abounded that Alexandra paid him a salary to tend the "lamps burning day and night before the holy icons" in the Alexander Palace chapel. There was no such position—and in any event Rasputin was too clever to ask for employment by the imperial couple. It was best for the empress to suppose that Rasputin was busy with God's work and his time was too valuable to be sold for wages.

In fact, when it came to money, Rasputin was constantly complaining that the empress was "stingy—it's terrible how stingy she is!" She usually failed to compensate him for railway and taxi fares, even when it was she who asked him to come to Tsarskoye Selo. Alexandra did shower Rasputin with clothing and icons and bric-a-brac for his home in Pokrovskoye. But she gave no thought to the economics of his life in the capital. On the rare occasions when the empress handed over a bit of cash, she did it begrudgingly—and she seemed surprised if he asked for more. Rasputin often "borrowed" funds from friends to pay his way to and from Alexander Palace. Alexis Filippov, his publisher and friend, thought that the situation was ironic and absurd: although

Rasputin himself was struggling for survival, he would fling "hundreds and even thousands of rubles a day to stray acquaintances who asked for his help."

Anna Vyrubova likewise claimed to have no idea of where (or how) Rasputin got his money. The charity of friends was helpful, but they were not rich. Peasants who sought his help gave the starets poultry, vegetables, and pastries, while poor people offered fish, fruit, and bread. Wealthier favor seekers came bearing icons, wine, and caviar. Akilina Laptinskaya supervised Rasputin's finances and collected money from those who sought his influence. She began as an early follower and in due course became Rasputin's secretary and lover. The last favorite of the last tsar suspected her of pocketing money, and on two occasions he drove her away. He also asked her to return. Laptinskaya was intelligent and organized, and Rasputin needed her as his life became steadily more complicated.

Rasputin's financial situation improved significantly by 1913. He learned to expect bribes from people who wanted him to intercede with officials on their behalf. Rasputin had gotten his first taste of this in 1910, when some businessmen paid him to secure state financing for an irrigation project in the Caucasus. Other "deals" followed as the word got around that Rasputin's influence was worth the price.

Rasputin was now walking on the dark side—this stage of his career added to his mystique. Newspapers published articles on "Rasputin—the Corrupt Holy Man" or "Rasputin—Wheeler and Dealer!" Rasputin professed indifference to this, but it bothered him. Journalists "always write horrors about me," he grumbled. The peasant toyed with the idea of starting his own newspaper. "The people need every living word," he claimed. "I've been thinking of bringing out the most genuine and true people's newspaper. People are giving me money for it; religious people are stepping forward. I'm getting good people together, believers, and if God wills it I'll ring the bell." The idea died when it became clear to him that few newspapers in Russia were very profitable.

Meanwhile the critics were unyielding. Although an editorial in the *Evening Times* did not refer to Rasputin by name, it complained that "a certain starets" should not be directing political policies or influencing church appointments. Rodzyanko showed a copy of the paper to Nicholas II, who claimed to be puzzled. "Who held such power?" the tsar asked. "There is but one starets of that sort in Russia," Rodzyanko answered, "and you know who he is. He is the sorrow and despair of all Russia."

Security procedures at Tsarskoye Selo added to the intrigue. When Vladimir Voeikov assumed this responsibility in 1913, he was surprised to learn that no effort was made to conceal Rasputin's comings and goings. Nicholas II's diary suggests that Rasputin saw the imperial family at least once a month. But Rasputin did not have an open pass; he was forced to wait each time he appeared while a sentry phoned for permission to admit him. Noting this provoked gossip, Voeikov had the peasant admitted immediately in the future.

Nicholas had little to say when Rodzyanko or anyone else tried to engage him in discussions about Rasputin. Since Alexis needed Rasputin, the peasant's position after Spala was secure. The tsar's diary notes that on July 16, 1913, his son's "right elbow began to hurt from waving his arms about too much while playing. He could not sleep for a long time and was in great pain, poor thing!" Rasputin arrived the next day. "Soon after his departure the pain in Alexis's arm started to disappear, he became calmer and began to fall asleep." What was there to discuss?

Ironically, the campaign against Rasputin was at odds with the mystical mood that was sweeping Russian society in these years. The creeping religious cynicism of earlier years had blossomed by 1913 into a full rebellion against established Christianity. Intellectuals were bored—they sought diversion in the obscure, the obscene, and the bizarre. Vasily Rozanov scoffed at traditional morality and preached that sex was the path to liberation. George Gurdjieff was attracting attention by synthesizing the great religions of the world into what he called "esoteric Christianity" or the "Fourth Way." Mysterious teachings from the east were becoming popular in fashionable society. A haunting sense that disaster loomed brought a frenzied embrace of pleasure. Peter Badmaev and his mysterious Tibetan herbs were entirely at home in salons where aristocrats passed cocaine to guests at the dinner table. Esoteric religion blended with drug addiction and the new sexuality.

Homosexuality was becoming common—it included church leaders, aristocrats, proletarians, and members of the Romanov family. The imperial couple held Vladimir Meshchersky in high esteem despite the fact that the prince was caught fornicating with a young Guards officer in what they (obviously) thought was a quiet corner of Alexander Palace. The empress once described Meshchersky as her husband's "help and counselor."

In some ways Rasputin reflected the new moods that were sweeping the capital. Even so, his triumphant autumn at Spala turned into a winter of discontent the following year. Alexis Filippov noted how Rasputin passed from "a mellow, spiritual tranquility to a period of doubt and painful disillusion with everything, especially the meaning of life." This was a true spiritual crisis, and it lasted to the end of his journey on this earth. Those who suppose it was caused by sex and alcohol may be confusing cause and effect. Rasputin's friends claim that he scarcely touched alcohol until 1912 or 1913. Then they noted the "great change"—the crisis. Rasputin was now drinking in alcoholic fashion. His sexual appetite also became stronger and more openly expressed from 1913.

Rasputin's worldly success had eroded his spiritual life. He was shaken when he felt his spiritual gifts slipping away. He confessed to his daughter Maria that he would have to start over again, like a novice on the spiritual way. But that was only a smoke screen—a sign of just how much he needed his daughter's approval. It did not mark a change in his behavior. Rasputin suddenly could not face the world without alcohol. He drank regularly and heavily, and his life became disorderly. Night time was the worst time: that was when he was left alone to wrestle with insomnia and nightmares. His solution was to escape into a world of alcohol, sex, and Gypsy music.

It was no coincidence that Rasputin suddenly needed instruction in hypnotism. As we saw in chapter 10, the police expelled the professional showman who agreed to teach Rasputin his secrets in 1913. But the starets did not give up. A police report dated February 1, 1914, notes that Rasputin "has been studying hypnotism from a certain Gerasim Papandato (nicknamed the 'Musician')." Lessons in hypnotism: how ironic! People often attributed Rasputin's gifts of healing to hypnotism. But when Rasputin feared he was losing those powers, he turned to hypnotism. If God's power failed, perhaps man's would prevail?

Rasputin never lost his faith or sense of religious mission. To the end he taught, prayed, and sought forgiveness. But the Rasputin of 1913 was no longer the wide-eyed wanderer who had arrived in Saint Petersburg a decade earlier. The pilgrim had become a profligate. As if to compensate for the damage that heavy drinking was doing to his life, Rasputin embraced temperance societies and their public crusades. He denounced vodka and insisted that the government should not profit from its distribution. Rasputin called upon people to abstain from alcohol even as he was finding it impossible to face life without it. "It's a

Rasputin from 1909 to 1913. When the picture on the left was taken in 1909, Rasputin was forty years old and was still bright-eyed and intense. By the time the center photograph was taken in 1911, Rasputin had attained spiritual serenity and the status of a respected teacher and a spiritual guide. The picture on the right, taken in 1913, shows the effects of a spiritual crisis that Rasputin had been suffering for about a year. The effects of his sudden heavy drinking are all too apparent.

matter of struggling against drunkenness, which is an old evil in Russia," he declared in a rare newspaper interview on May 29, 1914. "It's a good cause, certainly," he continued. "What we need is a change of hearts and attitudes towards the general welfare, that's the only way we'll succeed."

If Rasputin's life echoed the new attitudes sweeping Saint Petersburg, he was totally at odds with public opinion on the question of war in the Balkans. As Turkey declined throughout the nineteenth century, Russia and Austria-Hungary jockeyed for control of the peninsula. Austria was interested in the area while Russia was protective of her fellow Slavs. When Serbia, Greece, and Bulgaria attacked Turkey in 1912, influential voices in Saint Petersburg called on Nicholas II to defend the Slavic cause and the Orthodox faith they shared. War fever was especially strong by the spring of 1913, just as the Romanov dynasty was celebrating three hundred years of its increasingly shaky greatness and glory.

As a peasant Rasputin had a keen understanding of what war would bring to Russia. As he saw it, the nobles had a vested interest in warfare—they relished the opportunity to command armies, lead the troops, and gain fat salaries and fine privileges. The peasants, on the other hand, got nothing but death, misery, and patriotic exhortations from the military machine. Even a Russian victory would be illusory. ("We're already the biggest country in the world," Rasputin once declared. "Why do we need more real estate?!") He also understood that Germany would defeat Russia—and her allies could not prevent it. Defeat would lead to revolution and the fall of the imperial system. The world that Rasputin cherished would be swept away in a torrent of fire and bloodshed. Millions would suffer and die.

Rasputin voiced some of these opinions to journalists in the fall of 1913. He told the *St. Petersburg Gazette* that "we should do away with the fear and discord of war and not encourage discord and hostility. We Russians should avoid conflict and build a monument—a real monument I say—to those who work for peace. A peaceful policy against war should be considered lofty and wise." He spoke well of the Turks and rejected the sentimental notion that Russia should defend the Balkan Slavs. "We have seen how our 'little brothers' behave. Now we understand everything."

Rasputin was equally direct with an interviewer for the *New Times*:

It's good for foreigners to come to us because the Russian people are good—our soul's the best. The worst Russian has a better soul than foreigners. They themselves feel this and they come to us for spirit. They have the machine but you can't survive with just the machine. It looks like everything around them is good, but there's nothing in the person. And that's the main thing.

He dismissed suggestions that Russians should support the Greeks because of their common faith. He observed a "lot of sin" at Mount Athos; they "don't live like monks should"—an ironic complaint considering the source. "Christians," he continued, "are getting ready for war, they preach it, work themselves up along with everyone else. War's bad but Christians run to it rather than submitting. It's not worth fighting, taking life and good things from each other, destroying Christ's teachings and killing the very soul from the outset."

A game of wits was in play during this interview. The reporter for the *New Times* was hoping to twist Rasputin's words into damaging statements: Rasputin did not appreciate the importance of Europe, he did not understand Russia's honorable tradition of defending the Balkan Slavs, et cetera. And yet, Rasputin's performance showed how sound his advice, at its best, could be.

In the end it was France's failure to support Russia that preserved the peace in 1913. Rasputin's views took a back seat to power politics. But ex–prime minister Sergei Witte paid tribute to Rasputin's courageous stand; the peasant "spoke decisive words at the time of the Balkans War. One must consider him therefore a fact of life." The *Bell*, a newspaper closely allied with the Russian Orthodox Church, noted, "Our savior from this most senseless bloodshed is said to be an inspired 'holy man,' a sincere prophet who dearly loves Russia and is . . . close to the helm of our highest politics."

Rasputin emerged from the crisis relieved but worried. He understood that his victory had been close—and it was precarious. "As long as I live, I will not permit war!" he declared. When an Italian journalist asked Rasputin if he thought that war was imminent, he replied, "Yes, they say there will be war, and they are getting ready for it. May God grant that there will be no war. This troubles me."

12

The Woman with the Missing Nose

I N THE SPRING OF 1914, Nicholas II suddenly turned against Rasputin and forced him to return home. The reason for this dramatic turn of events is not entirely clear, although the events themselves suggest an explanation.

Nicholas II accepted Rasputin as a voice of the people, and he drew strength from their conversations. He believed in the power of prayer and was open to the possibility that miracles occur in modern times. Experience convinced him that Rasputin had spiritual gifts. But the tsar was jealous of his authority as the ruler of Russia, and he probably resented the way his wife was constantly injecting their friend into political issues. Everyone realized that conflict was again brewing in the Balkans; Nicholas knew that his wife and the peasant still opposed war, and he might have resented their never-ending pressure to avoid war. (If this was an irritant, at least he could strike out against Rasputin.) Tensions in Alexander Palace obviously exploded when Gregory met with the imperial family on March 14, 1914. Nicholas ordered the Siberian mystic and healer to leave the capital. When Leonid Molchanov dropped in for a visit shortly after this blowup, he found that his old chum was "extremely upset" at the unexpected turn of events. "It's a bad thing," Rasputin explained. "All of a sudden I have to go to my town of Pokrovskoye for good."

Rasputin's father, Efim, happened to be visiting his son, and they traveled together as far as Tyumen. Newspapers noted that Rasputin was wearing a beautiful fur coat and beaver hat—but they did not realize that he was being exiled from Saint Petersburg. It is clear that Nicholas II stood up to his wife in making this decision, and it is interesting to note that when he did that, she accepted it. The 75,000 rubles Alexandra gave Rasputin from her own private chancery at the moment they parted had all the earmarks of a farewell gift—a goodwill offering that would end her family's relationship with the peasant on as pleasant a note as possible.

But the empress would not give up in such instances—that was the second half of the story. In May 1914, Rasputin returned to the capital. It seems likely that Alexis suddenly needed Rasputin, although later events suggest that the tsar got a concession: an agreement that would keep the peasant out of public affairs. Nicholas's diary notes that Gregory visited the imperial couple on May 18 and June 17. The three old friends probably acted as if Rasputin's recent return home had resolved what had simply been an unfortunate misunderstanding.

Nicholas and Alexandra had a full schedule, starting with an official visit to Romania in June 1914. Upon their return, they received the king of Saxony; the British First Battlecruiser Squadron weighed anchor at Saint Petersburg on June 20 and stayed there ten days. Raymond Poincaré, president of France, paid a much-anticipated state visit in late July. The imperial couple received Rasputin on Tuesday, June 17, just before he left to spend the summer in Pokrovskoye. That date was June 30 on the Gregorian calendar; two days before that, a member of the Black Hand killed Archduke Franz Ferdinand and his wife at Sarajevo. Few people—Rasputin included—expected the assassination to lead to war. Indeed, the peasant offered his thoughts on the tragedy to a reporter just before he left for Siberia:

Well, brothers, what can Gregory Efimovich say? He's dead. Cry and shout as much as you want, it won't bring him back. Do what you will—the result will always be the same. It's fate. But our English guests in Petersburg [Rasputin is referring to the visiting squadron] can't help but be glad. It's good [for them]. My peasant mind tells me it's a big event—the beginning of friendship between the Russian and English people. It's a union, my dear, of England with Russia, and if we find friendship with France as well, that's no trifle but a powerful force, really good.

So the tirades about "Russia's greatness" that Rasputin vented dur-ing the Balkans crisis in 1913 were gone—that was probably part of the compromise that brought him back to Saint Petersburg. Now Rasputin was telling the world how much he valued the allies. This time the Siberian mystic and healer was not embarrassing his royal master.

Diplomatic tensions grew over the next two weeks as Austria moved to punish Serbia for her support of the Black Hand. The Serbs looked to Russia for support while Germany stood behind Austria; France made clear that this time she would fight at Russia's side. A localized war would be a thing of the past. An Austrian attack on Serbia would trigger a general European conflict.

Alexandra sent an urgent telegram to Rasputin: "It is a serious moment, they are threatening war." The cable arrived at Pokrovskoye just before three o'clock in the afternoon on Monday, July 13, on the Gregorian calendar. A messenger rushed it to Rasputin's house. Rasputin gave him a tip and started to go back into his house, reading as he went. Then he moved to stop the courier and dictate an immedi-ate reply. "I came through the gate of my house to the street," Rasputin recalled, "when an unknown woman approached from the left side of our wicket fence. Her mouth and face were veiled so that I could only see her eyes. I did not know her name." Supposing that she was a beg-gar, Rasputin reached into his pocket for some coins. "At that moment a dagger flashed in her hand and she stuck it once into my stomach, near the navel. And I could feel the blood pouring out of me." Stunned, Rasputin turned and ran toward the church, "holding the wound with both hands. The woman came after me with the dagger." Only the crowd attracted by Rasputin's cries prevented his assailant from strik-ing another blow.

Rasputin was carried to his house, bleeding profusely. A telegram to Tyumen sent Dr. Vladimirov and two assistants scrambling. Racing through the night, Vladimirov urged the driver on, promising him a bonus "for vodka" if he got them to Pokrovskoye before midnight. It took the team eight hard, bumpy hours to reach their destination. The nurse recalled that "we found Rasputin lying on a bench, covered by a sheep-skin coat . . . wrapped in towels." The wound was two centimeters long and a centimeter wide; the intestines had not been injured, but his condition was serious, and the doctor warned his family that the patient might die. "We performed the operation right in the house," the nurse continued. The surgery was by candlelight, and Maria Rasputin recalled that her father refused an anesthetic. Rasputin insisted that he would survive—he urged the doctor not to worry. Then he fainted. Rasputin called for a priest when he regained consciousness to hear his last confession.

Rasputin also fired off a telegram to Alexandra, telling her "that hunk of carrion struck me with a knife, but with God's help I'll live." Rasputin was drifting in and out of consciousness by the time Alexandra's reply arrived: "We are deeply shaken"—"praying with all our hearts." On July 2, she wrote, "Our grief is beyond description, we hope for God's goodness. Alexandra." A first-class doctor was dispatched to Siberia to oversee Rasputin's medical care. Nicholas II also directed the minister of the interior to see that Rasputin's security would henceforth be a matter of top priority.

"That woman hit me a good one in the gut, but it's not so bad," Rasputin assured the empress in another wire. "Saved by a miracle. I'll live for us all. The Virgin's tears weren't wasted. They sent for a doctor." By July 3 he had stabilized sufficiently to be moved. The steamship *Lastochka* carried Rasputin, Praskovaya, and Maria to Tyumen, where the court physician assumed direction for his care at State Hospital #649. The journey had been difficult: by the time he arrived Rasputin was drifting in and out of consciousness, mumbling, "I'll pull through! I'll pull through!" Rasputin sent another cable that night, warning Alexandra that he faced another operation and it "will be quite serious. I'll be in bed three weeks." Rasputin actually spent forty-six days in the hospital.

The doctor operated the next morning, repairing the internal damage and suturing the wound. Everything went well, and the doctor told Rasputin that he would probably be released within two weeks. Then his temperature rose to 103 degrees, and it fell a few hours later. Cables kept the empress briefed on developments. On July 7, Rasputin told Alexandra that the "stitches came out OK, I'll recover." There was a turn for the worse on July 12: "Lost a lot of blood today, I'll have to stay longer in the hospital." Then he rebounded, although he confessed that "I have been deceiving you; the illness was very dangerous, the loss of blood was great and the stench was terrible."

An artist's sketch of Rasputin survives from those days. It reveals a chastened man who had barely survived a brush with death. Rasputin's

Rasputin recuperating in State Hospital #649 in Tyumen in the summer of 1914. The sketch is by an unknown artist.

head is bowed, and his hands are clasped. The inscription in his own hand reads: "What of tomorrow? You are our guide, Lord. How many Calvaries must we cross in life?" Letters, telegrams, and expressions of concern came in from every part of the empire. Akilina Laptinskaya rushed to Siberia with gifts from the faithful, intent on keeping vigil at Rasputin's bedside. Bishop Varnava visited, as did various female friends.

Rasputin had no proof, but he was convinced that Iliodor was behind the attack. He told the police that Iliodor was "abnormal":

He's separated from God, from the holy Church. I was with Iliodor four years ago in Tsaritsyn . . . I lived with him in a friendly way and shared all my thoughts with him. I helped him, but when I stopped helping him he turned on me. . . . Our quarrel came from the fact that I didn't let him have his way with pilgrims on the Volga and I was against giving him money for his paper, *Thunder and Lightning*. Iliodor was with me just four years ago at Pokrovskoe and he stole an important letter which he gave to powerful enemies. I can't say more than this.

Rasputin felt well enough at one point to take a break from the hospital and visit Tobolsk. He traveled by steamship, arriving to a welcome by Bishop Varnava, who offered a Te Deum aboard the vessel. The ship buzzed with rumors that Rasputin was near death, although the police kept curious people from his cabin. Every now and then a female admirer emerged to fetch something for "Papa." Rasputin ordered them not to wear corsets—that quickly got around the ship. The large crowd waiting at the dock when he returned to Tyumen saw a curious spectacle: Rasputin getting off the ship clad in a woman's long, white dress with a matching bonnet.

Rasputin's presence disrupted the sleepy routine of State Hospital #649. "Peasants and admirers from the intelligentsia are here," a newspaper noted, "along with journalists and photographers—but only family and very close acquaintances saw the patient. They say that the starets requested that journalists and photographers not be admitted to the hospital within the range of a cannon shot." Rasputin's supporters asked that he be moved to a private room to avoid curious stares; but the hospital administrators, exasperated by their notorious patient, refused these requests.

The attack on Rasputin triggered a new burst of attention from the press. Articles suddenly appeared about his background, teachings, and followers, as well as his love life and "connections with high personages," to use a phrase that suddenly became common in Russian newspapers. It was an eloquent testament to Rasputin's hold on the public imagination. Rasputin was also agitated by the inaccuracies and prejudice he found in most of the stories.

Although the censor mandated that journalists could not link Rasputin's name to a member of the imperial family, the press enjoyed a freedom in discussing Rasputin that is striking. "The whole authority of the mighty Russian Empire," the *Voice of Moscow* informed its readers, "crawls on its knees before Gregory Rasputin." The *St. Petersburg Courier* told its readers that

rumors are circulating in Petersburg that Rasputin is not normal in sexual matters. Our associate turned to Professor S. Ya. Kulnev of the Women's Medical Institute to clarify this matter.

Kulnev spoke of cases of sexual discontent which happens "very often" among women, but is also "not rare" among men . . . when they are fully-grown, about 40 or older. "I and most doctors view these illnesses as psychological, nervous disorders. This illness is extremely dangerous to the sick person and it is quite difficult to cure. A long and stubborn struggle is common. Isolation is often desirable."

The editor of *Speech* confessed that he had known for some time that "Russia is a country of endless possibilities. Nothing is a surprise, anything can happen with us. Even so I cannot accept the significance accorded to Grishka Rasputin by leaders of every category from lower officials to ministers, and not just from hysterical women and bootlicking officials but from broad circles of the intelligent, newspaper reading public."

Press accounts of the attack in Pokrovskoye on that fateful afternoon were imaginative, to say the least. One paper quoted Rasputin as saying: "I grabbed a birch stake and was thinking, 'when do I split her head open?' Then I felt sorry for her and struck her pretty lightly on the shoulder. She fell down, people grabbed her by the arms—they wanted to tear her apart. I stood up for her, and then my strength failed me and I fell down." Radzinsky and Nelipa accept these stories at face value, although police reports and other archival materials suggest that journalists ground out reams of fanciful copy based on the rumors that were floating about Pokrovskoye in those tumultuous days.

The crowd that had rushed to save Rasputin dragged his assailant to the police. She cut her left wrist when someone pushed her to the ground—but she was otherwise unhurt. When the police questioned the suspect in the file room of the District Administrative Building, they learned that she was Khioniya Kuzmina Guseva, an unmarried, thirty-three-year-old woman originally from Simbirsk Province—the same region that gave the world Vladimir Lenin and Alexander Kerensky. She lived at Tsaritsyn with her sister and worked as a seamstress and servant. The police described Guseva as "barely literate"; she was Orthodox and owned no property. Under "Special Characteristics" the arresting officer noted, "Nose absent, irregularly shaped hole in its place."

Guseva had been driven by loyalty to Iliodor. The police described her as one of the "simple, uneducated, unskilled laborers" who formed his ever-shrinking circle of followers at Tsaritsyn. The police treated

Khioniya Guseva in a rare police photograph. Note that
the suspect's nose was missing or at least deformed. This
photograph is now in TFGATO, along with most of the
police documents related to the crime.

Guseva well, and the mayor's wife saw to her personal needs. Guseva
said that she shared Iliodor's hatred for Rasputin. She was proud of the
six rubles she earned daily as a servant and seamstress; some might have
considered the sum paltry, but she gladly contributed it to the common
fund, saying that the "little father [Iliodor] has to be fed with something."

Guseva had no previous contact with Rasputin, and she swore that
the plan to assassinate him was entirely hers. The newspapers had
persuaded her that Rasputin was (in her words) a "profligate and false
prophet." She remembered the day she read I Kings 18:40—it was
May 18, 1914—and she found it to be a powerful summons to what
she realized *she* had to do. If Elijah was justified in slitting the throats
of 450 false prophets, could anyone object if Khioniya killed only
one? Lowly and disfigured, Guseva probably thought that eliminating
Rasputin would give her a unique place in Iliodor's world. If someone
had to be sacrificed to rid the world of this monster, let it be her—not
some beautiful, young person with a hopeful future.

Guseva's choice of a weapon showed how little she knew about murder: instead of a medium-sized blade that a woman could use to good effect at close range, she chose a fifteen-inch dagger with a white bone handle designed for a man's grip. Guseva stalked her prey with this unwieldy blade from Yalta to Saint Petersburg to Pokrovskoye. There she rented a room, telling her landlord that she had come to meet the "perspicacious starets." The police learned that Guseva was spotted several times on the steps of the District Administration Building, perched on a spot with a clear view of Rasputin's house.

Although Guseva insisted that Iliodor was not involved, the police were suspicious. They did not think it was coincidental that he fled to Norway just before the attack. Investigators doubted that Guseva could have gone so far on the thirty-nine rubles that she claimed had financed her jaunts across the empire, even if she traveled fourth class as she claimed. (She still had ten rubles when she was arrested.) Guseva was talkative and defiant; refusing to apologize, she admitted hoping that Rasputin would yet die. The questions of her interrogators invited Khioniya to claim insanity or—as we read in the interrogations—to being in the throes of "religious ecstasy." She probably understood that such claims might mitigate her guilt and bring a lighter punishment. But Guseva insisted that she was entirely rational, and there is really no reason to doubt that.

Newspapermen descended on Khioniya's cell after she was placed in the local jail. The journalists quickly came to respect her. They characterized her as a simple, uneducated woman—though "numerous travels to holy places and associations with various people" would suggest that she was a "cultivated woman who has seen and knows much." They described Guseva as quite religious.

One of these journalists was Benjamin Davidson, a reporter for the *St. Petersburg Courier*. Since he could not explain why he "just happened" to pop up in Pokrovskoye on what proved to be the eve of the assault, the police moved to expel him—but their superiors in the capital refused the request. According to rumor, a confederate in Tyumen told Davidson when to arrive. The fact that he had an interview with Khioniya at the ready suggests that a high authority in the police department knew about the plot, and he was glad to let events unfold as they might. Efforts of the local police to take such an elementary precaution as expelling Davidson were quashed. This "high authority" or his underlings apparently helped Davidson prepare his story even before it took place.

Davidson was not the only one who invented stories about Guseva. The inaccurate accounts in the newspapers have confused historians. It was not true, for example, that Rasputin and Guseva had been lovers—that he had wronged her and she was seeking revenge. Rasputin and Khioniya saw each other the first time on the day she attacked him. What of the report that Guseva was angry because Rasputin raped Xenia, a beautiful young nun at the Balashevskaya Convent in Tsaritsyn? There was indeed a nun by that name at the cloister, and she confessed to admiring Iliodor—which probably meant that she disliked Rasputin. But Xenia declared in a court deposition that she saw Rasputin only twice, both times at a distance. She had no experiences, good or bad, with the peasant.

Guseva's missing nose added to the mystery. Journalists and historians assumed that the terrible disfigurement was caused by syphilis, that she got the disease from Rasputin and was seeking revenge. Guseva insisted that she lost her nose at thirteen when she suffered an unfortunate reaction to medicine.

It is also a myth that Rasputin showed sympathy for Guseva or that he tried to protect her from the villagers who flocked to save him. Rasputin called her the "slut who stuck a knife up my ass!" Although he was furious, Rasputin sensed that it was not in his interests for the world to learn why a total stranger hated him enough to kill him. Rasputin did not want her brought to trial. Lacking evidence against Iliodor for what the police called the "crime of June 29, 1914," the courts could proceed only against Guseva. The doctors concluded that she was "irresponsible" and should be spared criminal punishment—as well as a trial. The Tyumen District Court declared that Guseva was "insane" at the time of the attack; she was in a "state of passion due to the influence of religious-political ideas, and so she remains at present." The presiding judge directed that Guseva would remain in a "special psychiatric clinic until she is well."

Guseva was sent to the Tomsk Regional Clinic for the Insane. To keep her from speaking to others bound for the same destination, she traveled on a special ship while another craft carried the other inmates to Tomsk. The court ordered her confined "for at least two months." Although Guseva was housed in a medical facility, she was isolated from the other patients and treated as a prisoner. Wishing to use her time constructively, she sought permission to sew shawls for charity, but authorities denied the request.

A psychiatric evaluation of Guseva eight months after the crime conceded that she did not display "delirious ideas or hallucinations" or "symptoms of any particular type of insanity." She was simply anti-social, demonstrating "a hysterical nature" by quarreling with people and pursuing "groundless complaints." Her doctor thought that these symptoms would probably recede or "not manifest themselves in a par-ticularly acute fashion" if she were transferred to a better facility. Her sister twice petitioned for Guseva's release, but the authorities refused; their goal was obviously punishment, not rehabilitation. Guseva was finally freed in February 1917 by the handwritten order of Alexander Kerensky, minister of justice in the government that replaced the tsar-ist regime. After giving a brief statement, Guseva disappeared into the pages of history.

Rasputin was discharged from the hospital on August 17, 1914, so he was absent from Saint Petersburg during that momentous sum-mer when Europe rushed to war. Yet the telegraph kept him in con-stant communication with an increasingly worried empress. "We don't have a war yet and we don't need one," Rasputin cabled from Tyumen. Following daily developments in the newspapers, he could imagine the complicated situation the tsar faced; even so the diplomats "should be able to keep the peace, even if they are leftists." He warned Nicholas it was important to conceal the "disorders" in Russia. (Rasputin was probably referring to the problems that he knew would create difficul-ties if Russia went to war with Germany.) "It's a pity I can't be with you," he added the following day. "Everything will pass," he promised on July 1. "We just have to get through it. But don't give [our enemies] a reason to start yelling again."

"Bad news," Alexandra told Rasputin on July 3. "These are horrible moments. Pray for us, I do not have the strength to struggle with the others." The same day Rasputin told Nicholas "not to worry too much about war—pretty soon we'll have to put some shit in their breeches, but not yet; when the moment comes, our sufferings will be rewarded." Three days later, Rasputin wired the tsar, "I believe and hope for peace and calm, but they are planning great evil. We who are part of your life know all of your sufferings. It's very difficult not to see each other. Those who are close to the heart are secretly wondering: how can they help you?"

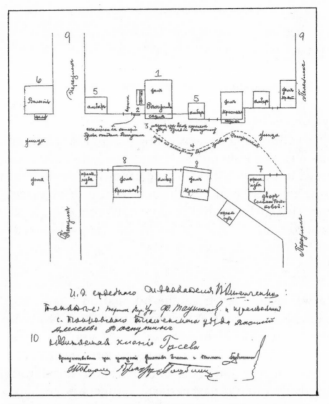

Police sketch of the "Crime of June 29, 1914." The top of the map is west, and the numbers indicate the following locations (the signatures of villagers at the bottom attest to the accuracy of the diagram): (1) Rasputin's house; (2) the bench where Khioniya sat while she waited for her victim to come out of his house; (3) the spot where Khioniya stabbed Rasputin; (4) the path Rasputin took to escape before he collapsed; (5) the barns on Rasputin's farm—Efim, his father, lived next door; (6) the District Administration Building—Khioniya sat here a day or more before her assault, studying Rasputin's house; (7) the house of another villager, where Rasputin collapsed (the police calculated that Rasputin ran 101 paces, and the sketch shows that); (8) a neighbor's house across the street; (9) an alleyway; (10) Khioniya's signature, which also confirms the accuracy of the diagram, though on the charges against her, the court automatically entered a plea of not guilty.

Rasputin realized that Alexandra was in despair to see peace slipping away—and he shared that view. Their greatest nightmare—a war with Germany—was unfolding before their eyes, and they were powerless to stop it. Former prime minister Sergei Witte thought that Rasputin was the only person who could "untangle the complex political situation at the present time." "Rasputin knows Russia better than anyone: her spirit, mood, and historical aspirations," Witte insisted. "He puts his own unique stamp on everything, but unfortunately he is not here now."

According to rumor, Rasputin tore his bandages when he read in the newspapers that Russia was about to mobilize her army. Seeing that his daily telegrams were not defusing the crisis, Rasputin sent the tsar what has come to be known as the "special telegram." He routed the message through Anna Vyrubova, ensuring prompt delivery and a defense of its views. The original has been lost, but Vyrubova recalled that it read, "Let Papa not plan war, for war will mean the end of Russia and yourselves, and you will lose to the last man." Anna said that the tsar was furious with this "almost unprecedented interference in affairs of state on the part of Rasputin." Nicholas insisted that "our domestic affairs are not subject" to the influence of others, and he spoke of putting Rasputin on trial for treason.

The tsar was also irritated to realize that the police had intercepted Rasputin's telegram and leaked it to key members of the Duma, hoping that it would discredit Rasputin and his pacifist views. Rasputin later told a friend that his enemies "wanted to hand me over for trial because of that telegram." The tsar defended his peasant friend—or at least he made clear that Rasputin's critics were out of line. The emperor insisted that "these are our family affairs; they are no matter for a court." But thanks to this leak, we have an alternate account of the contents of the "special telegram." Alexander Kerensky was a member of the Duma at the time; he saw the document, and he recalled that it said, "Don't declare war—fire Nicholasha[, the bellicose commander of Russian armies in the west]. If you declare war evil will fall upon you and the Tsarevich."

Nicholas II wavered in these July days. He was caught in the middle of conflicting forces: his own instincts, Alexandra's pleas, Rasputin's insistence on peace, and finally the pressure from his officials and generals to mobilize the army and prepare for war. Alexandra was horrified when she learned that her husband had authorized mobilization—people at the time regarded it as but one step away from firing the first shot. "War!" she mumbled to Anna. "And I knew nothing of it. This is the end of everything."

Germany announced war with Russia on August 1, 1914. (It was July 19 on the Julian calendar.) Nicholas II responded with his own declaration the following day, and it brought an enormous crowd to the Winter Palace. Just after three o'clock in the afternoon Nicholas appeared on the balcony, followed by the empress. A wave of energy passed through the people, and a mighty "Hurrah!" pierced the air. The tsar's subjects fell to their knees. People in the front rows tried to hush the others so that Nicholas could speak, but the excitement was uncontrollable. After a few moments they began singing the Russian anthem, "God Save the Tsar."

It was a moving sight: Nicholas II and his people were united—finally. This was a defining moment, and it pointed directly to the future. If Russia were victorious, history would forgive Nicholas for all the dark moments of his reign; Khodynka Field, the Russo-Japanese War, as well as Bloody Sunday and the suppression of the popular uprisings that followed it. And what if he failed? Much as Russians did not want to talk about that, the possibility hovered in the background like a ghost at a joyous feast. For the moment, their leader was standing on the balcony, savoring the outpouring of patriotism in the square below. Who would have suspected that within a few months this inspiring moment would give way to the "Reign of Rasputin"? Not even Rasputin would have dared to contemplate that.

13

Disaster Lurks in Moscow

W AR FEVER SWEPT RUSSIA in August 1914. In keeping
with the nationalist spirit, Nicholas II changed the name
of the imperial capital from Saint Petersburg to the more Slavonic
Petrograd. Thousands of his soldiers paraded to cheers, patriotic songs,
and waving handkerchiefs, unknowingly on their way to oblivion. Russia
launched an immediate offensive that drove three hundred miles into
East Prussia. But the Germans, better organized, led, and equipped,
reinforced their armies and counterattacked. The Russian First Army
perished at Tannenburg in August while the Second Army was defeated
and driven from East Prussia by mid-September. Over 30,000 Russians
died in the first thirty days of the fighting, while an incredible 225,000
men were taken prisoner. The Russian army was suddenly found to lack
munitions and arms, and the initial hope of a quick victory vanished.
Soldiers starved; artillery shells and even bullets were rationed. Rasputin
had been right: conflict brought misery—just that and nothing more.

Rasputin returned to the imperial capital a changed man. Guseva's
attack left him shaken, frail, and in constant pain. At times he found it
difficult to even stand. A friend recalled that Rasputin "walked around
hunchbacked in a gown because his wound was still bandaged and he
could not wear ordinary clothes. He was very depressed."

Rasputin after his return to Petrograd. This is how the
starets appeared in 1914, after Guseva's attack left him
frail and shaken.

Nicholas II had been furious with Rasputin for opposing the
war, and Rasputin was worried about his standing with the tsar. Anna
Vyrubova arranged a reunion on August 22, 1914, a few days after
Rasputin returned to the capital. "The meeting took place in my house,
and I heard every word of the conversation," Anna recalled. Nicholas
was "dejected and pessimistic" and turned to Rasputin as a friend he
needed at this hour. The tsar noted military difficulties and admitted
that he was worried by heavy storms and problems in transportation.
Rasputin had long championed peace, but now he told the tsar that
Russia must have total victory. Vyrubova recalled him saying that the
"country that held out the longest against adverse circumstances would
certainly win the War."

It was not just Rasputin's former pacifism that made the situation
difficult. He had always relied on Anna to arrange meetings, express
his opinions, convey messages, and alert him to potential threats.

But the friendship between Alexandra and Anna had cooled considerably at this point. The empress had come to notice that her friend was flirting with her husband. Since Alexandra was so often depressed, Vyrubova joined Nicholas for tennis and walks. The tsaritsa trusted her spouse but was beginning to doubt her best friend. In Anna's words, the empress was "ill, very low-spirited and full of morbid reflections." Alexandra found Anna to be "crude" and "unkind"; the empress suddenly was now referring to Anna as the "Cow" or the "lovesick creature."

It took a near-death experience to heal the breach. On January 15, 1915, Anna was traveling on a train that crashed; her legs, spine, shoulders, and head were severely damaged. Nicholas and Alexandra rushed to the hospital to find her unconscious and, apparently, near death. Rasputin likewise raced to her bedside. "Father Gregory!" Anna moaned as he entered her room. "Pray for me!" Rasputin called out her name and took her hand. After some intense moments of prayer, he pronounced that "she will live but she will always be a cripple!" as he fainted into a chair. Rasputin was right: Anna survived but from that day she walked only with the aid of a "stout stick." At the time Anna believed that Rasputin had worked a miracle, but she softened that position in her memoirs, perhaps to avoid appearing gullible.

And so the ladies' friendship was restored and Anna's house was again the place where Rasputin met Alexandra when Nicholas was not home. The empress's letters note these encounters: "Will go to Ania this afternoon and meet Our Friend, who wishes to see me"; "Our Friend was not long at Ania's yesterday, but very dear. Asked lots about you"; "Went to Ania's till 5, saw Our Friend there—thinks much of you, prays, we sat and talked together—says God will help."

On the eve of the war Rasputin settled into the apartment that would prove to be his home for the rest of his life. He had gone through seven different addresses in his decade in the capital, but in May 1914 he finally rented his famous flat at 64 Gorokhovaya Street. It was not a fashionable location: the area was swarming with lower-class people that must have provided Rasputin with grim memories of his peasant past. But it had the advantage of being only a few minutes from the train station that connected the capital to Tsarskoye Selo.

The building still has a distinctive oriel window and a broad arch-
way that leads to the inner courtyard. The staircase gives access to
apartments on its five floors. Rasputin occupied number 20 on the
third floor of the center section. The double doors of his flat opened
into a receiving room and corridor that led to the other five rooms.
Rasputin's daughters shared a bedroom to the right when the holidays
gave them a break from the exclusive Steblin-Kamensky Gymnasium.
This school represented something of a compromise: according to
rumor the empress wanted Maria and Varvara to attend the fashionable
Smolnyi Institute for Young Ladies of Noble Birth, but the director
rejected their application.

Massive oak furniture stood in the dining room. The small kitchen
at the end of the hall was filled with boxes of produce and opened to
the rear staircase. Three rooms were located on the other side of the
corridor. Rasputin's study featured a large desk littered with papers
and leather armchairs and a sofa for the ladies. The spacious reception
room finally permitted Rasputin to receive large numbers of people. It
also had oak furniture; lithographs decorated the walls while a samo-
var and telephone stood on the side table. (Rasputin's phone number
was 646-16.) His bedroom was at the end of the hall. Anna Vyrubova
gave him the red fox skin that covered his narrow bed; the walls were
festooned with icons, biblical prints, and pictures of Nicholas and
Alexandra. Akilina Laptinskaya moved in to serve as Rasputin's secretary while Katya Pecherkin came from Pokrovskoye to cook and clean.

Nicholas II increased Rasputin's security after Guseva's attack in
1914. Twenty-four agents now guarded Rasputin day and night. A
detective was always on the street, in the common vestibule, and at the
stairway leading to the apartment. Rasputin appreciated the protection
but not the spying that went with it. He resented being followed and
often darted down the back stairs or ducked into a nearby building
to lose the men on his trail. The alternative was to risk assassination.
Special Okhrana operatives Terekhov and Svistunov guarded Rasputin
at close range and remained his favorites even as the number of detectives surrounding Rasputin grew.

The police carefully recorded the name or description of every
person who came to Rasputin's apartment. A hundred or more people
seeking his favor began gathering before sunrise each day. The lines
often trailed down the stairs and onto the sidewalk. "You have all come
to me for help," Rasputin told a typical crowd as he returned home
from a night on the town. "I will help you all!" A friend compared

these scenes to "a movie—each time something new." An English visitor dismissed them as sycophants "anxious to secure appointments for themselves or their protégés." Many were peasants who needed help in lawsuits; they rubbed shoulders with ladies hoping to save the men in their lives from military duty. Students stood next to officers who hoped for a promotion or a transfer. Rasputin was especially friendly to beautiful young women and Jews, most of whom were illegal residents facing expulsion from Petrograd. Shady contractors expected to pay for the favors they sought. Not that this made Rasputin rich. A foreign observer was amazed to see "rich ladies push bundles of notes into his hand," but he never even bothered to count what he received. "When he saw a poor supplicant, he merely handed out the money just as he had received it."

One visitor was a woman whose husband and sons were killed in the early days of the war. She came to Petrograd, hoping for a pension that would help provide for her late husband's mother and sisters. When her requests were denied, she came to Rasputin as a last resort. "Got to make 'em listen," he mumbled. "All they do is scribble away. They're stupid—busy with their own stuff." Rasputin demanded money from each well-dressed gentleman who was waiting to see him. "Come on! Fork it over!" he barked. "You can part with a little bit of cash!" At the end he gave the money he had collected to the woman, saying, "Take this, dear lady! Be on your way—be careful—don't lose it!" On the street the woman counted 23,000 rubles—more than an imperial minister's annual salary. As she walked off the police heard her say, "What a man!"

Rasputin often wrote notes to help his petitioners. These messages became famous and developed a cash value. A typical note had a small cross at the top with a text that read something like, "Dear Friend, be so kind—do it for me. Gregory." Most were scrawled in Rasputin's hand, but he eventually had them typed up, ready to be signed and distributed. One note in the Moscow archive asks an official in the ministry of finance to help a woman named Margarita Leshch. It is handwritten on cheap school stationery and still has an envelope bearing the official's name, P. M. Vittorf. A second note simply informs "the bishop" that Annushka is arriving. A third note has an envelope and a letter addressed to "Sir [G]eneral Yuetu"; it read, "Dear one, forgive me for disturbing you but find work to help her gospodin [sir]." None of these messages has a date, and the last reminds us that Rasputin spelled certain words his own way: God (*bog* in Russian) was "bokh";

general (*general*) was "eniral"; revolutionary (*revolyutsioner*) was "lyutsoner."

The usefulness of Rasputin's notes varied. Sergei Sazonov, minister of foreign affairs, claimed that he threw the ones he received in the trash. Fearing Rasputin's influence, some recipients granted the requests. Rumor spoke of a woman who was denied permission to see a certain general until she took out the "precious square paper" with Rasputin's signature. She was then admitted, and her request was supposedly honored. Rasputin often sent people who needed money to Jewish millionaires he had befriended. Heinrich Schlossberg complained that these petitioners "cost me dearly, for the people who asked for my help really did need it."

A person who wanted Rasputin's help had to ask for it in person. Kuzma Chshtichev, an obscure minor official who lived in Yekaterinodar, tried to rely on the mail, but Rasputin ignored his pleas. His letter is a remarkable indication of the public perception of Rasputin's power.

"Father Gregory! What does it mean that you are completely silent?" Chshtichev wrote in despair on November 24, 1916. "We have written many letters to you, we have sent candy with stamps but you have not answered a single word. If you do not have the time to write, instruct Anna [his intermediary?] to write a couple of words. . . . Our case is progressing, there will soon be a trial, we are in despair [and are about] to lay hands on ourselves. [A suicide threat?] We plead with you, we believe in you, and know that you can do everything, that you can save us from the court, from prison. Our case does not fall under military authority, but under the city's jurisdiction. One word from you to minister of justice Makarov, and something in general to the great Alexandra Fedorovna [would save us]. You can do everything. . . . [Y]our strength and influence are all powerful." Chshtichev offered Rasputin 45,000 rubles in cash plus "gold items—everything, everything, . . . only save us from the court and prison. Write our answer, write Anna." The envelope was addressed "To Petrograd/to father starets Gregory Rasputin," with a 10-kopeck stamp (canceled) on the back. Chshtichev also wrote on the front, "The exact address is known to the post. To his own house."

Rasputin often warned petitioners that his notes might hurt their causes. He once sent an aspiring opera singer to an official with a note that read, "Fix it up, she's all right." The official could only tell the lady that the matter was beyond his jurisdiction. Rasputin sometimes directed his petitioners to friendly officials, but the ultimate source of his influence was at Alexander Palace at Tsarskoye Selo.

"I have heaps of petitions Our Friend brought here for you," Alexandra wrote to her husband on January 26, 1915. This became a common theme in her letters. On August 30, 1915, she wrote, "I enclose a petition from Our Friend, you [could] write your decision upon it, I think it certainly might be done." On January 6, 1916: "I send you a petition from Our Friend, it's a military thing. He only sent it without any word of comment." Rasputin also handed petitions to Nicholas when they met. But the tsar was irritated by reports that Rasputin was acting as a "fix-it" man, and he often challenged those requests. Rasputin retreated in such instances, claiming that he was simply acting on behalf of a friend.

Rasputin, never primarily interested in acquiring wealth, was always concerned about improving his financial position. On the eve of the war he considered backing a British armaments merchant. He also looked briefly at an opportunity to invest in a new cinema in the capital that promised to bring sound to the silver screen. Alexandra became more generous to Rasputin on the eve of the war—this might have been connected in some way with the 75,000-ruble "parting gift" Gregory received in 1914. The empress was now paying some of Rasputin's expenses from her private treasury. This included an annual allowance of 10,000 rubles plus the 1,000-ruble monthly rent on his apartment. But most of Rasputin's income came from bribes.

Documents in the archives tell of Rasputin's transactions with several shadowy entrepreneurs. N. A. Gordon, a foreign industrialist, paid Rasputin 15,000 rubles to act as a "consultant" to his firm. A Russian merchant, who was a woman, won his support for a two-million-ruble contract to provide the army with underwear. We do not know how much Rasputin netted from that deal, but he received 50,000 rubles from Dr. Peter Badmaev to facilitate a transaction in October 1916. Rasputin was paid 20,000 rubles to expedite the probate of a will. He charged 250 rubles to free an imprisoned forger; 2,000 rubles to keep a soldier from the front; and 5,000 rubles to secure the freedom of a political prisoner. He agreed to spring three hundred Baptists from prison for refusing military service; they were each to pay him 1,000 rubles, but they delivered a total of just 5,000 rubles.

Rasputin obviously needed a business manager to help with such transactions. Ivan Dobrovolsky, a corrupt ex–school inspector, handled some of Rasputin's finances until Aaron Simanovich replaced him. But

Simanovich's claims to have been Rasputin's secretary seem to have been exaggerated. Akilina Laptinskaya actually played the leading role in conducting the peasant's financial affairs.

Many of Rasputin's wealthy friends were Jews. Simanovich insisted that he led Rasputin to become an advocate of Jewish rights, but this seems exaggerated. It would be more accurate to say that Rasputin transcended his own prejudices when it was in his interests to do that. His closest Jewish friend was Dmitry Rubenstein, a short, vivacious man of humble origins who became a wealthy banker. Rasputin presented "Mitya" to Alexandra, and she was soon telling her husband that this multimillionaire would donate 500,000 rubles to support research on aircraft technology if he received the honorary title of Actual State Counselor. This would have been a high honor for a Jew in imperial Russia. Rumors also claimed that the empress used Rubenstein to funnel money to her relatives in Germany during the war. Mitya was thought to be a German agent. When he was arrested for illicit financial transactions in the summer of 1916, Rasputin saved him from trial. (The Siberian mystic and healer probably feared that the inquest would embarrass him.) When Rubenstein was released he flooded Rasputin's apartment with 500 rubles worth of flowers.

Rasputin made a highly publicized trip to Moscow in March 1915 to humor Alexandra. The empress felt the need to shore up Rasputin's image as a holy man. Her plan called for him to pray at holy places in the Kremlin and other parts of the city. But an incident at the Yar, an ancient and famous Gypsy restaurant, easily overshadowed the spiritual dimensions of the visit. It was a dramatic and outrageous episode that became an integral part of the Rasputin legend. We need to examine it closely, since some historians have recently claimed that the entire "affair" was fabricated.

On the night of March 26, 1915, Rasputin went to the Yar in Moscow. He was drunk when he arrived, and he dined in a private room on the second floor. There was much eating, drinking, singing, and dancing. Rasputin scribbled improper notes to the female Gypsy singers and tried to grab several. Their angry rejections triggered an alcoholic rant. According to the official report Rasputin "became sexually psychopathic" and began bragging of his sexual prowess, hinting at an improper relationship with Alexandra. "See this belt?" he bellowed.

"It's Her Majesty's work. I can make her do anything." Drunk, filled with his ego, and not knowing when to stop, he made obscene gestures, referring to the empress as "the Old Girl."

By now other diners were attracted to the commotion coming from Rasputin's party. When someone questioned if this fool was really *the* infamous Rasputin, Rasputin proved his identity by dropping his pants and waving his penis—its size was already legendary—at the startled spectators. British agent R. H. Bruce Lockhart happened to be at the Yar that night. He heard "wild shrieks of women, a man's curses, broken glass, and the banging of doors." Waiters ran back and forth, and Colonel Semenov of the Moscow police appeared. He tried to calm Rasputin but hesitated to do more. The police finally arrested Rasputin around two o'clock in the morning and led him away—as their report put it—"snarling and vowing vengeance."

Rasputin was released upon "instructions from the highest quarters." He returned to Petrograd the next morning—a crowd of women saw him off at the train station. What happened next is not entirely clear, but apparently General Alexander Adrianov, chief of the Moscow police, shared his files on the episode with Vladimir Dzhunkovsky, assistant minister of the interior and police director. Dzhunkovsky reported to Nicholas on June 1. He had just returned from Moscow and briefed the tsar on the recent anti-German riots before turning to Rasputin. Dzhunkovsky assured the emperor that he had no desire to interfere in his private affairs, but he feared that Rasputin's behavior was threatening the dynasty. Dzhunkovsky handed Nicholas a report on the "Yar Incident." The tsar took the papers, put them in his desk, and asked Dzhunkovsky to keep the matter confidential.

Rasputin was summoned to the palace on June 9. He later told Stephen Beletsky that the tsar was angry and demanded an explanation. Rasputin fell back on the familiar excuses: he was "a sinful man" who fell victim to wine and temptation. He denied exposing himself or slandering the empress. He subsequently admitted to A. T. Vasiliev (an ally who eventually became assistant minister of the interior) that he had indeed "misbehaved" at the Yar, although he provided no details.

Revisionist historians have argued that Rasputin was not even at the Yar that night, that Dzhunkovsky fabricated the charges and concocted a false report to discredit the Siberian holy man. What of Beletsky and Vasiliev, who claim that Rasputin himself told them about his misdeeds that night? They were lying, apparently in a conspiracy to destroy the starets. The revisionists stress that the Okhrana account of Rasputin's activities on the date in question—March 27, 1915—is missing. They suggest that it disappeared because it would reveal that Rasputin did not go to the Yar that fateful evening. The revisionists note that the official report is dated June 5, nine weeks after Rasputin's alleged visit; they think that this indicates it was a clumsy forgery. It is also possible that the report was written at Dzhunkovsky's request after his visit to Moscow (on May 31) or following his audience with the tsar (on June 1).

The traditional account of the Yar episode claims that Rasputin was accompanied by Anisya Reshetnikova, a seventy-six-year-old widow who was his hostess in Moscow, along with a younger woman and a shady journalist. The revisionists note that this was unlikely company for a man who was planning a wild evening. They claim that Rasputin never associated with journalists and did not go to restaurants after Guseva's attack. In fact, Rasputin was friendly with some journalists in these years, including Alexis Filippov. The police chronicle his constant forays to hotels, restaurants, and nightspots in Petrograd throughout the war. According to information the French ambassador Maurice Paléologue got from one of General Adrianov's relatives, Reshetnikova protested Rasputin's behavior, demanded the bill, and left the restaurant before the worst excesses occurred.

The revisionists claim that the British observer Gerard Shelley visited the Yar just after that evening and learned that "no one at the restaurant knew anything about the matter." A waiter supposedly told the Englishman that the story of a raucous evening was *yerunda* ("bunkum"). Shelley also claims that Rasputin was a "tall, huge" man who hated Jews and never took bribes! Shelley claims to have heard teachings from Rasputin's mouth that do not reflect the way he spoke in public or the words that he used to express himself. Shelley imagines that imperial protocol permitted the empress to "drop in" on folks in Petrograd. He tells us that Alexandra came by Rasputin's flat and favored him with an interview. That is simply preposterous. Shelley was a silly, poorly informed partisan of Rasputin's; he is not reliable on anything pertaining to the Yar.

One piece of evidence, however, is ambiguous. The tsar sent Captain Nicholas Sablin, commander of the imperial yacht *Standart*, to Moscow to investigate the Yar incident. One source tells us that Sablin found no evidence that Rasputin had visited the Yar, and General Adrianov assured him that Rasputin had not been there. Sablin did not visit the restaurant or question its employees, however.

The official report certainly existed at the time of Sablin's visit. According to Paléologue—who often relayed gossip—the captain confirmed Rasputin's misbehavior. It is difficult to say what this inquiry proved.

The evidence supports the traditional view that Rasputin behaved outrageously at the Yar, although questions remain. The incident certainly damaged Rasputin. It also led to Dzhunkovsky's downfall: the police director was anxious to discredit Rasputin, so he showed his report to members of the imperial family, including the tsar's cousins Nicholasha and Dmitry Pavlovich. The empress was outraged and railed in letters to her husband against "my enemy Dzhunkovsky" and his "vile, filthy paper." He "acts as a traitor & not as a devoted subject who ought to stand up for the Friends of his Sovereign."

Nicholas fired Dzhunkovsky and made Stephen Beletsky assistant-minister of the interior on August 19, 1915. Russians were outraged to see an enemy of Rasputin punished while one of his allies was elevated to high office. Since Nicholas still fancied himself to be an autocrat, it would have been beneath his dignity to explain that Dzhunkovsky was being dismissed because he had violated a confidence—not because he opposed Rasputin. Only the people in Nicholas II's circle would have known that. The anger increased all the more on September 26, 1915, when Nicholas appointed Alexis Khvostov—another of the peasant's cronies—as minister of the interior. The "Reign of Rasputin" was about to begin.

14

The Tsar Takes Charge and Loses Control

Having done quite a lot to provoke the Great War, Nicholas II threw himself energetically into winning it. Factories ran at full capacity, and trains rushed soldiers to the front while his generals stunned the world by staging two grand offensives. The tsar appointed his cousin Nicholasha as commander-in-chief. Standing six feet, seven inches tall, the grand duke was an imposing and highly respected figure. The emperor overlooked Nicholasha's hostility to Rasputin in the widely shared expectation that he would lead the army to victory. But the German war machine was so powerful that when it counterattacked, the grand duke was forced to preside over what Russians called the "Long Retreat." From the outset Nicholasha was hampered by shortages in war matériel and constant quarrels with Vladimir Sukhomlinov, the not-very-competent minister of war.

Nicholas II had a mystical conviction that a tsar's place was with his troops. He had always regretted not assuming command of his soldiers in 1904, when Japan attacked Russia. In 1914 his advisers convinced him to place Nicholasha in charge of battlefield operations. The tsar reluctantly agreed. But he was determined to make frequent visits to Stavka, the Slavonic term for general headquarters. It was initially located at Baranovichi, a railway station between the German and Austrian fronts. And so Nicholas bade his family farewell on September 19, 1914, and left on the first of many trips to headquarters.

"I am so happy for you that you can at last manage to go," Alexandra wrote, "as I know how deeply you have been suffering all this time—yr. restless sleep has been ever a proof of it." She thought that Nicholas had best not be "at the head of the army" but should limit himself to inspecting troops and visiting hospitals. He charmed and impressed everyone on these occasions. Although the last tsar was a short man, he had a regal bearing, and many were struck by the fact that he somehow seemed "taller than anyone else in the room." He moved "with an extraordinary dignity" through hospital wards, his eyes establishing an "almost mystical sense of contact" with the patients he met. The emperor inspired loyalty and dedication in subjects of every rank and station, at least at the beginning of the conflict.

Alexandra flourished during the war. A need to serve had always characterized the empress, and now she was able to engage in the sort of practical work that she found important. She organized several hospitals and many Red Cross trains. Alexandra joined her daughters, Olga and Tatyana, and Anna Vyrubova in training as nurses and spending hours each week in the hospital that she established at Tsarskoye Selo. Alexandra assisted in operations and comforted sick and depressed soldiers. Rasputin encouraged these efforts. He believed that such work pleased God and inspired patriotic fervor. But some complained that these energies were misdirected. They insisted that an empress should limit herself to appearing at patriotic events and fostering wartime charities. Anyone could empty bedpans or assist in operations: Alexandra debased her position—or so their reasoning went—by focusing on such menial tasks.

When Nicholas and Alexandra were apart they poured their thoughts, feelings, worries, and advice into the remarkable stream of over 1,600 letters and telegrams that has come to be known as the "Nicky-Sunny" Correspondence. These communications give a unique insight into their complex marriage, revealing the deep passion they felt for each other, their family, and Russia. The letters were written in their customary English. The telegrams are in Russian. These documents also reveal the ever-increasing influence of Alexandra—and Rasputin—over the affairs of state.

●   ●   ●

Russian defeats in 1915 brought new and ugly accusations. Looking for scapegoats, people noted that many officers and high officials bore German names. People imagined that spies were lurking in restaurants and public places. This paranoia claimed an innocent victim in Colonel Sergei Myasoedov, an intelligence officer close to Minister of War Vladimir Sukhomlinov. Myasoedov was rumored to have been Madame Sukhomlinov's lover, "and all three were said to be in relations with Rasputin." The colonel was tried, convicted, and hanged—all in a single day. News of the execution broke on March 20, 1915, just before Easter Sunday.

Suspicion fell heavily on Rasputin—the man who before the war was always praising German power and calling on the tsar to back down in a crisis. Millions were convinced that Rasputin was working for Russia's defeat. They took for granted that he was on the kaiser's payroll and working for a "separate peace" that would betray the allies and join Russia's fortunes to those of her enemies. In fact, Rasputin never failed to support his country in this, her greatest struggle. He insisted that a victorious Russia must occupy Constantinople, although Wilhelm II should remain on his throne, for he was—as Rasputin put it—"the Lord's anointed for the Germans."

Rasputin never had much discretion, and he made friends with people who were obvious German agents. The police knew that some of the visitors to Rasputin's apartment were decidedly "fishy." At the top of the list was Arthur Gyulling, the son of a Finnish senator. (The Finns wanted to break away from the Russian Empire, so most hoped for a German victory.) Gyulling met Rasputin in July 1916 and began to frequent his apartment. He often appeared just before or after Rasputin visited Tsarskoye Selo, and he used the peasant—as well as Anna Vyrubova—to communicate with the emperor. Russian intelligence agents believed that Gyulling was a German spy: he commanded a steady stream of money, and his secretary had an Austrian wife. Gyulling offered to pay Rasputin a million rubles if he could facilitate the sale of a large number of Russian ships to a Swedish firm that was obviously a German front.

"Doctor" Carl Perren was another friend of that sort. Traveling on a U.S. passport, he practiced hypnosis and the "mystical arts" as a cover. Perrin befriended Rasputin and used him to meet certain ministers, much to the horror of the police. When the Russian government finally expelled Perren in July 1916, Rasputin intervened (vainly) on his behalf. Perren relocated to Sweden and Norway, but he soon returned to Petrograd with forged documents, continuing to meet with Rasputin and gather information for his German handlers.

There is no evidence that Rasputin passed information to Gyulling, Perren, or any other German agent. But perception was more important than reality. Millions of the tsar's subjects were convinced that Rasputin was a traitor, and their suspicions included the empress. Many assumed that since Alexandra was from Hesse, she was pro-German. She was famous for scorning Russian high society—that proved she hated Russia. A persistent rumor had the empress in contact with Berlin by way of a hidden telegraph at Alexander Palace. Who could doubt that Alexandra was working for the Central Powers?

The wave of animosity included other members of the imperial family and—to some extent and at certain times—the tsar himself. An ugly demonstration erupted in Moscow in May 1915. Angry crowds demanded the arrest of Alexandra's sister, Elizabeth, accusing her of being a German spy and hiding her brother, the grand duke of Hesse, in her convent. Some of the placards demanded that Alexandra be sent to a convent while others called upon Nicholasha to take the throne.

These sentiments were not limited to a single demonstration, and they did not go unnoticed at Tsarskoye Selo. Alexandra loathed Nicholasha. Not only was he Rasputin's persistent enemy, the empress believed that he was using his position to promote himself and diminish her husband. Nicholas II knew that such suspicions were unfounded: he and his cousin loved each other and enjoyed an excellent relationship. But Nicholasha did present certain difficulties: he was tactless; he undercut civilian authorities; and he spread confusion throughout the power structure. Nicholas Nicholaevich's greatest liability, however, was that he was losing the war.

Russia took Galicia from the Austrians in early 1915. But the Central Powers launched an offensive in May 1915 that slaughtered 100,000 Russian troops and took 750,000 prisoners. Russian territorial loses now stretched from Galicia to the Baltic and Warsaw. The Russian army was in retreat, and the situation was critical. A million and a half Russian soldiers had died in the first year of the conflict, and thousands more joined them each week.

This was a true crisis, and it forced Nicholas to consider firing his cousin and assuming direct command of the army. The change would have several advantages: the tsar hoped that it would lift morale. It would consolidate the civilian and military authorities and send a signal to the allies that Russia was committed to remaining in the war until victory. Nicholas would reside at Stavka, but he did not intend to direct military operations. The emperor had his eyes on General Michael Alexeev for this task—and in fact, he proved to be an excellent chief-of-staff.

But such changes would also bring problems. Russian defeats were likely to continue for the foreseeable future, and the full blame for them would now fall upon the new commander, Nicholas II. The tsar would need someone to administer state affairs while he was absent at Stavka. Such a scheme might have worked if the emperor had assigned this responsibility to an intelligent minister who was strong enough to stand up to Alexandra and Rasputin. But the tsar intended to assign this task to his wife. That was, in fact, the whole idea. The war was taking its toll on Nicholas: he was getting weaker, and he knew—although he might not admit it to the world—that he needed Alexandra's strength and self-assurance. Incredible as this might seem in terms of the events that followed, he trusted her judgment. The emperor would make the key decisions, but the ministers would report to the empress and accept her direction. Apparently Nicholas never quite understood why this plan horrified nearly everyone. The tsaritsa appealed to his aspirations—and vanity—by urging him to fulfill his destiny by taking this historic step.

Alexandra could not forgive Nicholasha for his hatred of Rasputin. She reminded the tsar that Nicholasha was "Our Friend's enemy & that brings bad luck." His "work can't be blessed nor his advice be good." Rasputin had opposed making the grand duke commander, and "when He [she capitalizes the pronoun] says not to do a thing & one does not listen, one sees one's faults always afterwards." God "would not forgive us our weakness & sin" if we failed to protect Rasputin.

These changes would make Rasputin the third most powerful man in Russia, and given his ability to control Nicholas and Alexandra, he might have been more than that. So he blessed and encouraged the plan. Nicholas saw the pros and the cons, and he knew it would be controversial—so he wavered. By encouraging the emperor to fire Nicholasha and assume the high command, Rasputin was playing a pivotal role in Russian history that we are only now beginning to appreciate. Alexandra fired off an urgent cable asking Rasputin to return to the capital to help her convince her husband to do what they knew was best. Even at this moment, Rasputin was *that* important.

Rasputin arrived in Petrograd on July 31, 1915, and was taken directly to Alexander Palace. He returned to Tsarskoye Selo four days later to urge Nicholas to follow his intuition; that is, yield to his wife's advice. The emperor finally agreed, and on August 5 Rasputin boarded the train to return to Siberia. Knowing that others would try to change the tsar's mind, Rasputin sent him seven telegrams in the next nine days. One proclaims that "firmness is a rock but wavering is death to all." Another adds that "in glory there is no dishonesty," while a third reminds the emperor that "victory will come through decisiveness and spiritual firmness and faith in God." Rasputin predicted that the "bells will toll everywhere" the moment Nicholas placed himself at the head of his army.

Nicholas II's decision to assume the supreme command showed just how dimly he understood history's demands of him at this difficult hour. It was logical to dismiss Nicholasha and Alexeev proved to be an excellent replacement. But the tsar's business was government—he could not delegate that task to anyone else. It took Nicholas to supervise his ministers and support his recent appointees, men who were new and promising but untested. The emperor had to be at the center of power. With all of his shortcomings Nicholas was the tsar. To put it kindly, Alexandra was not an adequate replacement for her husband.

Nicholas informed the minister of war, General Alexis Polivanov, of his decision on August 4, 1915. Nicholas did not realize that his ministers had been secretly meeting for some time to discuss the crisis the empire was facing. They flew into pandemonium when Polivanov brought them the news. Even Ivan Goremykin, the emperor's loyal prime minister, agreed that his master's plan was misguided. The ministers instantly realized that the change would put Rasputin in charge. In an unprecedented display of unity, they went to the tsar as a group on August 20 to ask him to reconsider. The ministers were polite, but it was quite a confrontation. Nicholas was pale and nervous, perspiring as he clutched a small icon for moral support. "I have heard what you have to say," Nicholas finally declared, "but I adhere to my decision."

Discouraged but undefeated, the ministers hit on a different strategy. Ten of the thirteen signed or verbally endorsed a letter dated August 22, reiterating their opposition to the tsar's plan. If Nicholas rejected their advice, they asked to be relieved of their posts. This was an unprecedented development—the servants were refusing to be treated as servants. Nicholas viewed this as a challenge to his imperial

Nicholas II and his son reviewing the troops. The tsarevich was
handsome and made a great impression when he accompanied his
father in reviewing the troops and visiting hospitals.

authority, and in a sense he was right. He angrily ordered Goremykin
to express his displeasure to the ministers and tell them that he would
not permit them to resign.

Nicholasha welcomed his cousin back to Stavka, and he made it easy
for the tsar to tell him about the changes that would soon be in place.
Nicholas made the grand duke viceroy of the Caucasus and commander
of Russian forces on the Turkish front. Rasputin sent Alexandra a wry
telegram proclaiming: "Light is growing, the beam of the Protector
shines though there is little sun in the Caucasus." Alexandra was ecstatic:
"Our Friend's prayers arise night and day for you to Heaven," she assured
her husband, "and God will hear them. It is the beginning of the glory of
your reign. He said so and I absolutely believe it."

•   •   •

A month after assuming command Nicholas decided that his son would join him at Stavka. This was a bold, inspired move—and it was reasonably successful as an effort to mold public opinion. It was also risky, given Alexis's health. Only two months into the war the tsarevich had suffered an encounter with hemophilia that brought Rasputin to his bedside. Alexandra agonized over letting her son move to General Headquarters, but she finally agreed.

Alexis had just turned eleven, and he was excited to don the uniform of an army private. The tsarevich had spent his whole life at the mercy of doctors and women—he welcomed the male atmosphere of Stavka. (It was now located at Mogilev.) His father was glad to have his son's company, but the decision rested on more than mere sentiment. Nicholas appreciated the propaganda value of his attractive children, and he knew that Alexis never faced real danger. The lad's appearance at army reviews and in hospital wards reminded Russians of the cause for which they were supposedly fighting. For his part the tsarevich was moved by the idealism and suffering that he witnessed.

But hemophilia was ever lurking in the background, and tragedy nearly struck when Alexis caught a bad cold in December 1915. His sneezing and coughing triggered a nosebleed that Dr. Sergei Fedorov was unable to control, and he decided that his patient should return to Tsarskoye Selo. The trip was a nightmare: the train had to be stopped several times so that doctors could change the blood-soaked bandages around the boy's nose, and twice Pierre Gilliard thought that Alexis had died. According to Anna Vyrubova, Alexandra sent for Rasputin as soon as her son returned home. Rasputin supposedly came to the tsarevich's bedside, made the sign of the cross over him, and said quietly, "Don't be alarmed. Nothing will happen." Anna claimed that the boy's condition improved so much the following day that Nicholas and his son returned to Stavka. According to Vyrubova the doctors "did not even attempt to explain the cure."

Anna tells a good story, but she does not seem to be telling the truth—she often does that in her memoirs. Nicholas and Gilliard (who were eyewitnesses) agree that the doctors at Tsarskoye Selo cauterized the tsarevich's nosebleed. The tsar's diary notes that Alexis had no further need for a bandage; his temperature returned to normal and once again, he was "in excellent spirits." Rasputin visited the palace the following day (December 6). Six days later Nicholas returned to Stavka alone.

This incident raises troubling questions about Anna's veracity, while Alexandra emerges as something of a coconspirator. She must have known that the doctors cauterized her son's nose and that the bleeding stopped before Rasputin appeared. But Gilliard notes that she "remained convinced that the boy had been saved thanks to [Rasputin's] intervention." Alexandra saw what she wanted to see and rejected the facts that interfered with that fantasy. She insisted on torturing a miracle from a series of events that in no way suggested a miracle.

Alexandra's faith in Rasputin as a messenger from God extended to military affairs. Nicholas rarely discussed military affairs with his wife, and he valued her opinions only when they agreed with those of the generals. His biggest concern was that Alexandra might share information with others—he must have had Rasputin and Anna Vyrubova especially in mind. "Please, lovy mine," he warned in a letter that discussed strategic plans dated August 31, 1915, "don't mention these details to anybody. I only wrote them down for you."

Incredibly, Alexandra defied his wishes. Their friend was "so anxious to know" about the strategy of the Romanian campaign. Rasputin was "praying & crossing himself about Rumania and Greece & our troops passing through." He "finds you need lots of troops there so as not to be cut off from behind." Rasputin's dreams were even important: "He saw in the night . . . that one should advance near Riga, . . . otherwise the Germans will settle down so firmly through all the winter, that it will cost endless bloodshed and trouble to make them move—[but a feint] will take them so aback, that we shall succeed in making them retrace their steps. [He told me that] I was to write it to you at once."

Rasputin's advice about the war was amateurish, but he was extremely perceptive about the "food question." He was never in want, but he always sympathized with people who struggled to put food in the pantry. He understood the pain of standing in line for hours to buy bread, only to learn that the day's supply was gone. He was constantly telling Alexandra that Siberia was "overflowing" with food. The army enjoyed top priority use of railway facilities—and Rasputin saw danger in that. He wanted the army's service reduced to three days a week; another three days should be devoted to transporting "flour, butter, and sugar" to urban centers. Rasputin also thought that food distribution in Petrograd could be improved if the shops weighed and priced their goods in advance. Under his scheme, a store would have several lines, with the clerks at each quickly handing out what each customer requested.

These ideas were awkwardly expressed, but the tsar would have been well advised to have his "experts" make them workable. As it was the problems were simply ignored. The crisis worsened as Russia's feeble and overworked railroad service continued to deteriorate. Nicholas did not lose his throne because of problems related to the army, which was battered but undefeated when a popular uprising swept him from power. Shortages in food and fuel led to the crisis in Petrograd in March 1917. The tsar's subjects in the countryside—by contrast—were warm and well fed.

Rasputin also argued that the responsibility for supplying the cities should be transferred from the minister of agriculture to the minister of the interior—he had the police at his disposal. When the Council of Ministers rejected this proposal in the autumn of 1916, Alexandra (and Rasputin) urged Nicholas to take it to the Duma. If it refused to act, Nicholas could prorogue the legislature and enact the changes by executive decree. Rasputin was furious with the tsar's high officials. "If a minister's a coward," he declared, "he's in the wrong spot!"

Alexandra and Rasputin were even more stunned by the Brusilov Offensive. "I beg you not to tell anyone of this," Nicholas wrote to Alexandra of the plan to shatter the Austrian army and force the Hapsburg kingdom out of the war. The Russian onslaught began in May 1916 and continued for four months. This was Russia's greatest military effort in the conflict and one of the most lethal battles in history. The empress heeded her husband's plea until the offensive began, when everyone could see that a major drive was under way, and the conflict stood at a turning point.

Rasputin was full of advice, and Alexandra faithfully relayed it to her husband. Rasputin thought it was "better [to] not advance obstinately as the losses will be too great." He "hopes we won't climb over the Carpath[i]ans & try to take them" since the "losses will be too great again." But the Russians forged ahead, demolishing the Austrian army and throwing it into total disarray. Minister of War Polivanov was so successful in improving the army that everything went well from a military standpoint. The Austrians suffered 750,000 casualties, including 380,000 prisoners. But the Russians sustained 1.4 million casualties. Alexandra confronted the results of the carnage in her hospital, and she was appalled. For weeks she (and Rasputin) had been calling for an end to the offensive; when that decision was finally reached, she disregarded her husband's pleas for secrecy and shared the good news with Rasputin. "He won't mention it to a soul," she assured her husband, "but I had to ask His blessing for your decision."

The Brusilov Offensive was magnificent—but was it a Russian victory? It saved the French at Verdun by forcing the Germans to pull divisions from the western front to save their Hapsburg ally. As for the Austrian army, it never recovered from the Russian assault. The Brusilov Offensive also decimated the Russian army, especially the officer corps. But its conclusion was also problematic. As soon as the Russian campaign reached deep into enemy territory, Nicholas ordered what seemed to be a sudden and premature halt, leaving his people demoralized. Rasputin and the empress were certainly well intentioned, and they might even have been right. At any rate, their opinions had no influence on military operations; even the tsar was a mere bystander. The end of the episode reinforced the notion that Rasputin and the empress were undermining Russia's war effort, and that damaged the prestige of the imperial throne.

Russians were wrong in thinking that Rasputin was responsible for the beginning or the end of the Brusilov Offensive. They would soon be blaming Rasputin for the next chapter of the story: the disintegration of the government. In this, unfortunately, they were not wrong.

15

Rasputin Conquers the
Russian State

I T WAS JUST AS RASPUTIN PREDICTED—the war was cata-
strophic for Russia. Optimism and the initial tendency to rally
around the tsar dissipated within a month, as soon as his armies were
defeated in East Prussia. The state was simply not prepared for the
problems it suddenly faced; the bureaucratic machine was slow, inef-
ficient, and error prone. As criticism mounted, Nicholas clung even
more tightly to his authority. He knew that the Duma would exploit
the troubled situation to increase its powers and diminish the powers
of the tsar. Nicholas and Alexandra were even suspicious of the "volunteer organizations" that in other nations so effectively harnessed their
industries, trade unions, and farms for victory. The imperial couple saw
reformers as enemies and often viewed even humanitarian questions in
political terms.

According to tradition, the tsar appointed all officials, and they
were responsible only to him; by the spring of 1915 his critics were
demanding a Ministry of Public Confidence. Under this scheme, the
Duma would play a role in selecting the ministers, and they would be
accountable to the legislature as well as the emperor. But Nicholas
regarded the Duma as an alien institution; he did not even consider
it to be part of "the government"; his wife (and Rasputin) encouraged
that view. "We must be firm," she insisted; the ruler of the Russian land

must "be his own master [and] not bow down to others." She called on her husband to "be more decided & self-confident." She repeatedly intoned, "Remember, you are the Emperor. . . . Be more Autocratic, my very own sweetheart, show your mind."

Alexandra lamented the fact that people were "still so uneducated" in Russia; she thought this justified autocracy. But she was convinced that the tsar's uneducated subjects were loyal to the throne. The empress savored the thought that Russia had "a real anointed" monarch. She insisted that the empire was "not ready for a constitutional government"; such an idea would "be Russia's ruin."

Eager to play a political role, Alexandra wrote to her husband, "Let me help you, my Treasure. . . . Surely there is some way in which a woman can be of help & use." In a revealing moment she wrote that "silly old wify [had] trousers on, unseen" and was ready to lead. Stronger in character than her husband and armed with a righteous mission, Alexandra would spend the war years badgering her spouse—pleading with him and demanding that he follow her advice. Her brother Ernie once commented that the "Tsar is an angel, but he doesn't know how to deal with her. What she needs is a superior will which can dominate [and] bridle her."

Alexandra repeatedly praised Rasputin. "Hearken unto Our Friend," she intoned, "believe Him, He has your interests & Russia's at heart—it is not for nothing God sent Him to us—only we must pay more attention to what He says [for] His advice is great. . . . I am haunted by Our Friend's wish, & know it will be fatal for us & the country if [it is] not fulfilled. He means what He says when He speaks so seriously." Nicholas should also "bequeath the realm to his son in its entirety. Alexis's son must receive it from him just as you received it from your father."

Biographers have told us that Rasputin manipulated Alexandra. That was true to some extent, but she often used Rasputin to promote *her* ideas. A symbiotic relationship developed between the empress and the peasant; each fed from the other. Rasputin rarely contradicted Alexandra or raised his own concerns—at least before the war. Rasputin usually listened to the tsaritsa; he would reinforce what he had just heard, restating it with a religious point of view that flattered Alexandra. She then turned to Nicholas, using "Our Friend's" opinions to bolster her own. "A country where a Man of God helps the Sovereign will never be lost," she wrote. "God opens everything to him. [We must] admire his wonderful brain, ready to understand anything."

Nicholas probably tuned out a lot of Alexandra's babble about Rasputin—her letters show that she suspected as much. Nicholas was constantly dealing with people who peddled all sorts of policies and programs; a taciturn manner and polite silence were useful in dealing with their blather. But Nicholas did not reject the artifacts his wife sent to Stavka; for instance, the vial containing a taste of the wine used to celebrate Rasputin's Name Day. Alexandra insisted that her spouse "pour it into a glass and drink it all up for His health." Then there was the comb that had rippled through Rasputin's greasy hair: "Remember to [use it] before all difficult talks & decisions"; it "will bring its help." Alexandra also sent a "stick (bird holding a fish), wh. was sent to him . . . [Rasputin] now sends it to you as a blessing [so if] you can sometimes use it, it wld. be nice."

What Nicholas really needed was help. Perhaps it was his fault, but the problems he faced baffled him. They seemed to appear so suddenly, and not knowing what to do, he did nothing. Then the critics thundered about "paralysis in government." The high turnover of leading officials, for example, became a terrible problem, as did the increasingly low caliber of the men who took their places.

The changes were not alarming at first. Nicholas replaced Vladimir Kokovtsov as prime minister in January 1914 with loyal, old Ivan Goremykin—no one was sure what, exactly, that indicated. The changes in the summer of 1915 were actually encouraging. The tsar fired four unpopular, lackluster ministers in a belated effort to appease popular opinion. He replaced Vladimir Sukhomlinov, the bumbling minister of war, with Alexis Polivanov, a talented field commander. Nicholas Shcherbatov and Alexander Khvostov became, respectively, minister of the interior and minister of justice. Alexander Samarin assumed leadership of the Holy Synod. The new ministers were able men who enjoyed public confidence. The most interesting fact in all this was that Nicholas demonstrated courage in standing up to his wife, for he knew the changes would displease her (and Rasputin). The tsar showed that he was capable of doing that.

He could not make it last, though. The situation took a sudden negative turn in the autumn of 1915 with a shake-up in the ministry of the interior. The men who were elevated to leadership positions in that bureau were some of the most incredible—and outrageous—scoundrels in Russian history. And they owed their good fortunes solely to Gregory Rasputin.

Michael Andronikov was the driving force behind these changes—not that he ever assumed an official position. "Misha" was born into a financially troubled noble family in 1875, and even as a boy, he imagined that one day he would become wealthy and powerful. Andronikov began his career as a low-ranking official at the Holy Synod; he had no salary, but the post provided an important benefit: the right to wear a uniform and attend social functions. From the outset young Andronikov displayed a genius at soliciting bribes, extorting funds, and peddling secrets.

Andronikov befriended the city's bicycle messengers, luring them to his apartment with money, food, wine, and sex. He encouraged them to take naps so that he could go through their delivery bags. Using gossip, Misha could often guess that an official letter from a certain office to a particular man was sent to notify him of a promotion; visiting him the next day, Andronikov would intimate that *he* was responsible for this good fortune. Misha might invite the gentleman to join his "circle," making clear what he expected in exchange for his goodwill. The prince soon became an influential figure.

Officers and cadets also found their way to Andronikov's immense apartment, although they had been warned that his flat was "off limits." Andronikov held gay parties—he moved freely among his guests, selecting the one who would share his bed that night. He loved filthy boys from the street, offering them what he promised would be extraordinarily delightful baths. A servant testified "that the Prince had more than a thousand young male conquests during my two years of service to him."

Andronikov and Rasputin met in 1914. The prince needed the peasant to get his allies installed as minister and assistant minister of the interior. (The man who held the second position was, ex officio, the police director.) Andronikov's objective was to head off investigations into his unsavory finances. Misha's choice to serve as minister was none other than Alexis Khvostov, the fellow Nicholas considered—and rejected—for the very same post in 1911. Khvostov had offended Rasputin on that occasion, but now he praised the starets and promised to see that the police would protect him from his enemies.

Andronikov's candidate for assistant minister was Stephen Beletsky, a hardworking professional policeman who had held the post until Vladimir Dzhunkovsky replaced him in 1913. Rasputin was initially wary: when Beletsky was police director, he provided the tsar with a lot of "unfortunate information" about the peasant's background and life. But Andronikov reminded Rasputin that at least he was safe when Beletsky was in charge. Dzhunkovsky, on the other hand, was a loud and determined enemy—and Guseva's attack occurred on his watch. Beletsky promised to be Rasputin's friend and defend him in the future. Rasputin was interested but noncommittal. Perhaps he needed a sign that would lead him to agree to Andronikov's proposal.

If that was the case, the Yar provided that sign. Andronikov pretended to sympathize with Rasputin; admittedly the starets got a bit tipsy and loud in the restaurant that night, but it didn't justify his arrest and a night in jail. Dzhunkovsky was his enemy—that was the problem. Prince Andronikov told him of his plan to capture the ministry of internal affairs. Misha spoke of a "Troika"—a team of three horses pulling a sleigh. Andronikov was the organizer; Khvostov would be the minister while Beletsky would serve as his assistant. But the Troika needed Rasputin to manipulate Nicholas into making these appointments. Andronikov assured Rasputin that he would be a full partner with a voice and great benefits. Rasputin finally agreed. He would be in Siberia in August 1915 when the plan unfolded—but that was no problem. Rasputin proceeded to tell Andronikov what to do to get his allies elevated to high office.

The prince should begin by visiting Anna Vyrubova, who was basking in the glow of her own ambitions after an accident in January 1915 restored her friendship with Alexandra. Anna's position was going to her head. She began linking her opinions to those of the imperial couple—declaring, "We do not agree" or "We will not permit," as if she were the third ruler of Russia. Anna also took to inviting ministers and high officials to dine with her. This actually bothered the empress, who complained to her husband that Anna "wanted to play a political role." "Our Friend always wishes her to live only for us," Alexandra continued, but "she is so proud & sure of herself, not prudent enough."

Andronikov charmed Vyrubova by deploring the fact that Nicholas Shcherbatov was an enemy of Rasputin's and a terrible minister of the interior. Andronikov assured Anna that he had a perfect replacement for Shcherbatov: Alexis Khvostov. When Andronikov presented Khvostov to her, Vyrubova was totally impressed. Of course she shared all this information with Alexandra.

The timing could not have been better. That very moment—August 27, 1915—found Alexandra writing to her husband that "Shcherbatov

is impossible to keep, better quick to change him." The following day
she told Nicholas that Anna had just seen Andronikov and Khvostov,
"& the latter made her an excellent impression. He is most devoted
to you, spoke gently & well about Our Friend to her." Anna arranged
a presentation of the proposed candidate to the empress, although
not before applying a thick layer of flattery. Alexandra reported that
Khvostov "looks upon me as the one to save the situation whilst you
are away & wants to pour out his heart to tell me his ideas." Rasputin
had blessed the proposed appointment—by telegraph—saying that it
would "be good."

This last point was crucial. In 1911 Nicholas had sent Rasputin to
interview Alexis Khvostov for the post when he was the governor of
Nizhnyi-Novgorod. Rasputin concluded that the young man did not
have the qualities needed in a minister of the interior, and Khvostov
did not get the position. Rasputin's opinion actually had nothing to
do with the decision—but Khvostov was not taking any chances. He
engaged in servile flattery—or as Alexandra put it in a letter, his "eyes
had been opened" about "Father Gregory." The empress was so enthusiastic after the interview that she wrote two letters the same day urging
Nicholas to make the appointment. She complained that all "men seem
to wear petticoats now" but Khvostov was a "man, no petticoats—will
not let anything touch us & will do all in his power to stop the attacks
upon Our Friend." Nicholas duly received Khvostov and within a few
hours made him minister of the interior. Rasputin returned to the capital the next day, September 27, 1915.

"We were struck at how much he had changed," an observer
recalled. "I gasped when Rasputin entered the parlor. His bearing was so
regal, his bows were dignified, he took people's hands so delicately—he
was a totally different man!" Rasputin told a friend he was "extraordinarily joyful" because he had just toppled several enemies and replaced
them with Alexis Khvostov, who was a "good man and a close ally."

Rasputin was invited to dine with the Troika the day after he
returned from Pokrovskoye, September 28, 1915. "Rasputin was self-
confident and assured," Beletsky wrote two years later. "He made clear
at the outset that he was annoyed that our appointments had taken
place while he was gone. He emphasized this to the Prince and made
clear that he blamed him for it." Andronikov thanked Rasputin for his
support and for "putting us on the right path and saving us from mis-
takes." Khvostov assured Rasputin that he would attend to Rasputin's
needs. Asking Rasputin to bless the fish soup, he then kissed his hand.

After the meal Andronikov took Rasputin into his study and handed him 1,500 rubles, explaining that Rasputin could expect the same sum each month if he "behaved himself." Such an allowance meant nothing—Rasputin often received and gave away ten times that amount in a single day. But Rasputin pretended to be pleased. Then when Andronikov's back was turned Khvostov and Beletsky took the peasant aside and—as in a comic opera—slipped him 3,000 rubles with the request that he be "favorably disposed" toward them. "He crumpled up the envelope [and] shoved it into his pocket."

A furor greeted the news that Khvostov—known to be an ally of Rasputin's—had been appointed minister of the interior. Nicholas was demonstrating one more time his indifference to public opinion. Once in office, Khvostov cultivated imperial favor: his reports emphasized what Nicholas and Alexandra wanted to hear while downplaying or ignoring unpleasant matters. Nicholas soon bestowed a high honor on the young minister: the Order of Saint Anna First Class. Success went to Khvostov's head, and he began to dream of becoming both prime minister and minister of the interior—just like Peter Stolypin.

By October 1915 it was obvious that Ivan Goremykin could not last much longer as prime minister. The Duma had booed and hissed the old man during his last appearance. Goremykin was dreading a repetition of this on November 1, when the Duma was scheduled to reconvene, and he asked the tsar to postpone the session. Khvostov, by contrast, was urging Rasputin to convince Nicholas that the Duma should open on schedule. In fact, Khvostov was giving Rasputin a crash course in new political realities—and it worked. Rasputin was soon telling Alexandra that the Duma was an important fact of life; it was a permanent fixture of Russian government, and the tsar had to learn to work with it. It should be convened on schedule. Incredibly, the empress was easily persuaded of all that—or so it would seem. On November 15 she wrote to her husband that "Our Friend loathes [the Duma's] existence (as do I for Russia), [but] one cannot again uselessly offend them." Yesterday's champions of autocracy had embraced a new vision: constitutional monarchy. Incredible!

But what to do about Goremykin? Rasputin advised the empress to "see the Old Gentleman and gently tell him if the Duma hisses him, what can one do, one cannot send it away for such a reason."

The tsar was actually thinking of replacing Goremykin with Alexander Khvostov, the uncle of Alexis Khvostov. When Rasputin learned of this, he asked the emperor to let him speak with Alexander, who did not even realize that he was being considered for a promotion. The letters that followed between Nicholas and Alexandra made clear that they were looking to the peasant to find a "worthy successor" to Goremykin. An uneducated peasant was wielding enormous power at this critical moment in Russian history.

Rasputin visited Alexander Khvostov and told the empress that he seemed honest but, compared to Goremykin, was "obstinate" and "very dry and hard." Nicholas decided to postpone the decision. Goremykin would continue as prime minister, and the tsar granted him his wish: the Duma would not meet until February 1916. The search for his successor continued. Alexandra and Rasputin finally chose an elderly, retired statesman with a clouded reputation who had disappeared from public memory.

Boris Sturmer was born in 1848 into a reasonably distinguished noble family of Austrian and Russian ancestry. He rose in the provincial bureaucracy to become a governor in 1895. Sturmer worked well with the *zemstvos*, the elected boards that Alexander II had created to deal with problems at the grassroots level. This gave Nicholas reason to hope that Sturmer as prime minister might work well with the Duma. In 1901 Nicholas had written in frustration that he wished "other governors would understand things so well and give as good an account" as Sturmer did in carrying out orders from Saint Petersburg. But Sturmer was a man of limited ability; he was ostentatious, obsequious, and generally regarded as a third-rate bureaucrat. Nicholas got him out of the way by appointing him to the State Council. Sturmer tried (and failed) to become ober-procurator of the Holy Synod in 1911 and mayor of Moscow two years later. As of 1914, his career seemed to be over.

The Russian ship of state was floundering by late 1915. Men of ability were increasingly unwilling to serve it—they expected the tsarist regime to collapse and were waiting to see what would follow it. Even a weak figure like Sturmer could suddenly hope to stage a comeback. Sturmer approached Pitirim, the metropolitan of Saint Petersburg and known to be a close friend of Rasputin's. The next step was to win Rasputin's support, but Rasputin found Sturmer to be quite mediocre. Another meeting plus Sturmer's assurances that he would be Rasputin's friend and heed his wishes finally carried the day.

Relying on Rasputin's recommendation, Alexandra wrote her husband an unusually important letter on January 4, 1916, touting Sturmer as "the right man [who] will work well with the new energetic ministers." Most of what Nicholas was hearing about the man was unfavorable, so it took some convincing. On January 7 Alexandra pointed out that Sturmer "very much values Gr.[egory] which is a great thing." She insisted that Sturmer "is suited best of all for the present time"; he was "a decided loyal man and will hold others in hand." Rasputin urged the tsar to act at once.

Nicholas II appointed Sturmer prime minister on January 20, 1916. Russians were stunned. Goremykin's departure was hardly a surprise, but people hoped that his replacement would be an improvement. Men who had known Sturmer recalled how he positioned himself in such a way as to appear awake while he slept through committee meetings. French intelligence described Sturmer as a "third-rate intellect"—mean-spirited, of low character, and of dubious honesty with "no idea of state business." Rasputin brushed all this aside: "He's old, but that doesn't matter. He'll do!"

Sturmer understood that he had to keep Rasputin's goodwill to remain in power, and within twenty-four hours of assuming his post he (secretly) met Rasputin to receive his blessing. Sturmer was reassuring, telling Rasputin that all his requests would be honored; but Rasputin saw distressing signs of independence in the next ten days. Rasputin confronted the new prime minister—a peasant was scolding the highest official in the land. "Sturmer had better stay on his string," Rasputin warned. "If he doesn't, his neck will get broken! If I say the word, they'll toss the old guy out!"

Rasputin also urged Nicholas to build a better relationship with the Duma. He should reconvene it and appear (unannounced) at its first meeting. The tsar did this when the legislature went into session on February 9, 1916. Nicholas stood pale and nervous throughout the ceremony, tugging his collar as he clenched and unclenched his fists. Cheers greeted his call for the "representatives of My People" to work with the throne. (This was new—Nicholas had always rejected any suggestion that the Duma represented "the People.") As the tsar was leaving, the president Michael Rodzyanko called on him to grant a Ministry of Public Confidence—a cabinet that would be responsible to the Duma as well as the tsar. Nicholas promised to think about it.

Meanwhile, greed and ambition were causing the Troika to unravel. Khvostov and Beletsky were angry with Andronikov for using

Rasputin having tea with friends and followers at his
apartment. Anna Vyrubova is the figure in the top row at the
right. Efim Rasputin is second to his son's right.

the ministry to enrich himself in ways that they thought undermined
their alliance. Beletsky told Rasputin that Andronikov was pocketing
shady funds that should have gone to him. Khvostov and Beletsky
ran to Anna Vyrubova, denouncing the prince. Andronikov retali-
ated by mailing a copy of a famous photograph taken in 1914 showing Rasputin surrounded by his admirers—including Anna—to the
dowager empress. This did not really affect Maria Fedorovna's opinions—she already loathed Anna—but it demolished the last elements
of friendship between the prince and the peasant.

The Troika collapsed when Khvostov learned that Rasputin was
opposing his efforts to become prime minister, but he claimed an idealistic motive—devotion to the imperial family. Khvostov referred

to a particular night when the police informed him that at that very moment Rasputin was boasting at a party that the empress and her daughter Olga were his lovers. Challenged on this by one of the guests, Rasputin reached for the telephone and called "Olga." A young woman promptly appeared and was arrested. She turned out to be a prostitute whose fur-trimmed coat would make country bumpkins think that she was royalty. Khvostov testified that this "incident convinced me that Rasputin had to go to save the motherland!"

Khvostov tried to get Rasputin out of the way by encouraging him to make a lengthy pilgrimage to the great monasteries of northern Russia. This amused Rasputin—he played along, pocketing 8,000 rubles plus expensive bottles of Madeira wine. Then he cavalierly told Beletsky that he had changed his mind and would not go. This episode persuaded Khvostov to take direct measures.

In January 1916 he tried to draw an Okhrana officer into the plot to kill Rasputin. Khvostov offered Colonel Michael Kommisarov 200,000 rubles to kill Rasputin. Ironically, Kommisarov was the agent responsible for Rasputin's safety and security. Shaken and unwilling to become involved in such a caper, Kommisarov turned to Beletsky for advice. The police director pointed out that the colonel was trapped: if he refused the assignment, Khvostov would probably come up with another plan that would make him the fall guy. Beletsky suggested that Kommisarov ask Khvostov to add him to the conspiracy. Beletsky and Kommisarov played along with Khvostov—the three set to work planning the assassination. Khvostov first suggested strangling Rasputin and burying his body on a frozen riverbank where the spring thaw would carry it out to sea. Kommisarov thought poison was a better option: he researched several and tested them on Rasputin's cats. Rasputin was furious; he blamed Andronikov and got him exiled to a remote town for a crime he did not commit.

Khvostov soon realized that Beletsky and Kommisarov were stalling—they had no intention of killing Rasputin. Khvostov tried to contact Iliodor in Norway to see if he could use his contacts in Russia to have the peasant murdered, but Beletsky had the minister's emissary arrested. The scandal now exploded onto the front page of newspapers throughout the Russian empire. The minister and his assistant each gave self-serving interviews to bemused journalists. Khvostov rushed to assure Anna Vyrubova that he was innocent, insisting that if anyone was out to kill Rasputin, it was Beletsky.

RASPUTIN

Anna arranged for Rasputin and Khvostov to dine at her home; the minister fawned before Rasputin and kissed his hand. The peasant, of course, was not impressed; he was observing how coarse a "gentleman" could be. Nicholas II granted Khvostov an audience on March 3. The tsar was typically polite and cordial, and Khvostov left believing that he had survived the crisis. A few hours later a letter from the emperor arrived, dismissing Khvostov from his position as minister of the interior. Beletsky was fired as police director and appointed to the Senate (a judicial organ) with an annual salary of 18,000 rubles.

Officials had repeatedly warned Nicholas II about Khvostov, but he rejected their advice. Consequently, a man who was known to be a scoundrel assumed this high post—only to behave like a scoundrel. Alexandra offered an apology in a letter of March 2, 1916: "Am so wretched that we, through Gregory, recommended Khvostov to you—it leaves me not peace—you were against it and I let myself be imposed upon by them." Or was she really to blame? "The devil got hold of him, one cannot call it otherwise." Their subsequent actions show that the tsar and his wife had actually learned nothing from this sordid episode.

The Khvostov scandal fell on a people battered by war and depressed by what was now being called "the Reign of Rasputin." People who had long supported Nicholas II were now deciding that he was out of his depth and unable to lead them to victory. They were shocked, as Beletsky said, to see the government "behave like the Mafia." Yet this scandal was minor compared to what Russians would witness in the next ten months.

16

The Church at the Feet of a "Low Hound"

RUSSIA WAS LOSING THE WAR by the summer of 1915. At the point Warsaw fell to the advancing German army on August 5, 1,400,000 Russian soldiers had been killed or wounded and almost a million were in POW camps. General Anton Denikin recalled the "retreat from Galicia as one vast tragedy for the Russian army." When the Germans counterattacked, their "heavy artillery swept away whole lines of our trenches and the defenders with them." The ill-equipped Russian troops were scarcely able to respond. "Our regiments, although completely exhausted, were beating off one attack after another by bayonet." Blood flowed, and the ranks thinned as the number of graves grew daily.

Nicholas II could do little to improve the situation—but at least he could shake up his government. In the previous chapter we saw that he replaced four unpopular and lackluster ministers in the summer of 1915 with able men who enjoyed the nation's confidence. The tsar had not intended to strike out against Rasputin, but the new ministers of war, justice, and the interior were notably unfriendly to the peasant. It was the new leader of the Holy Synod, however, who had the most immediate impact on Rasputin.

• • •

Alexander Samarin came from a distinguished family—his father Dmitry was the celebrated Slavophile philosopher who had worked with Alexander II to abolish serfdom in 1861. Alexander was extremely conservative, but his sterling character made him admired even by people who disagreed with his opinions. The British observer R. H. Bruce Lockhart called him "one of the very best representatives of his class." Nicholas had invited him to head the Holy Synod in 1911, but Samarin demanded assurances that Rasputin would be excluded from any role in church affairs. The tsar was unwilling to do that, and the appointment went to Vladimir Sabler, who rapidly acquired the reputation of being subservient to Rasputin. "I am sure that [Samarin's appointment] will not please you," Nicholas conceded in a letter of June 15, 1915, telling his wife of Samarin's appointment. But these "changes must happen now & one must choose a man whose name is known in the whole country & who is unanimously estimated." The empress was furious—she bristled with anger: Rasputin was "in utter despair" at the news; his enemies "are ours," and Samarin would undermine the throne. "I am so wretched ever since I heard [the news] & cant get calm."

Samarin's appointment opened a floodgate of anger at Rasputin's influence in the Russian Orthodox Church. The *New Times* declared that seminaries and schools were in chaos; priests were abandoning their parishes, and the clergy enjoyed little respect. There was a "weakening of belief among the population and a growing indifference to the Church." The paper insisted that all this was because of Rasputin. "How has an abject adventurer like this been able to mock Russia for so long?" it asked. "Is it not astounding that the Church, the Holy Synod, the aristocracy, ministers, the Senate, and many members of the State Council and Duma have degraded themselves before this low hound? The Rasputin scandals seemed perfectly natural" in the past but "today Russia means to put an end to all this."

Samarin was soon receiving reports that Rasputin was a "horse thief" and a "heretic." They characterized his ally Bishop Varnava as an unbalanced fanatic. In fact, Varnava had been preaching a series of sermons claiming the war had been caused by abortion, which he fancied had been introduced into Russia by the Germans. His critics commented on the bishop's "boundless self-love" and ambition. In 1914 Varnava had first suggested the canonization of John Maximovich, a Siberian metropolitan of the eighteenth century, claiming that this would heighten religious devotions and bring financial rewards. A new saint would attract pilgrims and money to the cathedral in Tobolsk, where John was buried.

The Holy Synod applied two criteria in considering canonizations: Was the body preserved without decay, and were miracles associated with the remains? Varnava's answer to these questions was sly: he told the Holy Synod that "by God's grace Saint John's body was not preserved but the entire skeletal frame has been well preserved." Actually, no miracles had been attributed to John Maximovich. Knowing that Nicholas and Alexandra (as well as Rasputin) were interested in this canonization, however, the new ober-procurator suggested a compromise: the question should be postponed until after the war ended.

Varnava was unfazed—he forged ahead, asking Rasputin to urge the tsar to use his own authority to secure the canonization. If miracles were what the Holy Synod wanted, now—suddenly—they were occurring at John's tomb. The people of Tobolsk loved their sovereign and wanted a new saint. The empress agreed. "Bishop Varnava comes from the people," she chirped. "He understands them." On August 29, 1915, she advised Nicholas to "give Samarin the short order" that you wish Varnava "to chant the laudation of St. John Maximovich because Samarin intends getting rid of him, because we like him & he is good to Gr[egory]." (Roman Catholics call *laudation* beatification; it preceded *glorification*—the recognition of full sainthood.) Alexandra had no need to worry: Nicholas had already acted and, for once, his course of action was even more reckless than what his wife suggested: she had been urging her husband to force the church leaders to authorize the canonization. Nicholas had decided to defy them.

The tsar telegraphed Varnava on August 27, 1915, giving him permission to "sing the laudation but not the glorification." Varnava rushed to obey. The bells of the cathedral tolled the very night the telegram arrived, summoning the faithful to a theatrical ceremony that would prove to be the "last event of its kind in Imperial Russia." The congregation was profoundly moved. It was also confused, for Varnava led the people to think that they were witnessing the proclamation of full sainthood—and nothing was done to correct that impression.

Samarin was furious—he summoned Varnava to Saint Petersburg. The new ober-procurator planned to use this act of disobedience to launch a campaign against Rasputin's influence in the Church. Varnava stood while his tormentors sat cross-legged, smirking and engaging in catcalls. Varnava showed great dignity; he warned the ober-procurator that it was not his task "to judge a hierarch." Then he played his trump card—he produced Nicholas's fateful telegram. Alexandra subsequently wrote to her husband that the Synod "nearly laughed at your telegram, disregarded it, and forbade [Varnava] to continue the glorification." Nicholas should "hurry with clearing out Samarin as he & Synod are intending to do more horrors & he [Varnava] has to go there again, poor man, to be tortured." Rasputin added his support. "God blessed what you did," he declared in a telegram. "Your word is peace and kindness for all, and your hand conquers everything through thunder and lightning."

The Synod invalidated the laudation and moved to force Varnava from office. But it was Samarin who would lose the battle, not the bishop of Tobolsk. Nicholas was turning against the ober-procurator. Samarin's popularity and the wide praise he drew touched the jealous streak in Nicholas's character. The young minister had also been foolhardy: he composed the letter on behalf of his fellow ministers protesting the tsar's decision to replace Nicholasha and relocate to Stavka. Rasputin knew what was coming; for weeks he had been bragging that "Samarin will not be ober-procurator much longer." Samarin had been in office for only two months, but Nicholas decided that he must go.

Samarin joined the other ministers for a conference at Stavka on September 15, 1915. Nicholas listened pleasantly as the ober-procurator reported to the group on the Varnava situation. In a private moment the tsar asked Samarin about his family, and they spoke of his time in the service. Nicholas then left and had Goremykin call Samarin from the table to tell him that he was being dismissed as leader of the Holy Synod.

Everyone knew that Samarin lost his post because of pressure from Alexandra and Rasputin. Samarin's fellow Muscovites were stunned and outraged: observers detected in their reactions the first organized sign of opposition to Nicholas. (From this time Russians would speculate on a "coup from the right" that never materialized.) Samarin's removal inflamed conservative public opinion; it fixed responsibility for this development on the "court," a term that included Alexandra, Anna Vyrubova, and Rasputin. People were coming to think that Nicholas II was inept—and could not change. Alexander Spiridovich was shaken to see that "everyone and everything seemed to be against the Government. The people of Moscow really seemed to hate Alexandra Fedorovna, Anna Vyrubova, and Rasputin."

Rasputin was extremely interested in Samarin's replacement. The wrong man might renew the campaign against Rasputin and his allies in the Church. The Synod treasurer, Nicholas Soloviev, and chief secretary, Peter Mudrolyubov, openly supported Rasputin. Another ally, Vasily Skvortsov, edited conservative newspapers that praised the peasant's influence in the church. Varnava's sister, Natalya Prilezhaeva, was the wife of a minor Synod official; she spied on the affairs of his office and shared critical documents with Rasputin. The new ober-procurator had to protect and defend the interests of this network.

Minister of the Interior Alexis Khvostov recommended Alexander Volzhin as a replacement for Alexander Samarin. Volzhin was a provincial bureaucrat with no special religious experience or ties to church leaders. He admired Rasputin and loved church music. He was distantly related to Khvostov, who expected to control him. Alexandra interviewed the candidate and reported that "he made me a perfect impression[;] one sees he is full of the best intentions & understands the needs of our church perfectly well." Volzhin also knew when flattery would be important: at the end he asked the empress to bless him, "wh. touched me very much." Alexandra urged her husband to make Volzhin ober-procurator, and he did so on September 26, 1915.

Russians might ignore controversies in Tobolsk, but Nicholas scandalized the nation by making one of Rasputin's allies the metropolitan of Petrograd in 1915. The man of the hour was Pitirim—one of the best known (and most disreputable) figures in Russia at this time. Born Paul Oknov, he took the name Pitirim upon entering the monastic life in 1883. Pitirim received a high distinction in 1891: he became rector of the Saint Petersburg Theological Academy. Although Pitirim ignored his monastic vows of poverty, obedience, and chastity, he had the support needed to become a bishop in 1894 and an archbishop in 1909. Pitirim openly installed his male lover in his mansion when he was the bishop of Tula; the two shamelessly plundered the church treasury. When Pitirim botched the laudation of a local proposed saint in 1911, his enemies got him demoted to a remote diocese where, they hoped, he would slide into obscurity.

That was not to be. Within a few months a Synod official was admitting that "Pitirim is one of the most shameful figures in our Church." It was Rasputin who rescued him. Hearing that Pitirim had once defended a group of heretics, Rasputin begged the empress to intercede on his behalf. Pitirim's homosexuality was obviously not a problem for Rasputin, although his daughter claimed that he found it to be "disgusting," at least when he was a young man. But time and experience had made Rasputin more tolerant. He had always been partial to religious dissenters; in 1913, he spoke up for Muslims and even defended the Turkish government. Although the Siberian mystic and healer grumbled about "Yids," he befriended Jews, especially businessmen and prostitutes. Rasputin always sympathized with marginalized people—this might even have been a reason for his defense of Pitirim. At any rate, Nicholas pressured the Holy Synod to promote Pitirim to archbishop of Samara. The local postmaster was surprised to see that Pitirim came to the post office to send Rasputin a wire congratulating him on his Name Day in 1913. The postmaster shared the news with the local governor, and the word spread that Pitirim was a member of Rasputin's circle.

When the exarch of Georgia died in 1914, Nicholas discussed his replacement with the ober-procurator. He was appalled when the tsar let it slip that he favored Pitirim, and he rushed to present a list of more suitable candidates. Looking it over, Nicholas wrote at the top "Pitirim." Since neither the emperor nor his wife had even met the archbishop, it seems that it was thanks to Rasputin that Pitirim became exarch. (He was now the fourth most prestigious bishop in the Church.) Alexandra was soon praising Pitirim as a "clever and large-minded man." The tsar was impressed when he finally met Pitirim—he told Alexandra that he wanted the man to become the metropolitan of Petrograd, which was the greatest honor a bishop could hold in the Russian Orthodox Church at that time.

Pitirim's opportunity for advancement came when the metropolitan of Kiev died in November 1915. Alexandra suggested that Vladimir, the current metropolitan of Petrograd (and a Rasputin foe) be demoted to Kiev, which was the third highest post. This would open the way for Pitirim to be promoted to Petrograd, which was the first. No metropolitan had ever been demoted in Russia. But Nicholas II had already demonstrated a willingness to break with tradition and sow confusion in the Church when it pleased him to do so.

Alexander Volzhin was ober-procurator at this point. He presented a report on Pitirim's unsavory activities, but Nicholas ignored it. By law and tradition the thirteen-man governing council of the Holy Synod had to approve such a promotion. They objected, but Nicholas insisted, and it was duly announced that Pitirim was the new metropolitan of

Petrograd. Officials at the Alexander Nevsky Monastery (the official seat of the metropolitan) were appalled. Only Pitirim's friends congratulated him on the honor he was receiving. The ministers boycotted the liturgies he celebrated on official occasions at Saint Isaac's Cathedral. When Pitirim paid a courtesy call on Michael Rodzyanko, he found the Duma president to be totally hostile, and their conversation was strained.

"Rasputin and men like him," Rodzyanko thundered at last, "must be expelled, and your own name cleared from the opprobrium of being looked upon as a nominee of Rasputin." Pitirim turned pale and asked Rodzyanko if he had ever spoken to Nicholas about Rasputin. "Yes, many a time," the president conceded. "As for you, Your Eminence, your very looks betray you."

Pitirim brought a handsome, charming, young homosexual priest named Antony Guriysky from Georgia to Petrograd. Rasputin was soon recommending him for promotion to vicar bishop in the capital. Alexandra was charmed when she met Guriysky—she praised the "cosy Georgian intonation in his voice—knows Our Friend longer than we do—was rector years ago at Kazan" Seminary. The empress also visited with Melchizedek, another gay priest in Pitirim's entourage; he became the bishop of Kronstadt. "Our Friend says he will be a marvelous metropolitan in the future."

Pitirim made Filaret father superior of the Alexander Nevsky Monastery. He was a crude man who had been expelled from previous posts for fighting with novices and stealing their property. Filaret brought his mistress into his house and demanded kickbacks from anyone who did business with the monastery. Auditors claimed that he stole over 100,000 rubles from the treasury in 1916 alone. The metropolitan was willing to overlook Filaret's indiscretions because Pitirim had so many of his own. His sexual partner was a handsome young layman named Ivan Osipenko. Pitirim debased the proud and ancient monastery by throwing it open to wild parties that included Gypsy choruses and dancing. Alcohol flowed as drunken revelers paraded through the gardens and grounds, terrorizing the ordinary monks. Rasputin was a frequent guest at these occasions, and they greatly amused him.

Isidor was another homosexual who profited from Rasputin's friendship. Isidor became a bishop in 1902, but his sexual conduct caused difficulties. He was transferred four times, and in 1911 was stripped of his rank for "unnatural conduct." It seems that Isidor had a penchant for seducing novices, including one who became his lover. Rasputin met Isidor in 1913 and got him restored as a bishop in 1916. Isidor was reunited with his lover, and they carried on as openly as before. Alexandra enjoyed the company of these gay clergymen. She told her husband on October 1, 1916, about the "quiet, peaceful" evening she spent with Rasputin, Isidor, and Melchizedek: "We talked so well & calmly—such a peaceful, harmonious atmosphere."

Rasputin also helped Palladi become a bishop. As a seminary inspector he had been responsible for monitoring the lives of his students, some as young as twelve. The assertions that Palladi engaged in "unnatural vice" were borne out by testimony from the nuns who laundered his bed sheets. He allegedly seduced a boy who was fourteen, the age of consent in Russia then and now. Palladi was accused of luring other young monks and laymen to his bed in exchange for promotions and favors. The case was never resolved because none of the alleged victims would testify against him. One youth admitted that he had destroyed the letters he received from the bishop.

In February 1916 there were rumors that Rasputin was planning to oust his remaining opponents from the Holy Synod. Supposedly the peasant's friends intended to eliminate "all the prelates, abbots and archimandrites" who were opposed—as the French ambassador Paléologue put it—to the "eroto-maniac-mystic of Pokrovskoye." They would be demoted and exiled to remote monasteries. At this point even the police seemed to be in service to Rasputin. When the police discovered that Archbishop Anthony of Kharkov was criticizing the peasant in letters, he was expelled from the governing council of the Holy Synod and assigned a post in Siberia. Archbishop Innocent of Irkutsk deplored Rasputin's influence and was immediately demoted. Rasputin insisted on selecting Innocent's replacement. He vetoed one candidate because he had once spoken critically of Rasputin before a church commission.

Rasputin expected the new ober-procurator to sanction his power at the Holy Synod—that was why he was chosen for the position. It was true that Alexander Volzhin flattered the empress and Rasputin when he was a candidate for office. In fact, John Maximovich received full canonization in the summer of 1916, and Varnava was promoted to archbishop in October. But Volzhin resented being taken for granted, and he was making a quiet decision to fight Rasputin and his "gang of supporters in the church." He was delighted to learn that the assistant ober-procurator was willing to support him in this effort. Indeed, the battle with Rasputin and his supporters took shape around the fateful question: Who would hold the number-two position at the Holy Synod?

Rasputin suggested that Prince Nicholas Zhevakov become assistant ober-procurator. He had befriended Rasputin and won the empress's attention by telling her of a vision in which he saw the Russian army score a great victory by bringing a certain icon to the front. When Volzhin objected to the suggestion that Zhevakov be elevated to this high office, Alexandra informed her husband that Rasputin "finds you ought to tell Volzhin you wish Zhevakov to be named his aide." Upon reflection, however, Nicholas realized that the scheme would trigger a scandal in the Duma, so he backed away from the appointment.

Pitirim ran to the empress to complain—ironically—that *Volzhin* was disreputable and should be removed from his post. In fact, Volzhin had earned Alexandra's enmity after just six weeks in office. As his hostility to Rasputin became apparent, the tsaritsa decided that he was "a coward & frightened of public opinion"; he was "too pompous" and "quite unfit" to lead the Holy Synod. But with Samarin's dismissal fresh in the minds of his angry admirers, Nicholas decided that it was best to leave Volzhin in office, at least for the time being.

Exhausted from the battles he was constantly fighting, Volzhin asked Alexandra to relieve him of his post on August 1, 1916. The empress had endured the man for nearly a year, and she was delighted to step up her search for his successor. Officials provided her with a roster of suitable candidates, but Rasputin and Pitirim offered their own list—men of limited attainments with weak wills that would ensure their cooperation with their benefactors. It did not take long for Rasputin and Pitirim to find their candidate.

Their choice for this honor was Nicholas Raev, a prominent man in the social life of the capital. Although his father had been the metropolitan of Saint Petersburg, Nicholas did not pursue a Church career. He served in the ministry of education and on various state commissions. He met Rasputin though Pitirim, who was grateful to Raev Senior for helping him become the rector of the Saint Petersburg Theological Academy. Nicholas was short and a bit comical. (People widely noted that he wore a wig.) Lamenting the fact that able men were not available for high office by late 1916, Alexandra admitted that Raev was the best replacement she and her friends could find for Volzhin. The words the empress used to jar her husband's memory of the candidate were significant: "You probably know him—has the kursissky [girls' school] under him & when there were rows in all the schools & universities [in 1905], his girls behaved beautifully. . . . [He] is so well versed in everything concerning our Church." Raev's most recent activity was running a high-stakes gambling club in Petrograd.

When Alexandra met Raev on June 27, 1916, she found him to be an "excellent man, knowing the Church by heart." After Volzhin resigned and the position actually opened up, Rasputin and Raev talked for over an hour—this was clearly the sort of moment that would make or break a career. Raev probably gave assurances that if he headed the Holy Synod, all of Rasputin's wishes would be carried out. At least Rasputin told the empress that Raev "is a real God's send," and Nicholas duly appointed him ober-procurator on August 30, 1916. Prince Zhevakov became his assistant on September 15.

Russians were upset at these developments. "The Orthodox Church is in peril, brothers—protect it!" a deputy thundered in the Duma. There was speculation about a coming schism between the Holy Synod (controlled by Rasputin) and the rest of the faithful. On December 2, 1916, the *New Times* lamented the fact that "laymen—ordinary Orthodox people—have been forced to defend the Church" against its own leaders. Leftist propaganda directed against Rasputin was demoralizing priests and seminarians. Many Russians were depressed. The peasant's enemies had been punished, while the empress celebrated his friends and allies. The Holy Synod was polarized by the autumn of 1916, and one official there recalled that its offices reeked of "carbon monoxide."

Rasputin was powerful because Nicholas and Alexandra permitted it. Thanks to them, unqualified candidates were being elevated to high offices in the Church. The tsar humiliated and undermined the Synod, first by elevating Maximovich to sainthood, then by advancing Varnava's career. It was criminal for the emperor, of all people, to undermine the most loyal of Russian institutions. Monarchy depends on order and respect, but they were rapidly collapsing in Russia throughout 1916. For months people had been watching what a perceptive observer called a certain "devilish talent" Nicholas had for discerning popular opinion and then flying in the face of it "with a sort of nasty joy." Nicholas obviously thought he could do this without negative consequences. He would soon learn that he was mistaken.

17

"Our Friend's Ideas about Men Are Sometimes Queer"

T HE YEAR 1916 BEGAN WITH RUSSIANS in an angry
mood—the result of horrendous losses on the battlefield plus
food and fuel shortages at home with an incompetent government and
a Church in total disarray. The Khvostov scandal showed just how
much damage Rasputin and Alexandra could inflict on the ship of state.
As for the "Reign of Rasputin," it worsened as the year progressed.

Rasputin took for granted that it was up to him to find Alexis
Khvostov's replacement. "Shcheglovitov wants it," he mused about the
minister of justice, "but he's a rogue. Kryzhanovsky's pushing me to
have dinner. He wants it, but he's a swindler. And then Beletsky wants
it. If I haven't been murdered so far, he's the one who'll do it for sure."
In the end he recommended that Boris Sturmer serve as minister of
the interior as well as prime minister. The tsar agreed, and it was done.

The government was headed for a period of instability marked by
"Ministerial Leapfrogging." Ministers were appointed and fired with
no apparent reason, hurting the empire and disturbing Russia's allies.
Sometimes they traded portfolios. Historian Michael Florinsky calls
it an "amazing, extravagant, and pitiful spectacle" that was "without
parallel in the history of civilized nations."

Russia saw four different prime ministers from September 1915 to
March 1917, as well as five ministers of the interior and four ministers

of agriculture. Six other ministries had three different heads in these eighteen months. Minister of Agriculture Alexander Naumov—a Rasputin foe—resigned in July 1916. The minister of foreign affairs got the ax the same month. Sergei Sazonov had been urging the tsar to shore up the loyalty of his Polish subjects by promising that Poland would receive autonomy after the war. Alexandra insisted that Sazonov be fired, although he was highly regarded by the allies. Nicholas added foreign affairs to Sturmer's responsibilities, which led Sturmer to hand over the ministry of the interior to Alexander Khvostov, the minister of justice and Alexis Khvostov's honest uncle. Alexander Khvostov surrendered the ministry of justice to Alexander Makarov, a gray but experienced official. The leapfrogging went on and on, growing ever more complicated. Public opinion blamed Rasputin for the situation, though in truth he had practically nothing to do with firing or appointing most of these ministers.

All these men were nonentities—their comings and goings were of little consequence except to bewilder Russians and their allies. The loss of the minister of war, Alexis Polivanov, however, was quite different. He was a capable and energetic general; Paul von Hindenburg thought that he saved the Russian army in 1915. But Polivanov had opposed Nicholas II, assuming the supreme command, and he was a bitter enemy of Rasputin's. The empress finally forced him out of office in March 1916; he was replaced by a nonentity.

Alexander Khvostov lasted a mere two months as minister of the interior. Because he opposed Rasputin, it should have been obvious that his days in office would be numbered. But the man who replaced him was worse than incompetent; he was dangerous.

Alexander Protopopov was born in 1866 into a powerful noble family in Simbirsk, the same region that gave the world Khioniya Guseva and V. I. Lenin. The talented and multifaceted Protopopov was fluent in several languages and studied piano under the great French composer Jules Massenet. Protopopov served in the Imperial Guards before resigning to manage his family's cotton factory and farming operations. After helping to crush local rebellions in 1905, he served as a bank director and president of the Cloth Manufacturers' League. Protopopov was a liberal conservative and a leading light of the Octobrist Party. He won a seat in the Third Duma and was elected vice president of the Fourth Duma. Protopopov was opposed to anti-Semitism; he befriended Jews and favored improving their legal rights.

Alexander Protopopov, who served as minister of the interior from September 16, 1916, until the March 1917 Revolution. When the Old Regime fell, he was probably the most hated person in Russia besides members of the imperial family.

With his polished manner and distinguished appearance, Protopopov seemed to be a gifted statesman, charming and self-assured. He joined a Duma delegation that toured Russia's allies in the summer of 1916 to assure them that Russia would stay in the war until final, absolute victory. Although Protopopov created a favorable impression, darkness lurked just under the surface. He held conversations with the icon on his desk, answering quizzical looks with a smile that insisted he was absolutely normal. Protopopov was actually a victim of syphilis that he had apparently contracted as an officer. He was going insane. He also became a drug addict thanks to the "arousing powders" supplied by Dr. Peter Badmaev. Protopopov mumbled, twitched, broke into sweats, and occasionally unleashed strings of invective that made worldly men blush. A nervous breakdown kept Protopopov confined to Badmaev's clinic for six months during the war.

Dr. Badmaev introduced Rasputin to Protopopov in 1913. Friendship between the peasant and the elegant nobleman deepened while he was convalescing at the clinic. Meanwhile, Dr. Badmaev was hatching a plot much like the scheme that brought the ministry of the interior under the control of Prince Andronikov. Badmaev likewise had a shady financial empire that he hoped to protect by installing an ally as minister of the interior. This plan featured Protopopov as the chief minister; Paul Kurlov, Badmaev's business partner, would serve as the assistant minister and police director. Rasputin was fully committed to the project because he honestly believed that Protopopov was the man who could save Russia at this difficult hour. All that Rasputin asked in exchange for his services was to be left alone.

Rasputin's assignment was to maneuver Nicholas II into making Protopopov minister of the interior. Rasputin began—as usual—with the empress. Alexandra had never met the Duma's vice president; but as soon as Rasputin mentioned him, her letters were brimming with glowing recommendations. Protopopov "likes Our Friend since at least four years," she noted. "I don't know him, but I believe in Our Friend's wisdom & guidance." Three more letters in the next four days urged her husband to name Protopopov minister of the interior.

Nicholas resisted. He agreed that the gentleman from Simbirsk was "good a man"—note the slip of the pen. But the tsar felt for obvious reasons that Protopopov was better suited to head the ministry of industry and commerce. Nicholas confessed that the suggestion that the erratic entrepreneur should become minister of the interior took him "quite unexpectedly": "I must think that question over," he wrote. "Our Friend's ideas about men are sometimes queer, as you know. One must be careful, especially in nominations of high people. . . . All these changes exhaust the head. I find they happen much too often. It is certainly not at all good for the interior of the country because every new man brings changes also into the administration."

Alexandra kept up the pressure: "Please take Protopopov as Minister of the Interior, as he is one of the Duma, it will make a great effect amongst them & shut their mouths." The empress was actually making a legitimate point: there was reason to hope that Protopopov as minister of the interior might encourage a friendlier relationship between the throne and the legislature. As usual, Alexandra had her way: "It shall be done," her husband cabled tersely. Paul Kurlov was appointed assistant minister of the interior and director of the police, although he was so unsavory that Nicholas did not put this in the form of an official announcement. Kurlov proved to be so tyrannical and unstable that even his allies turned on him. He lasted a mere three months in office.

"God bless your new choice of Protopopov," Alexandra exclaimed. "Our Friend says you have done a very wise act in naming him." But as soon as Protopopov settled into the office, it was clear that he would represent the tsar to the Duma, not vice versa. This outraged his former colleagues—they shunned and slighted him. Protopopov began talking to himself, sobbing and answering the voices that raged in his head. The problem of supplying food and fuel to Petrograd worsened as the winter approached. Newspapers called for Protopopov's resignation. Constantly on the verge of nervous collapse, the gentleman from Simbirsk could be seen speeding across the city to Badmaev's clinic for more of the "arousing powders" that permitted him to function.

Protopopov's appointment added to another problem: Sturmer's increasing unpopularity. His policies had totally alienated the Progressive Bloc in the Duma. Sturmer's German name posed difficulties, as did suspicions—confirmed by documents published after the war—that he was secretly investigating the option of a separate peace with Germany. Nicholas II was concerned; he warned his wife that the situation was "much worse than last year" with Ivan Goremykin. Disregarding her wishes, Nicholas fired Sturmer on November 9, 1916.

His replacement was Alexander Trepov, a strong, forceful man with conservative views that would ordinarily have appealed to Alexandra. But Trepov was an enemy of Rasputin's. When Nicholas made him minister of communications the previous year, Alexandra informed her husband that "Our Friend is very grieved at his nomination as He knows he is very against him [Rasputin] . . . & he is sad you did not ask his advice." This time the tsar acted without seeking his wife's counsel. Trepov became prime minister on November 10, 1916. Nicholas acted with admirable resolution, although he did not anticipate the barrage of hostility that was about to come from the Duma.

If Sturmer was ridiculed, Trepov was hated. When the new prime minister first appeared before the Duma, the whistles and insults were so loud that he was unable to deliver his speech. But later he astounded the deputies by agreeing with their demands for a responsible ministry. He conceded that Russia had suffered far too long under "Dark Forces," a code term for the empress and Rasputin. He admitted that Protopopov had to go, and the tsar agreed, although he knew that this would infuriate Alexandra. The tsar wrote that Protopopov was a "good, honest man, but he jumps from one idea to another & cannot stick to his opinion. I remembered that from the beginning." He added that the unfortunate man was "not normal" owing to "a certain illness"; it would be "risky, leaving the Ministry of the Interior in such hands at such times." Certain of his wife's response, he ended, "Only please don't mix in our Friend! It is I who carry the responsibility [and] I want to be free to choose accordingly."

Alexandra traveled to Stavka to plead her case in person. Behind closed doors, the empress relentlessly impressed her views on her husband. Nicholas admitted that "these days spent together were indeed hard ones." He praised his wife's "staunch and enduring" arguments defending Protopopov. Incredibly, it was the tsar who apologized to his spouse: "Forgive me if I have been cross or impatient, sometimes one's temper has to get through." The historian Robert K. Massie notes that this was the "only evidence in the whole of their correspondence of a serious, personal quarrel."

Some of Nicholas's anger probably stemmed from the fact that Alexandra ignored his plea and told Rasputin of her husband's decision to fire Protopopov. Four telegrams from Rasputin warned the tsar of the dire consequences of doing that. One was 238 words long—the peasant had been stirred into writing at such unprecedented length. He insisted that the minister "is a true person" who should not be sacrificed. Rasputin made an interesting admission: Protopopov had guaranteed to leave Rasputin alone, and stripping the minister of his office would leave Rasputin—in a peasant's turn of speech—like a turnip without teeth. "Let reason come to you," Rasputin implored.

The empress followed her visit with a series of important letters, each blazing with the certainty that she knew what was best for her husband and Russia. Alexandra insisted that Protopopov was their "truest friend," while Trepov was trying to "frighten" the tsar with unwise advice. Nicholas would be well advised to have the "deepest faith in the prayers & help of Our Friend, for it was his power that has kept you where you are."

Nicholas capitulated: Protopopov stayed in office. Trepov was so angry with the tsar for breaking his promise that he tendered his resignation. But Nicholas refused to accept it. "I order you to carry out your duties with the colleagues I have thought fit to give you," Nicholas barked angrily. Trepov was desperate. His brother-in-law, Alexander Mosolov (director of the Imperial Secretariat), knew Rasputin. Trepov authorized Mosolov to offer Rasputin a deal: if Rasputin abandoned his political intrigue, he would get a house in Petrograd plus 200,000 rubles and permanent bodyguards. Mosolov had the feeling that his offer might be rejected—and it was. Rasputin was furious at the suggestion that money could corrupt him. As for Nicholas II, he was only using Trepov to master the Duma; Trepov not only failed in that—he agreed with the deputies' demands for a Ministry of Public Confidence.

Trepov was dismissed as prime minister after forty-seven days in office. Nine days before that, Rasputin had been murdered.

The main events forming the end of the tragedy quickly unfolded. The uprising in Petrograd that toppled the imperial regime began on February 23, 1917. Nine days later, Nicholas abdicated. In the early morning hours of July 17, 1918, the former tsar and his family together with three servants and the family doctor were shot in the basement of the "House of Special Purpose" at Yekaterinburg. An executioner used his rifle butt to crush the skull of Jimmy, the spaniel.

18

Shadows Come at Twilight

Rasputin drank in alcoholic fashion throughout World War I. In part this was because he was in constant pain after Khioniya Guseva's attack. It also came from the spiritual crisis that he had been suffering for two years before that. Rasputin never resolved the issues that were involved in that conflict; it bewildered him so much that he might not have even been certain of what they were. When he felt that his prayers were not being answered, he turned to alcohol, just as he had done before his conversion at Verkhoturye in 1897. He grew defensive when Maria tried to talk to her father about his use of alcohol. "Why shouldn't I drink?" he asked. "Am I not a man, like all the others?"

Rasputin's days followed a set routine. He got up late—scarcely a surprise given how he spent his nights. After eating breakfast, he telephoned Anna Vyrubova to learn about the latest developments at Tsarskoye Selo. Although his callers began gathering before dawn, Rasputin was spending less and less time with them. After pulling himself together, he sat in his study from eleven o'clock in the morning until one o'clock in the afternoon as they filed through his apartment. He took a nap after lunch or visited the baths.

Rasputin's nights would have tested a man half his age. He visited friends and attended parties at the capital's most fashionable restaurants and hotels. He was a regular fixture at Donon's Restaurant (on the Moika Canal) or the Hotel Astoria, as well as the Hotel Rossiia and the Hotel Europa; above all he relished the atmosphere of the gypsy clubs. He passed entire nights at Massalsky's Gypsy Chorus and at the Villa Rode, drinking and eating, singing and dancing.

Joseph Vecchi, manager of the French Restaurant at the Hotel Astoria, left an account of a party honoring Rasputin that he oversaw one night during the war. Vecchi watched as a princess and twelve elegantly attired ladies—some with young daughters—arrived and disappeared into a private room. Vecchi was struck by Rasputin's "dirty" and "untidy" beard, "surmounted by a hooked nose like the beak of some terrible bird of prey." Strands of hair fell across Rasputin's forehead, while his hands were "grimy, with bitten, blackened nails." His aura was "evil and sordid." Although Vecchi's impressions were negative, he could see that Rasputin was "undeniably powerful" even if "alien to the rest of mankind." It was "disgusting" to see Rasputin at the table—he ate "like a beast, using his long, talon-like fingers in lieu of knife and fork, grabbing the food on his plate and stuffing himself in a vulgar way." Although Rasputin drank throughout the meal, he never seemed to be drunk. He used "the most vulgar language in the presence of his hostess and the ladies." Shortly after three o'clock in the morning, the peasant slipped into a waiting vehicle while the ladies departed in an opposite direction to keep from "being connected with Rasputin."

Alcohol fueled Rasputin's evenings, and the police reports describe how it affected him. He came back to his apartment "very drunk" with a female companion on November 14, 1915. "They left again directly," and he reappeared alone at two o'clock in the morning "completely overcome with drink." On November 25, "Rasputin came home at 5 AM." On December 3, he spent the night with the actress Vera Varvarova and returned to his flat the next day completely drunk. On December 7 he dined at Donon's; he then joined two ladies at the Hotel Rossiia before leaving to spend the night with Varvarova. Two days later Rasputin picked up two women at two o'clock in the morning. They found the Villa Rode closed and were not admitted, even though Rasputin banged on the door and pulled the bell. The group ended up at Massalsky's Gypsy Chorus, where they remained until ten o'clock in the morning. Then the revelers, still drunk, moved on to a friend's apartment for the rest of the day. Rasputin's guards developed a terminology classifying their charge's states. Their reports describe him as "slightly inebriated," "inebriated," "fairly drunk," "drunk," "very drunk," "completely drunk," "dead drunk," and finally, "totally overcome with drink."

Rasputin was observed fleeing from a residence at ten o'clock in the evening on May 14, 1915, chased by two men after accosting a female guest. On June 2 Rasputin returned home and made drunken advances to three female residents; he tried to kiss the porter's wife before Dunya, the maid, dragged him away. One morning two women loudly exited his flat calling him a "scurvy peasant" and telling detectives that once they had seen him running about the Villa Rode, "dressed only in his shirt." On the morning of January 14, 1916, Rasputin broke a large pane of glass in the entrance door of his building. Four days later he returned at seven o'clock in the morning "completely drunk"; after "singing loudly in the streets," he spent the morning "shouting and stomping" about in his apartment.

Rasputin never let the empress see him drunk, but sometimes he was forced to appear at Tsarskoye Selo while he was hung over and shaky. He once received a telephone call asking him to come to Alexander Palace. Trying to get ready, he only managed to stumble around his apartment; friends who were visiting warned him that if the empress saw him in that condition, it would "ruin everything." They persuaded him to take a nap before boarding the train; they shook their heads and whispered, "Our *starets* is indulging himself far too much these days." On another occasion Rasputin was at the Tsarskoye Selo train station, drunk. He staggered about the platform, and Michael Kommisarov—the Okhrana colonel who monitored his behavior—barely saved him from a fall. Rasputin began referring to Alexandra in terms that shocked even the worldly Okhrana officer. Kommisarov shook Rasputin and made it clear that he was not going to talk that way about the imperial family.

Sex was an important part of Rasputin's life. He often demanded sex from the women who came to him for help. Many fled his embrace. One was halfway down the staircase when Rasputin's maid begged her to return, calling out, "He feels lonely." A soldier's wife asked that her husband be kept in a hospital and not returned to the front. Rasputin had her undress; he fondled her breasts and told her to kiss him. Although she submitted to his demands, Rasputin asked her to return the next day. Apparently she did not do that.

Rasputin had an obvious crush on an eighteen-year-old seamstress named Katya who lived in the same building. The police recorded how he was constantly asking to see her, knocking on her door when drunk and offering her 50 rubles if she would visit his apartment. He had a lengthy liaison with the actress Varvarova, and—as mentioned earlier—they often spent their nights together. Rasputin saw a prostitute named Vera Tregubova with some regularity. Some of his paid liaisons did not go smoothly: Rasputin once locked a prostitute in his bedroom for the entire day until a servant intervened.

Alexis Filippov was a journalist and friend who published Rasputin's *Thoughts and Meditations* in 1911. He and Rasputin spent much time together and spoke of many things. Filippov often tried to engage Rasputin in a discussion about women, but Rasputin was always evasive. Filippov was surprised to see that "if someone took up a more or less sexual theme, Rasputin would quickly and playfully change the subject." Rasputin also made clear that he did not care for anti-Semitic jokes and subjects.

Filippov and Rasputin often went to the baths together, and the publisher left a description of his friend's naked body. Filippov contradicts what others had to say about Rasputin and hygiene—even in this the starets was an enigma. "Rasputin was exceptionally clean; he often changed his underwear, went to the baths, and never smelled bad," Filippov testified in 1917. "His body was exceptionally firm, not flabby, [it was] ruddy and well proportioned, without the paunch and flaccid muscles usual at that age . . . and without the darkening color of the sexual organs, which, at a certain age, take on a dark or brown hue." These were the only "physical peculiarities" Filippov noted. He says nothing of the "enormous sexual organ" celebrated in the Rasputin legend. In Radzinsky's words, Rasputin was "a very clean peasant with a young-looking body—and that's all."

On January 23, 1912, the police began to guard Rasputin in a new and systematic way. Agents now tracked the peasant's every move—and their reports shed light on the public aspects of his life. We learn, for example, the importance of prostitutes in Rasputin's routine. "He seldom appears on the street alone," we read in one report. "But when he does that, he turns to a street where prostitutes gather, he selects one and takes her to a hotel or a bathhouse." Another tells us, "He hired a prostitute on Haymarket Square." Elsewhere: "He went to Nevsky [Prospekt], hired the prostitute Petrovna, and went to a bathhouse with her." "He visited the family baths on Konyushenny [Avenue] with a prostitute he hired near the Politseisky Bridge." "He went with the prostitute Anna Petrovna to the same place." Radzinsky quotes nineteen police accounts of this sort.

Sometimes Rasputin hired several prostitutes in the course of a single day. One report says: "He visited the baths *twice* with an unidentified prostitute." Another says he went with a prostitute to a hotel, "where he stayed for twenty minutes." A different report notes that he spent one-and-a-half hours with Zinaida Manshtedt, a follower and a very respectable lady; then he visited an "unidentified woman, possibly a prostitute, and came out again twenty minutes later." After spending two hours with Maria Sazonova, he "hired a prostitute and they went to her apartment, from which he soon emerged again." Apparently the contrast between "good" and "fallen" women energized Rasputin in some way. The difference between longer periods with the society ladies and shorter times with the others might also have been significant.

Rasputin's sex life was complicated, and we might not entirely understand it. His behavior would lead us to suppose that Rasputin was constantly seeking sex—but that might not have been the case. At least one prostitute who knew Rasputin thought he was impotent. In two cases we know what happened after Rasputin and the woman he hired closed the door, and that was, in the words of one police report, "most mysterious." In the first instance, "Rasputin bought [the prostitute] two bottles of beer, though he did not drink himself. . . . [He] asked her to undress, looked at her body, and left." The second involved a prostitute who was the peasant's regular client in these years. Her name was "Peach," and she was an old woman when Radzinsky interviewed her in the 1970s.

Peach was seventeen and wearing a tight-fitting coat the first time Rasputin picked her up. He promised her so much money that she wondered where a peasant would get such a sum. Maybe he had killed somebody. As if reading her thoughts, her client said to her, "Little fool! Don't you know who I am? I'm Grigory Efimovich Rasputin." He took her to a cheap hotel, and sat, watching silently, as she undressed. His face suddenly grew white, as if all the blood had left it. At this point, Peach had actually become quite frightened. Rasputin said something else to her, but she did not understand it because "it was cold in the room—it was winter—and I was sitting naked and all hunched up." He handed her some money and left. He took Peach to the same hotel another time. He even lay beside her, although he remained dressed and did not touch her. Peach saw Rasputin again, but she was glad to observe the mysterious peasant engaging the services of other women. Rasputin frightened Peach; he seemed mentally deranged, and she was afraid he would stab her. Such things happened to women of her profession.

Sex was sometimes not the purpose of these encounters with prostitutes. The challenge for Rasputin on those occasions was to *resist temptation*—to *transcend the carnal* by facing it. He was hiring those prostitutes to attain a religious experience.

Police reports from 1912 contain a fascinating detail. A detective notes that "the Russian [a code name for Rasputin], *while walking alone, talks to himself* and waves his arms and slaps himself on the body, thereby attracting the attention of passers-by." Was Rasputin talking to himself? Or was he rebuking Satan?

Praskovaya accepted her husband's relationships with other women in silence. In fact, Rasputin's family life seems to have been happy except for his dealings with Efim. This father-son relationship had never been easy, and the police witnessed a terrible brawl in Pokrovskoye that showed Efim's true feelings. Both were "exceedingly drunk" when the older Rasputin began cursing his son "in the foulest language." Rasputin was infuriated—he jumped from his chair, threw his father out of the house, knocked him to the ground, and began beating him. "Don't hit me, you scoundrel!" Efim howled. Only with some difficulty did a detective separate them. Rasputin punched his father so violently that one of Efim's eyes was swollen shut. He called his son an "ignorant old fool who only knew how to fondle Dunya's soft parts!" This triggered a new assault, and Efim punched back, injuring his son's hip.

When Efim died in 1916, Rasputin was in the capital. Rasputin spoke of returning to Pokrovskoye for the funeral, but he did not do so—he hinted to Beletsky that the imperial family needed him in the capital. The police director expected Rasputin "to alter his style of life, if only in those first days which are so sharp for anyone who has lost a near one." But if Rasputin mourned his father, he concealed it. His usual behavior continued. "Everything was the same," Beletsky noted, "the same drunkenness, the same carousing, the same relationship to women."

Rasputin and his son also had a distant relationship, although it does not seem to have been stormy or difficult. Dmitry was a peasant to the core, and Rasputin did not push the advantages of city life on him. Dmitry received only a rudimentary education at the village school in Pokrovskoye. Rasputin was upset when Dmitry was drafted in the autumn of 1915. Praskovaya admitted that she wondered if she would ever see her son again.

"Our Friend," Alexandra wrote to Nicholas, "is in despair [that] his boy has to go to the war, the only boy, who looks after all when he was away." The tsar could have excused Dmitry from military service, and that was what Rasputin hoped for—he had little faith that "his wretched, nearly feeble-minded offshoot" would survive life at the front. But Nicholas II refused to spare members of his own family, some of whom fell in combat; nor was he willing to extend such favors to Dmitry Rasputin. But the tsar and his wife were not unfeeling; the empress knew that the young man would never see combat. Alexandra got him assigned as a medical orderly to her hospital trains. The son was probably at Tsarskoye Selo as much as his father, although they saw different people. Dmitry showed character in obeying the call to duty. "The number of men who reported 'sick' was enormous," an English observer wrote of this moment in Russian history. "Any excuse was good enough to get away from the front. They said there was no good in their fighting, as they were always beaten."

"I felt quite sad because it was so grey," the empress wrote while the Rasputins were agonizing over Dmitry's fate. "But now the sun is trying to pierce its way through the clouds. The colouring of the trees is so lovely now, many have turned yellow, red & copper. Sad to think summer is over & endless winter awaits us soon."

Rasputin decided to go on a pilgrimage in August 1916. He could have traveled in luxury to any place in the empire, but he chose Verkhoturye, the place where he was converted in 1897. When he set out for the cloister, he probably did not suspect that this would be his final visit.

A ten-year-old girl named Tamara Shishkina also happened to be traveling to Verkhoturye. Years later she still recalled the excitement that swept her crowded train car as a rumor made the rounds that Rasputin was on board. The others were forced to wait while he disembarked—alone and hidden from the view of other passengers. Rasputin was an honored visitor at the cloister; Shishkina noted the "plush red carpet fit for the Tsar" that was waiting at the door of the church. Nothing was too good for the Last Favorite of the Last Tsar.

The church was filled with light—rays streaming from the candles and chandeliers bounced from the silver icon covers and the gold sarcophagus that held the relics of Saint Simeon. Rasputin stood on a rug at the place of honor in the middle of the congregation. His hair

Rasputin as the object of public hostility in cartoons. Cartoonists of this sort evaded the censor by issuing their work as broadsides that sold cheaply at newsstands. The image on the left suggests a sexual relationship between Rasputin and Alexandra—it was pornographic by the standards of late 1916 to early 1917. The caricature on the right shows Nicholas and Alexandra as the puppets of their master, Rasputin. It shows the tendency of hostile artists to show Nicholas as agreeable and passive and his wife as a shrew. The caption to this image reads "The Russian Tsar's house."

was combed back in a straight part. A sash with large tassels blended tastefully with his bright yellow *rubashka*—he was wearing loose velvet trousers and lacquered boots. Rasputin prayed fervently, crossing himself in a broad fashion. Shishkina recalled that "his face was peaceful, concentrated and kind."

The cross was finally taken from the altar and placed in the midst of the packed congregation, inviting the people to come and venerate it. Rasputin was the first to kiss the cross, followed by his entourage. There was a sudden crush "to reach the cross—to be closer to Rasputin, to see and touch him. I was thrown just under his right hand, and the 'starets' made the sign of the cross over me."

The three days Shishkina spent at Verkhoturye were unforgettable. Her mind was filled with memories of the "solemn Liturgies in the churches" and the "loud gatherings" that greeted Rasputin throughout the monastery. After the peasant and his party left, the other pilgrims stood in "noisy little groups," discussing their encounters with the infamous Gregory Rasputin.

•   •   •

Few Russians shared these friendly attitudes. "Obscene pamphlets of the Empress and the monk" began circulating—illegally, of course—in Petrograd in late 1916. Cinemas featured "disgusting and faked pictures" showing Rasputin in intimate poses with Alexandra and her daughters. Cartoons also appeared showing Rasputin as a puppet master who held Nicholas and Alexandra on his string.

The anger of Russians against Rasputin reached a high point in the autumn of 1916. Joseph Vecchi, restaurateur extraordinaire, described Rasputin as a "vulture" whose "wings were casting shadows all over Russia." People believed that he "was the actual ruler of the country," and the accusations of treason were inevitably directed against the empress as well. Paul Milyukov railed in the Duma against the "Dark Forces" threatening Russia. In what would prove to be one of the most influential speeches of all time, the liberal historian and politician cited terrible examples of Russian corruption and incompetence connected with the war, asking rhetorically at each point, "Is this stupidity, or is it treason?" And yet some observers believed that the "rumors of Rasputin's influence were undermining the monarchical principle much more effectively than all the revolutionary propaganda combined."

The crusade was unrelenting, and it shook Rasputin. "Satan spreads fear in the newspapers," he told Alexandra, and "nothing good will come of it." Alexis Filippov was the only journalist who defended Rasputin; he spoke up for his friend in six pamphlets, but they did little to shape public opinion. The *Siberian Trade Gazette* charged that Rasputin had been a horse thief in his youth—that clearly struck a nerve. Rasputin fired off a telegram to the editor: "Tell us where, when, and from whom I stole a horse as published in the paper. You are very informed. I will wait three days for your answer. If you don't answer, I know to whom to complain and what to say." The editor published the communication along with a flippant commentary calling Rasputin a half-educated peasant. But there was no retraction.

Rasputin was threatened and assaulted several times during the war. An outraged officer beat Rasputin one night at the Villa Rode when he made insulting references to the empress. Three officers set upon Gregory and sent him to the hospital for a similar indiscretion. Gunfire forced Rasputin to flee a party one evening; when he learned that several of the guests had wanted to murder him, Rasputin turned pale and seemed to age visibly. A troika on Nevsky Prospekt almost ran over the starets one night; on another occasion a car rammed into his sleigh, leaving him bruised. A pile of timber tumbled into the path of Rasputin's oncoming car one afternoon. The police nabbed the man responsible: he was a peasant from Tsaritsyn, Iliodor's former power base.

Some of these "incidents" might have been rumors or exaggerations, but the message was clear: many people hated Rasputin and his life was in danger. Gregory responded by asking that his security be increased. "No doubt they'll kill me!" he said. "They'll kill all of us. They'll kill Papa and Mama also."

Rasputin received threatening letters that were anonymous or signed with such threatening names as "the Avenger." "Our Fatherland is in peril!" one announced. "There is even talk of concluding a dishonorable peace. The very fact that you receive coded telegrams from Stavka proves your great influence. Thus we, the Chosen Ones, ask that you arrange matters so that the People are granted Ministers responsible to them and that the State Duma is reconvened . . . so that Our Country is saved from ruin. If you do not comply with our order we shall kill you. No mercy will be shown to you. Our hands will not shrink, as did Guseva's hand. Wherever you go, death will follow you. The die has been cast."

"They are thinking of assassinating me," Rasputin told his detectives in early 1916. He was tired and depressed. Teffi, the stylish female writer who admired him from afar, thought that a "power he tried—and failed—to master was sweeping him off his feet and carrying him away." A female follower recalled that the atmosphere in his apartment was "increasingly tense. . . . On the surface the same bazaar was in progress—the telephone constantly rang. . . . Women of every age came and went, pale and in mascara—bearing heaps of candy and flowers with all sorts of boxes strewn about. . . . Rasputin himself was weary; he gazed about searchingly and often seemed like an exhausted wolf. The routine made his life hectic and unsteady; everything seemed improvised and unstable, as if some sort of blow was looming over that dark, inhospitable building." Rasputin was fatalistic: "Do you think I don't know that the end's coming soon?" he asked.

The snows of winter fell over Petrograd, enveloping the weary and disillusioned city in a blanket of white. On December 2, 1916, Rasputin received a summons to meet the imperial couple. He spent the day preparing for the visit. He did not touch alcohol; instead he went to the bathhouse and then to church before boarding the train to Tsarskoye Selo. A waiting automobile took him along the snowy streets to Anna Vyrubova's lemon-yellow house. The imperial couple had already arrived, and the old friends took tea as usual. When it came time to leave, Rasputin was tense. Nicholas asked Rasputin for his customary blessing. Rasputin replied quietly, "This time, it is for you to bless me, not I you." In less than two weeks, Rasputin was dead.

19

The Assassin

PRINCE FELIX YUSUPOV was an unlikely murderer. Sole heir to what was rumored to be the greatest fortune in the world, Yusupov was a pale, effete dilettante given to transvestite escapades and scandalous affairs. It is difficult to imagine him as a cold, calculating assassin. His reasons for killing Rasputin are mysterious, although he published several detailed accounts of the crime after fleeing Russia in 1919. Even so, his role in the murder has been recently called into question. Yusupov was proudly defiant about his actions, insisting that his only desire was to save Russia from the revolution. The prince enjoyed his notoriety and the air of mystery that surrounded him after the events of December 1916.

Yusupov was born in 1887 in the immense residence on the capital's Moika Canal where Rasputin perished four decades later. The sprawling, neoclassical palace was a gift to the family from Catherine the Great—it included ballrooms, salons, art galleries, and a private theater. The Yusupovs were of Tatar origin. From the time a Muslim ancestor converted to Orthodoxy for political reasons, members of the family were regular fixtures at the Russian court. The Yusupovs became incredibly wealthy; their estates were so vast and far-flung that no one in the clan had ever visited more than a few.

Yusupov's childhood was a study in indulgence and conflicting influences. His mother, Zinaida, was beautiful, artistic, and sociable, and she doted on Felix. His father, on the other hand, was gruff and distant. Count Felix Sumarokov-Elston had been a penniless Guards officer as a young man. When he married Zinaida, he won Alexander III's permission to assume the name Yusupov Sumarokov-Elston so that his family name would continue after he died.

Young Felix learned to negotiate his parents' conflicting influences through manipulation and avoidance. He realized that his mother had desperately wanted a girl and was disappointed to learn that she had another son. Zinaida kept her son in dresses and curls until he was five, which was actually a fairly common practice among European nobles at the time. The father considered Felix to be weak, effeminate, and odd. Spoiled and selfish, the answer to Felix's demands was seldom, "No!" He blossomed into a strikingly beautiful youth, and at twelve he began dressing in his mother's gowns. His older brother, Nicholas, took him to fashionable restaurants and cafes, where Felix learned to bask in the excitement that men showered upon him. His father was horrified at these adventures, but Felix would not give them up. Like many of the high society folk of Saint Petersburg, he was soon dabbling in mysticism, opium, and anything that whispered of forbidden pleasure.

Felix thrived on intrigue, and he unwittingly played a key role in his older brother's death. Encouraging Nicholas's liaison with a married aristocrat, he facilitated secret meetings and urged the affair on until the lady's outraged husband killed her lover in a duel. Suffering from guilt, Felix turned to Grand Duchess Elisabeth Fedorovna ("Ella"), the empress's sympathetic sister, who became a nun and headed an order of sisters after her husband was murdered by revolutionaries. Ella assured the young prince that he was free of blame and should not be ashamed of his homosexuality. In 1909, Felix Yusupov enrolled at Oxford, although he spent much of his time at parties and living as extravagantly as possible.

Felix was back in Russia by 1913, pursuing the hand of Irina, the daughter of the tsar's sister, Xenia, and her husband, Alexander Michaelovich. Despite Yusupov's flamboyant past, the couple married in February 1914. Russia's ruling dynasty was united with its wealthiest family—it was the social event of the season. The bride arrived in a gilded carriage wearing a lace veil that had belonged to Marie Antoinette; Alexandra showered them with a fabulous collection of diamonds. The marriage proved to be reasonably happy. Although a daughter—also named Irina—was born in 1915, Felix never abandoned his pursuit of beautiful young men.

•   •   •

Prince Felix Yusupov and his wife, Irina. Yusupov was heir to what was rumored to be the greatest fortune in the world. Irina was the daughter of Nicholas II's sister, Xenia, and the tsar's cousin, Grand Duke Alexander Michaelovich. In this famous photograph, Irina seems warily watchful of her notoriously wayward husband.

Yusupov and Rasputin first met in 1909. Gregory was much taken with the handsome young prince—he even gave him a pet name, Malenkaya, the "Little One." Yusupov, on the other hand, had an instinctive aversion to Gregory, although he gave him little thought until 1913, when Zinaida began railing against Rasputin's influence at court. Zinaida made the fatal mistake of expressing her views to the empress, and she was sent from the Alexander Palace in disgrace. In 1915 Yusupov's father was fired as governor-general of Moscow, because he failed to control the anti-German riots that convulsed the city in May. The Yusupovs were unable to recognize the old prince's limitations and failures; they were convinced that somehow Rasputin was to blame for these misfortunes. Indeed, young Felix was coming to believe that Rasputin was destroying Russia thanks to an unstable empress and her weak husband. These sentiments cascaded into hatred for Rasputin, and Yusupov's conviction that his task was to destroy the man who threatened Russia.

Yusupov was consumed by the thought that "not a single important event at the front was decided without a preliminary conference" between Alexandra and Rasputin. He was certain that Rasputin was a German spy or at least acting in concert with those seeking a separate peace with Russia's enemies. Yusupov believed that public affairs revolved around Rasputin's whims: ministers came and went on his recommendation, and his favorites were destroying the Orthodox Church. Since Nicholas II was unable or unwilling to stop it, someone else had to save Russia. And that someone, in Yusupov's fevered imagination, was himself.

At least this was the idealistic face Yusupov presented to history. Some observers have been more than skeptical. They noted that Yusupov had an insatiable need to be at the "center of attention"; he was the sort of man who dreamed dreams of glory. Killing Rasputin would make him the "Savior of Russia."

Yusupov's character, however, was at odds with the profile of a cold, calculated killer, and some have suggested that the plot originated elsewhere. Alexander Bokhanov proposed that Vasily Maklakov, a renowned lawyer and member of the Duma, played that role, but there is no evidence that Maklakov acted in anything other than an advisory capacity to the assassins. Recent theories have fixed responsibility on the British Secret Intelligence Service. As will be seen in chapter 22, Yusupov probably discussed his plans with a British operative. But there is not much evidence that Rasputin's death was a piece of "dirty tricks" on the part of British counterintelligence.

Some have proposed that the tsar's cousin Nicholas Michaelovich (known to the family as "Bimbo") instigated Rasputin's death. The grand duke was a distinguished historian and man of letters who railed against Nicholas II's incompetence—and he loathed Alexandra. The feeling was mutual; the empress apparently blamed Nicholas Michaelovich for Rasputin's demise.

Three outstanding historians—Alexander Kotsiubinskii, Orlando Figes, and Margarita Nelipa—have developed this line of thought, pointing to Bimbo's frequent meetings with the conspirators and their high degree of respect for him. Perhaps he prodded Yusupov into action and advised him in some way. But Jamie Cockfield, the author of an impressive biography of Nicholas Michaelovich, dismisses the notion that he masterminded the plot. The grand duke was a loquacious busybody who craved attention; had he been behind Rasputin's death, it is unlikely that he would have kept it a secret. Nicholas Michaelovich did not know of the murder until after it occurred, and the details that he recorded in his diary are erroneous. No circumstantial evidence, even, suggests that Bimbo masterminded the murder.

In the end, an enormous body of evidence points to Felix Yusupov as the man who hatched the plot and carried it out. His candid memoirs were corroborated by the other conspirators. It is true that these accounts contain inconsistencies, but experts in crime expect that from even the most conscientious eye witnesses. The clumsy way the assassination was carried out shows that it was the work of an amateur. There was a unique and naive quality in Yusupov's approach. He obviously delighted in the intrigue and thrilled to its mysterious secrets. In his imagination, Yusupov relished the moment when a grateful nation would herald him as Russia's savior—always remembering that even egotistical people may be driven by idealism. Murder was so out of the prince's character that one is forced to accept, if grudgingly, that on some level his motives were patriotic.

In putting together his plan, Yusupov first went to Michael Rodzyanko, president of the Duma, and a longtime Rasputin foe. By setting forth a plan of action, Felix was calling Rodzyanko's bluff, and it immediately became clear that the fattest man in Russia was all noise and bluster. Rodzyanko suddenly recalled all of the reasons for doing nothing, even if the target was Public Enemy Number One. Yusupov next turned to Vasily Maklakov, a member of the Duma and a leader of the liberal Kadet Party. Yusupov naively assumed that liberals were revolutionaries; since revolutionaries were also terrorists, it followed that Maklakov would be glad to murder the peasant. Maklakov was stunned—and offended.

"Do you think I keep office for assassins?" he asked. Maklakov also advanced political objections: Rasputin was destroying the credibility of the tsarist regime, and when it fell, a democratic government of the sort he was demanding would arise from its ashes. Rasputin was actually fostering this revolution. It would be a mistake to kill him; in any event, the empress would quickly find someone to take Rasputin's place.

Yusupov chastised Maklakov; the prince pointed out that the distinguished attorney believed that Alexandra could replace Rasputin because he did not appreciate "supernatural forces." "But I'm involved in the occult," Yusupov continued, "so I know the truth. I assure you that Rasputin has a power you find only once in a hundred years. . . . The Empress would land in an asylum within two weeks if Rasputin were killed today. Her spiritual equilibrium depends entirely on Rasputin; she would fall apart as soon as he toppled. And if the Emperor were freed of the influence of Rasputin and his wife, everything would change; he would be a good constitutional monarch."

Yusupov visited Maklakov on subsequent occasions. The prince needed to use someone who was not involved in the conspiracy as a sounding board. Yusupov was also worried; if he was willing to risk his neck, he also hoped to escape detection. Maklakov suggested killing Rasputin and making it look like an automobile accident. Yusupov thought that was too complicated. Asking Maklakov about weapons, the Kadet leader handed him a rubber-coated dumbbell to batter the peasant. Yusupov took the weapon, although the idea of beating Rasputin to death horrified him. Although Maklakov subsequently denied it, the prince also claimed that the attorney gave him a box of cyanide crystals.

Yusupov now turned to a man he needed for emotional support, Grand Duke Dmitry Pavlovich. The young man was the tsar's cousin, the son of Nicholas II's uncle Paul. After Paul's wife died, he entered into a morganatic marriage and was exiled from Russia. Dmitry began spending a great deal of time with Nicholas and Alexandra, who looked upon him as something of an adopted son. It was even rumored that Dmitry would marry the tsar's oldest daughter, Olga, and that Nicholas planned to alter the succession law so that the throne would pass to Dmitry if Alexis died. It is not surprising, then, that Dmitry agreed to strike a blow against Rasputin, given his conviction that Alexandra and her peasant "friend" were destroying Russia.

Did Yusupov and Dmitry have a homosexual relationship? Yusupov was certainly filled with admiration for Dmitry, and some people suspected that they were lovers. The empress fretted over Dmitry's association with Yusupov and the way they ran with what she called the "fast set." There is no evidence that Dmitry was gay, although he certainly loved Yusupov as a friend. Given their friendship, it was natural that Yusupov would pull the younger man into the conspiracy. It also showed a strategic foresight that was rare in this plan. As a grand duke, Dmitry was immune from prosecution; only the tsar could punish him. "If it hadn't been for my presence [in] the December drama," Dmitry later wrote to Yusupov, "you would probably have been hanged as a political criminal."

●   ●   ●

Dmitry believed that the "murder should be clearly done by true monarchists for the salvation of the monarchy." Another man Yusupov recruited in November was Vladimir Purishkevich—and he was certainly a "true monarchist." Born in Bessarabia in 1870, Purishkevich won election to the Duma with the goal of undermining it, for he believed that a parliament was alien to Russia. Purishkevich despised Rasputin, and on November 19, 1916, he gave a fiery speech charging that "all evil proceeds from those dark forces, from influences headed by Grishka Rasputin." He called the tsar's ministers a "dozen sleeping beauties," ineffectual and corrupt. To save Russia, they must awaken and take action. "If the ministers place duty above their careers . . . they must go to the Tsar, throw themselves at his feet and ask him to open his eyes to the terrible reality!"

The chamber cheered these words. Yusupov was in the gallery, listening as Purishkevich denounced Rasputin. He was, according to one observer, pale and trembling, as if overcome by some "uncontrollable emotion." Yusupov called on Purishkevich the following day; he praised the speech but expressed the fear that it would make no difference. Yusupov proposed killing Rasputin. Purishkevich claimed that he had once actually considered the idea, and he agreed to join Yusupov's conspiracy.

When Purishkevich arrived at the Moika Palace the following evening, he was introduced to Dmitry Pavlovich and a fourth conspirator, Sergei Sukhotin, a twenty-nine-year-old lieutenant in the elite Life Guards Infantry Regiment. Sukhotin apparently met Yusupov while convalescing in a hospital that the prince's family operated at Tsarskoye Selo. Inevitably, some have wondered if Sukhotin was one of Yusupov's sexual partners. There is no proof of that, although it is true that Sukhotin was partial to conspiracy theories. He believed that Rasputin and Anna Vyrubova were German spies and that removing the peasant would save Russia. Apparently Sukhotin's task was to handle the body, an undertaking that was beneath the dignity of his aristocratic colleagues. Purishkevich brought a fifth man into the conspiracy: Dr. Stanislaw Lazovert, a French-educated Polish physician who joined the Russian army on the second day of the war. Lazovert directed Purishkevich's medical organizations and operations at the front. He had been wounded three times, and his decorations included the Saint George Cross.

The conspirators planned to lure Rasputin from his apartment and the security men who followed him throughout each day.

Rasputin's enemies would kill him in the Moika Palace. This forced
Yusupov to befriend Rasputin, and that was a prospect that the prince
found repugnant. Since no other solution presented itself, Yusupov
arranged to meet the peasant at a mutual friend's apartment on
November 20, 1916.

Yusupov was amazed to see just how much Rasputin had changed:
his face was "puffy" and he had grown "lax and flabby." He no longer
wore a "plain peasant's coat" but sported a pale blue silk blouse and wide-
cuffed velvet trousers. The prince claimed to be in bad health and in need
of Rasputin's healing skills. Yusupov played to the peasant's vanity by
confessing that the finest doctors had been powerless to help him.

"I'll cure you," Rasputin boldly replied. "Doctors? They don't
know a thing. All they do is stuff you with medicines, anything will do.
And you just get worse. But I know better, My Dear." Rasputin invited
Yusupov to come to his apartment for a "healing session." Yusupov
continued:

> The *starets* had me lie on the sofa. Standing, he gazed intently
> into my eyes and began to stroke my chest, neck and head.
> Suddenly he knelt—and, it seemed—began praying, placing his
> hands on my brow. He bent his head so low that I could not see
> his face. He remained in this position for some time. Then he
> suddenly jumped to his feet and began to make passes [with his
> hands over my body]. He was apparently familiar with certain
> hypnotic techniques. His hypnotic power was enormous. I felt it
> subduing me and infusing warmth throughout my whole being.
> I grew numb; my body seemed paralyzed. I tried to speak but
> my tongue would not obey and I seemed to be falling asleep, as
> if under the influence of a strong narcotic. Rasputin's eyes shone
> before me with a certain phosphorescent light.

Yusupov struggled to break the spell and Rasputin, sensing he had lost
control of the situation, cheerfully announced that the session was at
an end. But he made the prince promise to return, and soon.

Rasputin and Yusupov began visiting the restaurants and nightspots
of Petrograd together. Although society buzzed over the relationship,
there is no reason to think—as Maria Rasputin later suggested—that
Yusupov found Rasputin to be sexually attractive. Yusupov's resolve
waned at times, but an event in the first week of December convinced
him to act. On December 3, following a stormy meeting with Alexandra

at Tsarskoye Selo, Grand Duchess Elisabeth rushed to tell Zinaida Yusupov of her sister's firm and unyielding commitment to Rasputin. "She drove me away like a dog!" Ella cried. Alexandra had previously humiliated Zinaida, Yusupov's mother, when she criticized Rasputin, declaring, when they parted, that "I hope I never see you again!"

Yusupov's mother and Grand Duchess Elisabeth were the most influential figures in Yusupov's life, and both had run afoul of the empress over Rasputin. Ella despaired over the situation, but Zinaida—as she later admitted—was "suffocating from hatred" and "could not take it any longer." Both knew of Yusupov's plan and encouraged him to act. In a letter to her son, Zinaida wrote that "peaceful means won't change anything." The humiliation of his mother and Elisabeth finally erased Yusupov's lingering doubts.

The plan called for Yusupov to invite Rasputin to come with him to the Moika Palace. There, in a secluded spot, Rasputin would be poisoned. The conspirators would stuff his body into a sack and hurl it into the Little Neva River, whose strong tides would carry it to the Gulf of Finland. With luck, Rasputin would simply disappear. There would be no body, and without a body, no one could be charged with a crime—or at least that was a widespread misconception that they shared. Dmitry Pavlovich's schedule set the date: he could not cancel any of his obligations without arousing suspicion, and his next free evening was Friday, December 16. This was the date that was agreed upon, and the conspirators moved toward their final preparations.

Prince Felix Yusupov experienced moral uncertainty as December 16 approached. He knew that it was wrong to extend friendship and hospitality to a man and kill him. A gentleman would not do that. To resolve this dilemma, Yusupov went to the Cathedral of Our Lady of Kazan and spent hours in prayer—or at least so he said. He emerged in a state of religious exaltation. Yusupov was about to save Russia—and that included Nicholas II and his family.

20

Murder at the Palace

S NOW FELL ON PETROGRAD throughout the night, and by dawn on Friday, December 16, the sky was clear and dotted with pink clouds. It was cold—Alexandra noted that her thermometer that morning stood at -10 degrees. Rasputin struggled out of bed after a night of unusually hard drinking. Following church and a visit to the bathhouse, he returned to his apartment to receive at least a few petitioners. He was shaken by an anonymous telephone call threatening his life. Rasputin had so much wine at lunch that he was unable to take a friendly (and important) call from Tobolsk. Although he slept quite a lot, his secretary, Aaron Simanovich, estimated that his boss consumed at least a dozen bottles of Madeira throughout the day.

The conspirators simply could not keep a secret, and for some time Petrograd had been awash in rumors that Rasputin would soon be murdered. Purishkevich told this in no uncertain terms to Samuel Hoare, head of the British Secret Intelligence Service in Petrograd. "At this time everyone was talking about the impending 'liquidation' of Rasputin," Hoare recalled. "Purishkevich's tone was so casual" that the English visitor dismissed his message. Simanovich claimed that he had a sense of foreboding and stayed with Rasputin until Alexander Protopopov arrived in the late evening. The minister of the interior had come to tell Rasputin about the latest rumors. Protopopov was concerned but not alarmed. As for Rasputin, he often told his followers: "It is a great thing to speak of the hour of our death." That was how he saw it: there was no need to worry about death since everything unfolds according to God's plan. Rasputin might have been concerned about his safety, but he faced each day with a resigned courage.

Anna Vyrubova had dropped in earlier that evening, around eight o'clock. Rasputin told her about his invitation to meet Yusupov's beautiful wife, Irina, at midnight. Rasputin explained that the young prince did not want his parents to know of the visit, hence the odd hour. When Anna later mentioned it to the empress, Alexandra was surprised. "There must be some mistake," she said. "Irina is in the Crimea, and neither of the older Yusupovs is in town." But the news did not concern them, and they dismissed it from their thoughts.

Felix Yusupov spent December 16 putting the final touches on his plans. A wooden staircase just off the study descended to the basement; halfway down, at the landing, a door opened onto a side courtyard. The prince selected the vaulted storeroom at the bottom of the stairs for the crime, knowing that its thick walls would deaden sounds. Yusupov had it arranged as a dining room with chairs at a round table. An intricately carved ebony cabinet held a gorgeous rock crystal crucifix; an enormous plush white bearskin rug covered the stone floor. A crackling fire burned in the fireplace; Moorish lamps hung from the ceiling, making the room sparkle with colorful prisms. This corner of the palace was quiet—it radiated an "air of mystery and a sort of detachment from the world. It seemed that whatever might happen here would be hidden from mortal eyes."

The other conspirators arrived about eleven o'clock in the evening. Yusupov led them to the basement where they set the scene, swirling wine in glasses, crumpling napkins, and leaving the table in disarray, as if a party had just taken place. Yusupov handed Dr. Stanislaw Lazovert the box of cyanide that he claimed Vasily Maklakov had given him. Dr. Lazovert put on gloves to crush the crystals into a fine powder. He then sprinkled the poison into six little cream cakes; the wine glass intended for Rasputin received what Lazovert thought was a dose of cyanide sufficient to kill several men. As soon as everything was ready, the conspirators retreated to Yusupov's study. They were ready to simulate the sounds of a party when the prince and his guest arrived for their grand encounter with destiny.

The police guards left Rasputin's apartment building at midnight. (He actually had no security from midnight to 8 a.m.) Maria and Varvara returned at 11 p.m. to find their father dressed in the light blue silk shirt that he reserved for special occasions. He was wearing dark blue velvet trousers and leather boots. A heavy gold chain with a cross hung around his neck, while a gold-and-platinum bracelet engraved with the Romanov double-headed eagle and the monogram of Nicholas II dangled from his wrist. He told the girls he was invited to the Yusupov palace and would go to his bedroom to rest. Aware of the rumors, they hid their father's galoshes—they hoped this might keep him from leaving. Rasputin was searching for his footwear when, just after midnight, the bell rang at the back entrance. It was Yusupov. He noted that Rasputin smelled strongly of cheap soap and had never before seemed "so clean and tidy." Rasputin apologized for the delay. "It's those children again," he said, finally locating his overshoes. "They don't want me to go out." Rasputin slipped on his famous fur coat and followed the prince down the rear staircase to face whatever the night would bring.

Much speculation has surrounded the events of that night. Prince Yusupov left two detailed published accounts that agree substantially with the story recorded by Vladimir Purishkevich. Additionally there were police depositions and statements. An account supposedly by Dr. Lazovert appeared in 1923, although it was entirely fictional. Since the other conspirators were silent, history owes what might be called the "accepted version" of the murder to Yusupov and Purishkevich. This is the story they told.

A gramophone in the study was playing "Yankee Doodle" as the prince brought Rasputin to the basement. When Rasputin asked about the music, Yusupov explained that his wife was upstairs entertaining some friends and would join them as soon as her guests left. Until then the two men would wait in the dining room that Yusupov had prepared for the crime. Removing his coat, the guest looked around. He was fascinated by the carved ebony cabinet and "took a childlike pleasure in opening and shutting the drawers" before taking a seat at the table. At first he refused the poisoned cakes, saying they would be too sweet; but he finally gobbled down several. Yusupov watched, expecting Rasputin to collapse at any second. But the peasant seemed unaffected; he downed several glasses of the poisoned wine and chatted away merrily. At times he put his hand to his throat, as if he had difficulty swallowing, and his voice grew low and muffled; there was no other noticeable change. Yusupov was horrified. After an hour spent in this fashion, Rasputin spotted a guitar in the corner. "Play something cheerful," he asked his host. "I like your singing."

Yusupov sang one song after another as his intended victim listened intently. At times Rasputin's head fell and his eyes closed; Yusupov imagined that the poison had finally taken effect—but Rasputin lifted his eyes and demanded another tune. As the prince's nerves reached a breaking point, he excused himself, saying that he had to check on his wife.

The other conspirators were waiting impatiently in the study above the death chamber. They were stunned to hear that Rasputin was alive and well. Dmitry Pavlovich suggested that Yusupov take Rasputin home and try another time, but Purishkevich objected to that idea. If Rasputin died at home in his apartment, an autopsy would detect the poison and the police would trace the cause to the palace. If the poison was not working, the conspirators would have to kill Rasputin in another way. They considered entering the room en masse and strangling him; but Yusupov was afraid that Rasputin would try to flee and cause a commotion. So the prince took a small Browning revolver from Dmitry and returned to the basement. It was a bold move—but the highly strung Yusupov was nearly hysterical after two hours of entertaining a man he hated. He was finally prepared to use a more direct method.

Rasputin was still seated at the table; his breathing seemed labored. "My head is heavy and I have a burning sensation in my stomach," he complained. "Give me another glass of wine." Yusupov complied, and Rasputin became much livelier, suggesting that they visit the Gypsies. Yusupov insisted that the hour was too late. Rasputin got up and walked to the cabinet and the crystal crucifix. He pulled again at the drawers, fascinated. The moment to act had finally arrived.

"Gregory Efimovich," the prince said, "you had best look at that crucifix and say a prayer before it." Rasputin seemed amazed by this statement; he approached Yusupov submissively as a trace of fear spread over his face. Yusupov was standing at Rasputin's left side when he took the revolver from behind his back and, after a moment's hesitation, fired a single bullet into the victim's chest. With a "wild scream" Rasputin collapsed onto the bearskin rug "like a broken doll."

The shot brought the other conspirators stumbling down the staircase. Rasputin lay on his back; his eyes were closed, his face was twitching, his fists were clenched, and his body was shaking with convulsions. Then the movements stopped. Blood was now spreading across Rasputin's blue silk shirt. To avoid staining the bearskin rug, Dmitry and Purishkevich dragged the body onto the cold stone floor.

They finally turned out the lights, locked the door, and returned to the prince's study.

The next stage of the plan called for Lazovert to drive "Rasputin" home. Sergei Sukhotin was to impersonate the peasant by wearing his coat and hat while Dmitry posed as Prince Yusupov. Anyone who happened to view the scene would suppose that the peasant was returning home from another late evening. Sukhotin exited the car and pretended to enter the apartment; actually, he crouched low and slipped back into the car, where he huddled on the floorboard. The automobile now proceeded to the Warsaw Railway Station, where the three conspirators planned to burn Rasputin's coat and hat on Purishkevich's private railway carriage. Then they would return to the palace to collect and dispose of the body. But Madame Purishkevich objected that the tiny fire of her stove could not destroy these objects, which even included one of the galoshes. So the assassins brought these items back to the Moika Palace.

By now the mansion was as quiet as a tomb. Purishkevich sat smoking a cigar, but Yusupov was agitated; he suddenly had an inexplicable but powerful need to see the body. He found Rasputin lying in the same position on the floor. Overcome with a terrible inner rage, Yusupov grabbed Rasputin by the shoulders and shook him. As he stared into Rasputin's face, first one eye and then the other suddenly opened; "greenish and snake-like, they fixed [the prince] with an expression of satanic hatred." Rasputin stumbled to his feet, "foaming at the mouth," roaring in anger and wildly clawing at the air as he rushed toward Yusupov. Blood dripping from his mouth, he grabbed the prince by the shoulder, ripping an epaulet from his uniform. Rasputin was repeatedly growling his tormentor's name in a low, guttural voice.

By now, Yusupov's terrified screams were ringing throughout the palace. Shouting, Yusupov ran up the stairs to warn Purishkevich, who grabbed his own pistol (a Sauvage) and headed below until he heard the door at the landing open. Rasputin was now in the side courtyard, stumbling through the snow toward the iron gates that would bring him to freedom.

"Felix! Felix!" Rasputin was shouting, "I'll tell the Tsaritsa everything!" Purishkevich fired twice at the peasant, missing him both times. A third shot hit Rasputin in the back, and he collapsed into a bank of snow near the gates. A fourth bullet struck the middle of Rasputin's forehead.

Purishkevich kicked Rasputin hard in the temple, and this time the peasant did not move. Yusupov had disappeared at this point, but two soldiers walking on the street came to the iron fence, wondering what was happening. Purishkevich proclaimed, "I killed Grishka Rasputin, enemy of Russia and the Tsar!" One of the men kissed him while the other cried out, "Glory be to God! It should have been done long ago!" But Purishkevich warned them to keep silent, saying that the empress "isn't going to reward us for this." The privates pledged to honor Purishkevich's request; they even carried the body back to the palace and hurled it onto the landing of the staircase that led to the cellar.

Two officers on duty at the two police posts along the canal near the palace also heard the shots. Constable Flor Efimov telephoned a report to the police station and headed toward Yusupov's home to investigate the gunfire. On the way he met Officer Stepan Vlasyuk, who also heard the firing. Efimov returned to his post but sent Vlasyuk in the direction of the palace. Vlasyuk was ready to dismiss the noises as car tires bursting against the hard snow when he spotted the prince and his butler in the palace courtyard. Yusupov explained that a guest was drunk and fired his revolver into the air. After he said this, the prince disappeared.

Purishkevich found Yusupov in a bathroom, pale, trembling, and spitting repeatedly into a washbasin. Purishkevich assured the prince that everything was finished as he led him back to the study. Yusupov was in a daze—he was muttering over and over, "Felix! Felix!" When Vlasyuk suddenly reappeared with new questions, he was brought to the study. Yusupov listened in stunned silence as Purishkevich spoke, asking the officer if he was a loyal Russian and an Orthodox Christian. When Vlasyuk assured him that he was both, the Duma member confessed that they had just killed Rasputin. The policeman agreed to keep this confidential, although he could not lie if he was placed under oath. But as soon as Vlasyuk returned to his post, he relayed everything to headquarters.

Nothing had gone according to plan and now, thanks to Purishkevich, the police knew of the crime. Rasputin's corpse was still lying on the landing of the stairs that led to the basement. When Yusupov saw the body again, he flew into hysterics. Clutching the rubber-coated, two-pound dumbbell that he claimed Maklakov had given him, he struck Rasputin's head again and again. "In my frenzy, I hit anywhere," he later said. "All laws of God and man were set at naught." The prince, Purishkevich thought, was "wild" and possessed by an "absolutely unnatural" rage. It was a "harrowing sight." Only with great difficulty was Yusupov pulled from the body. He promptly fainted and was carried away to his bedroom.

The conspirators struggled to put Rasputin back into his fur coat, and, when this proved impossible, they wrapped the garment around his legs. The body was rolled in a piece of dark blue curtain, secured with a rope, and carried to a car waiting in the courtyard. Purishkevich, Dmitry, Lazovert, and Sukhotin drove across the city, accompanied by one of the soldiers. The car rattled along the bumpy and slick roadways toward that area known as "the Islands," a marshy archipelago where the Neva empties into the Gulf of Finland, although at this time of the year it was frozen. Their destination was the Great Petrovsky Bridge, which was used to cross the branch of the river known as the Little Neva to Krestovsky Island.

Dmitry stood guard while his colleagues dealt with Rasputin's body. (Fortunately for them, the sentry guarding the bridge was asleep.) The assassins threw the corpse over the railing, directing it toward the hole in the ice they spotted earlier that day. A dull splash told them they had achieved their objective. But Purishkevich was irritated when he realized that they had forgotten to use the weights and chains that would have sent the body to the bottom of the river. One of Rasputin's galoshes was also on the bridge. They cast it over the wood railing, not noticing that it landed and remained near the break in the ice; its mate was in the car, temporarily forgotten. Having accomplished their task and still hopeful that the river's current would carry the corpse to the Gulf of Finland, the conspirators climbed back into the car and returned to Moika Palace. Yusupov, exhausted, hysterical, and totally overcome by the events of the night, had retired. The others said hasty farewells and departed. It was nearly six in the morning. "No one noticed us when we returned," Purishkevich confided to his diary. "Everyone about us was sleeping as in a dead sleep."

21

The Aftermath

RASPUTIN OFTEN REMAINED OUT ALL NIGHT, but the morning of December 17 found Katya, the maid, somehow alarmed that he had still not come home. Rasputin's daughters telephoned Anna Vyrubova, but she could tell them nothing. Munya Golovina felt that he would soon return, but the hours passed without any sign of Rasputin. He had vanished.

The police immediately connected Rasputin's disappearance with Moika Palace. Yusupov was staying at his father-in-law's home when the police arrived to question him. He feigned innocence. He admitted that Rasputin had called the previous evening suggesting a visit to the Gypsies. Yusupov claimed that he had refused as he had guests, including several ladies whose names—as a gentleman—he could not reveal. The gunfire and bloodstains in the courtyard were due to the fact that Dmitry Pavlovich had gotten a bit tipsy and shot a stray dog. As for Vladimir Purishkevich, he was quite intoxicated—anything he babbled about killing Rasputin was nonsense. "If people murdered Rasputin," Yusupov insisted, "they planned to connect the crime with me and my party!"

When the police subsequently arrived at Yusupov's home, he showed them a dead dog lying in the snow. Yusupov was horrified to see that the police, acting on the empress's orders, were beginning to search his home and question the servants. "My wife is a niece of the Emperor," Yusupov declared, pointing out that only the tsar could order such an investigation, and the police left. In a panic by now, Dmitry Pavlovich telephoned the empress, asking her to receive him for tea. Anna Vyrubova, speaking on Alexandra's behalf, refused the request. Yusupov then called to tell the tsaritsa that he wanted to give her a "true account of what had occurred." Alexandra's message (again through Anna) was, "If Felix has anything to say, let him write it to me."

Everyone took for granted that Yusupov was responsible for Rasputin's disappearance. Grand Duke Nicholas Michaelovich had gotten a confused version of what happened in two phone calls early that morning. Knowing that Yusupov was staying with Alexander Michaelovich, the grand duke appeared at his brother's door and began peppering Yusupov with questions. The prince maintained his innocence, but Nicholas Michaelovich hoped to ferret out information, claiming, "I know everything, every detail—even the names of the women who were at the party." As this statement shows, the grand duke actually knew very little, but he entered an inaccurate statement from Yusupov into his diary.

Purishkevich had already left Petrograd for the front on his famous hospital train, while Yusupov decided to join his wife and family at the Crimea on Sunday, December 18. Acting on Alexandra's orders, the police prevented him from boarding the train. They escorted him back to Moika Palace where the empress illegally had him placed under house arrest. Alexandra was depressed and agitated. She knew that Rasputin's disappearance was connected with the crimson-stained snow at Yusupov's home, and she sent agonized telegrams and letters to her husband at Stavka. Nicholas II received the news impassively. He quickly set off for Tsarskoye Selo, although his mood stood in sharp contrast to that of his wife. "I almost got the impression that the Tsar was relieved," one observer recalled; another noticed signs of "serenity" and even "happiness" on his face. Nicholas assured his wife, however, that he was "anguished and horrified."

Petrograd was joyful at the news that Felix Yusupov and Dmitry Pavlovich had killed Rasputin. People burst into the national anthem, strangers embraced each other on the street, and shops exhibited photographs of the presumed assassins. Forbidden to print Rasputin's name, the papers referred to him as the "person living on Gorokhovaya Street." But the *Stock Exchange News* defied the censor by publishing an article late Saturday afternoon (December 17, 1916) boldly proclaiming the "Death of Gregory Rasputin in Petrograd." It was twenty-five words long, set in large, 12-point type: "This morning at 6 o'clock Gregory Rasputin suddenly passed away after a party at one of the most aristocratic houses in the center of Petrograd."

As yet there was no body. But early on the morning of December 17, two workmen crossing the Petrovsky Bridge reported dark red stains along the edge of the roadway and on the railings. The police began a search. At two that afternoon they found a man's galosh and a dark brown Tregolnik shoe (size 10) wedged into a bridge support. (How this occurred remains one of several mysteries of the crime.) Rasputin's daughters tearfully identified the footwear as belonging to their father. Police divers sprang into action the next day, but it was so cold that the pump that sustained the breathing tubes constantly froze and malfunctioned. On Monday, December 19, a wider sweep disclosed an object just beneath the surface: it proved to be the sleeve of a fur coat frozen into the ice some 250 yards from the bridge, toward Krestovsky Island. Axes and picks uncovered the body, and a grappling hook finally ripped it from the river's icy embrace.

The frozen body of Gregory Rasputin. When Rasputin's body was ripped from the ice, his torso was still bound by rope but his arms were free and extended, the right a bit further than the left. Rasputin's fingers were held in such a position as to invite the notion that he was making the sign of the cross as he died. Actually, Dr. Kosorotov's autopsy established that there was no water in his lungs; the third bullet caused instant death.

Police laid the corpse on planks of wood and photographed it. Rasputin's arms were slightly raised, and his knees were bent. This kept the frozen corpse from fitting into the coffin supplied by a local undertaker. The police finally located a large wood packing case to hold the body. At six o'clock that Monday evening, a Red Cross truck brought Rasputin's remains to the Chesmensky Charity Hospital, five miles outside the center of the city. Rasputin had often whisked past this building on his way to and from Tsarskoye Selo; he was now in the chapel, thawing, awaiting the autopsy.

The discovery of Rasputin's body triggered public celebrations throughout the Russian Empire. Samuel Hoare informed his government that "all classes speak and act as if [Rasputin's death] is better than the greatest Russian victory in the field." But a society lady who did volunteer work in a military hospital was shocked to find that her lower-class patients were not pleased with the news. When she tried to explain the significance of the deed, a soldier replied, "Yeah! One peasant got to the tsar and the nobles killed him!" An aristocrat from Kostroma reported that the peasants in his region of the Volga thought Rasputin was a martyr. Eyewitnesses often noted that peasants in these days asserted that Rasputin "let the Tsar hear the people's voice and he defended the people against the people at court, [that's why] they killed him."

Officials tried to keep details of the impending autopsy a secret, but the news leaked out, and a small crowd braved the dark, cold weather to peer into the windows of the Chesmensky Hospital. Dmitry Kosorotov, Petrograd's senior autopsy surgeon, performed the postmortem. What did the autopsy reveal? How did Rasputin die?

Only now are the answers to those questions becoming clear. The accounts in the existing literature on Rasputin have long been confused and confusing. Some historians have relied on the articles in contemporary Russian newspapers. But the information they provided was so inaccurate as to make people think—even at the time—that there must have been *two* autopsies. Great and enduring myths developed from all this. Supposedly, the first autopsy established that Rasputin had water in his lungs. That reinforced another misconception: Rasputin was alive when he hit the water—and thanks to his superhuman strength, he fought free of his bonds. He finally succumbed to the icy waters of the Little Neva and died.

Alexandra was supposedly unhappy with these findings because, we are told, the Russian Orthodox Church teaches that saints will not die of drowning. So a grumpy empress was said to have insisted on a second postmortem proclaiming that Rasputin died from the bullets that entered his body. In fact, the Eastern Church has no opinion on saints and drowning, and there is no evidence that the empress believed it for other reasons. There was only one autopsy.

But the report disappeared after the Bolshevik Revolution—although some black-and-white photographs associated with it have survived. The best account of the original autopsy available to us comes from an interview Kosorotov gave the journalist I. Kobyl'-Bobyl' after the tsarist regime collapsed and people were able to speak freely. Kosorotov's interview appeared in *Russkaya Volya* (Russian Liberty) on March 13, 1917. Professor Vladimir Zharov and his colleagues conducted a reassessment of the autopsy in 1993, relying on the March interview and the surviving photographs.

The French writer Alain Roullier published what he claimed was "the autopsy" in a book about Rasputin that appeared in 1998. His version claims that water was found in Rasputin's lungs, so he died of drowning. Some of the later books on Rasputin repeated that claim, although others went back to the Kosorotov interview that correctly established that the postmortem made no such finding. Margarita Nelipa, author of *The Murder of Grigorii Rasputin: A Conspiracy That Brought Down the Russian Empire* (2010), has done scholarship a great service by basing her discussion of the autopsy on Kosorotov's original interview.

Kosorotov had planned to conduct his autopsy on Wednesday morning, December 21, 1916. Tracking him to a restaurant, the police all but took the doctor into custody, forcing him to begin his postmortem at ten o'clock on the night of December 20. Even at that, officials kept pressing Kosorotov to finish his work as quickly as possible. Conditions at the hospital were worse than primitive: since the electricity had been turned off, the only light for his delicate, sensitive work came from two oil lamps and a lantern held by a policeman. The eerie scene continued for four hours.

Rasputin's body before the autopsy. Note the bullet hole to his forehead, which Dr. Kosorotov believed caused instant death. Vladimir Purishkevich, in his *Diary*, claims to have fired that shot while Rasputin was running away, but the evidence indicates that Rasputin was actually lying on the ground, dying.

"I often had to perform difficult and unpleasant autopsies," Kosorotov recalled in the interview of March 13, 1917. "I have strong nerves and have seen a lot of what there is to see. But I seldom had an experience as gruesome as the one of that terrible night. The body made a terrible impression. The goat-like expression of the face and the enormous head wound were hard even on my experienced eyes."

The autopsy disclosed that Rasputin was five feet, nine inches tall, forty-seven years old, and in such good physical condition that Kosorotov thought that Rasputin could have lived into his eighties. Members of the autopsy team noticed a strong smell of alcohol, indicating that Rasputin was drunk when he died. His hair, beard, and mustache were disheveled, and his clothes were covered with bloodstains. The right side of the head had been smashed in—the result (Kosorotov thought) of Rasputin hitting the supports when he was thrown from the bridge. The area of the right eye was blackened; the right ear had been torn and dangled uselessly. The large gash on the left side of the torso was possibly the result of "some type of sword or cutting object." Kosorotov noted other blows to the face, and the nose was crushed.

The doctor concluded that "many of these injuries were posthumous in nature." Yusupov probably inflicted some of the injuries with the rubber-coated dumbbell. Other damage might have come when the body hit the foundations of the bridge or still later, when the tides moved it about. The gash and the damage to the right ear might have resulted from the grappling iron that freed the body from the ice.

Kosorotov found that Rasputin's brain was of normal size and reeked of alcohol, as did the viscous liquid in his stomach. But what was missing was even more significant—and problematic. Although Dr. Lazovert supposedly put cyanide in the wine and pastry that Rasputin consumed, Kosorotov detected no trace of poison.

Rasputin sustained three gunshot wounds. Kosorotov could not establish the caliber or types of weapons used or the order in which they had been fired. One bullet penetrated the left side of Rasputin's chest, passing through his stomach and liver before exiting the body. A second bullet struck the right side of his lower back and passed through his right kidney. Either of these wounds, Kosorotov said, would have "produced a rapid decline in strength" and would have been fatal within twenty minutes. He thought Rasputin was standing when the shots were fired. The third gunshot was to the center of Rasputin's forehead. Kosorotov thought that Rasputin was on his back at that moment; the muzzle was no more than eight inches from his head, leaving a gunpowder residue around the entrance wound. The bullet that penetrated his brain caused immediate death.

Spurious accounts of the autopsy have claimed that Kosorotov established the calibers of the three guns used in the shooting. In fact, he made no such finding. The chief prosecutor of Petrograd also noted three shots, stressing that it was impossible to identify the type or caliber of the weapons in question. The case investigator who attended the autopsy agreed that no determination could be made as to the guns used. Dr. Zharov studied the records in 1993 and conceded that no one could verify the number of weapons or their calibers.

Unreliable versions of the autopsy invented other injuries. Rasputin's right eye, for example, is often described as having been dislodged from its socket. Supposedly it dangled or was found resting on his cheek—but the photographs refute this idea. Similarly, Kosorotov did not find that Rasputin's genitals were crushed, as is often alleged.

• • •

After the autopsy Kosorotov released the body to Akilina Laptinskaya, Rasputin's devoted follower, who washed and dressed it in a white linen shroud for burial. She sent the cross and bracelet to the empress. The corpse was placed in a heavy zinc coffin with an Orthodox cross on its lid and was brought to Tsarskoye Selo for burial the next morning.

Rasputin's body might have been shipped to Pokrovskoye, but the authorities feared the corpse would be stolen and/or desecrated. Protopopov spread rumors that the coffin *was* sent to Siberia, hoping to place distance between the imperial family and Rasputin and to confuse any would-be body snatchers. Anna Vyrubova was building a small church dedicated to Saint Seraphim of Sarov in the park at Tsarskoye Selo; its foundations had been dug, and Alexandra decided that Rasputin should rest there. Apparently neither Praskovaya, who was rushing to Petrograd by train from Pokrovskoye, nor his daughters, who were in the city, had any say in the matter.

Alexandra even kept Maria and Varvara from their father's burial. Why she acted so callously is not clear. Perhaps she had never really liked the girls very much. But the empress allowed Anna, Lili Dehn, Akilina Laptinskaya, and even one of Anna's servants to attend the service. Maria Rasputin still recalled the sorrow and anguish of that time years later.

The burial was as odd as everything else in Rasputin's life. It was bitterly cold on those early hours of December 21, and the ground was frozen; workers could dig only a shallow grave in the church foundations. A little after eight, a police van brought the coffin to the grave. "It was a glorious morning," Lili Dehn recalled, "the sky was a deep blue, the sun was shining, and the hard snow sparkled like masses of diamonds." Anna appeared, in a sleigh with incongruously jingling bells; a car arrived with the imperial family. Alexis was unwell and did not attend, but Nicholas stepped out of the limousine, followed by Alexandra and her four daughters, all clad in mourning. The empress nervously clutched a small bouquet of white flowers; Dehn recalled that she was "pale but quite composed," although she began weeping at the sight of the coffin.

Metropolitan Pitirim wanted to sing the funeral service, but he was so overcome with emotion that he could not do it. The honor fell to Bishop Isidor. The normal Orthodox rite was modified: a simple *litiya* replaced the customary *panikhida*; the cold made it impossible to kneel during the prayers, and the usual psalms were omitted. The hymns were truncated or omitted. Alexandra and her daughters and Anna signed the back of an icon of the Mother of God; this and a small bouquet of flowers were placed in the coffin before the service. At the end, Alexandra distributed flowers, and the mourners tossed them on top of the coffin. It was over in fifteen minutes. Nicholas II usually avoided emotion in his diary, but on this occasion he wrote, "My family and I witnessed a sad scene, the burial of the unforgettable Gregory, assassinated by monsters at the home of Yusupov."

Nicholas II now turned his attention to the "monsters." The tsar's children were upset. "I know that he did much harm," Olga said with tears in her eyes, "but why did they treat him so cruelly?" Alexis supposedly asked his father, "Is it possible that you will not punish them? The assassins of Stolypin were hanged." Actually, the public mood forced the emperor to proceed cautiously. He did not dare punish Purishkevich—his considerable popularity soared to new heights in the wake of Rasputin's murder. Felix Yusupov and Dmitry Pavlovich were fair game, but the wisest course of action against them was not clear. If they were tried, the court might find them innocent or hand down a punishment so light as to be a rebuke to the throne. Nicholas banished Yusupov to his family's estates in central Russia while Dmitry was assigned to Russian forces in Iran. Stanislaw Lazovert and Sergei Sukhotin were not punished at all.

Dmitry received a mere slap on the wrist, but even that was too much for the other members of the Romanov clan. Indeed, they seized this opportunity to show their opinion of Nicholas. Sixteen members of the family signed a petition noting that Dmitry was "physically ill and deeply shaken, depressed." He had always been filled with "warm love" for the tsar and Russia; Nicholas was advised to consider his "youth and truly weak health," as well as the "very difficult conditions our regiments in Persia face with epidemics and other scourges of mankind." If Dmitry were sent to that distant land, it "would be the same as outright death." He should receive the same punishment as was dealt to Prince Yusupov: exile to one of his estates. Nicholas was furious. He believed—and with good reason—that his own family was siding with critics who had become enemies. "I am filled with shame," Nicholas declared, "that the hands of my kinsmen are stained with the blood of a simple peasant." His decision stood. When Rasputin was alive, he strained Nicholas's relationship with his family; in death, Rasputin destroyed it.

Many people expected Alexandra to collapse in hysterics over her loss, but that did not happen. Nicholas and his wife, according to Captain Nicholas Sablin, accepted Rasputin's death as a "sad fact, but nothing more." The empress grieved for her friend; she often slipped away to his grave. To the end the tsaritsa regarded Rasputin as a man of God, a voice of the people—a messenger sent by God to save Russia and her son. "If I die or you desert me," the starets supposedly declared, "you will lose your son and your crown in six months." Nicholas abdicated on March 2, 1917, seventy-five days after Rasputin was murdered.

22

Who *Really* Killed Rasputin?

T HE MYTHOLOGY THAT SURROUNDED Rasputin's death was as astonishing as his life. The legend depicts a powerful, hulking peasant who fought poison, bullets, and beatings, only to succumb to drowning—though not before fighting free of the ropes that held him prisoner. His last act (supposedly) was to make the sign of the cross as he died. The truth is not at all amazing. No one could have escaped those ropes, and that included Rasputin. He was actually a rather small man, and he was still frail and shaken after the attempt on his life in June 1914. As for the cause of death, Dr. Dmitry Kosorotov, the autopsy surgeon, thought that the first two bullets that struck Rasputin would have taken his life within a short time, but the third bullet (delivered to the forehead) killed him instantly. Serious questions remain about Rasputin's death, however, and they deserve careful examination.

Some have suggested that the story of cyanide-laced wine and cakes was invented to portray Rasputin as an evil—if not satanic—man who had the power to resist death. It is more likely that the conspirators were telling the truth. Poison offered the advantage of killing Rasputin in a quick, quiet way; when the potion failed to work, shooting him became the preferred option. Perhaps Kosorotov failed to detect poison because he was not looking for it, or seeing no need to analyze the contents of Rasputin's stomach, he missed something that was in plain view. The poison might have lost at least some of its strength. When Dr. Vladimir Zharov reviewed the original autopsy seventy-seven years later, he theorized that the sweet cakes diminished the toxicity of the potassium cyanide. He thinks that at the end, Rasputin displayed symptoms of "light poisoning": dry throat, difficult breathing, headache, and a raspy voice. Zharov concluded "that a small dose unable to cause lethal poisoning affected Rasputin."

Rumors also spread that several of the prince's brothers-in-law had participated in Rasputin's murder or that women were present when Rasputin was murdered. Felix Yusupov fed the latter by telling the police that ladies attended the party at his home that night. That was a lie, but gossips swore that Vera Karalli (described as an actress, a singer, and a ballerina) or Dmitry Pavlovich's stepsister Marianna Derfelden was on hand. But no evidence supports this idea.

Edvard Radzinsky suggests that Grand Duke Dmitry, not Purishkevich, fired the fatal shots and that the conspirators lied to protect his succession to the imperial throne. Another nominee for this honor was Thespé, Yusupov's Ethiopian servant. Then there was Patte Barham's claim that Yusupov, angry with Rasputin for rebuffing his sexual advances, cut off Rasputin's penis. This relic supposedly ended up in an icebox in Paris, where it was venerated by a group of Rasputin's devotees. More recently a museum in Saint Petersburg has proudly displayed an item that they have assured the public was Rasputin's missing member. The museum has not explained satisfactorily how this enormous artifact came into its hands.

A more recent and interesting theory is that agents of the British Secret Intelligence Service (BSIS) organized and carried out Rasputin's murder—and that suggestion has captured international interest. Oleg Shishkin, Andrew Cook, and Richard Cullen have produced books arguing for the "British Theory." The motive of His Majesty's government would have been to remove an adviser who was urging Nicholas II to make a separate peace with Germany. The British and the French were exhausted by late 1916. If Russia withdrew from the war, Germany could have transferred enough divisions to stage a knockout blow in the west that would have ended the war before the United States even entered it. Actually, Rasputin did not favor Russia turning against her allies; Rasputin told Nicholas that to save his throne, he must stay in the war until victory. But admittedly, if the British did not know that, they had to act on the basis of what they believed to be true.

In 1916, the British Foreign Office sent Lieutenant-Colonel Samuel Hoare to head its intelligence mission in Petrograd. The three men central to the British Theory on Hoare's staff were Stephen Alley, John Scale, and Oswald Rayner. Rayner was Yusupov's friend from their Oxford days. Trained as a barrister, he spoke Russian fluently and had been posted to the intelligence mission in Petrograd in 1915 to serve as a communications censor.

Muriel Scale said that her father, Rayner, and Alley were "all together" in their work and in their private lives in Petrograd—they felt they "had to do something" to help their nation achieve victory. Proponents of the British Theory suggest that this "something" was to kill Rasputin—leader of the "Dark Forces" that were supposedly working for a German victory.

"I know my father was with the people who planned his murder," Scale's daughter insisted. The diary of William Compton, an English chauffeur in Petrograd, gives important evidence that supports the theory that BSIS was involved in Rasputin's assassination. Compton's records show that he brought Rayner to the Yusupov palace six times from late October to mid-November 1916. John Scale accompanied him the first four times, but on November 11 Scale left Russia to help with a crisis in Romania. Bucharest had finally entered the war on the Entente's side in August 1916. Despite Russian assistance, the Romanians were quickly defeated, and the enemies' advancing armies were about to seize their oil fields. The British began to bomb and neutralize those facilities, and Scale had gone there to help with that effort.

Rayner also visited Yusupov the morning after Rasputin's murder and was constantly at the prince's side for the next twenty-four hours. "He understands everything that has happened," Yusupov recalled, "and is most anxious on my behalf."

Grand Duke Nicholas Michaelovich—himself (unconvincingly) depicted as the architect of the assassination—thought that some "very skillful Englishmen" were behind the deed. His suspicions were driven by a phone call he received at five-thirty on the morning of the murder from George Buchanan, the British ambassador in Petrograd, telling him that Rasputin was dead. It has been suggested that this early knowledge reveals British complicity in the murder.

Several members of the British Intelligence mission knew that Rasputin's assassination was in the works. Vladimir Purishkevich told Samuel Hoare of the plot, while Rayner and Scale probably heard details about it on their visits to Yusupov's home on the eve of the murder. A communiqué from Alley to Scale nine days after Rasputin's

Oswald Rayner. Felix Yusupov knew Rayner from
their student days at Oxford, although they attended
different colleges. Rayner joined the British Secret
Intelligence Service station in Petrograd in 1915.
Some writers have argued that he and his government
were deeply involved in Rasputin's murder.

death suggests that British agents were doing more than exchanging
information. The letter deserves to be quoted in full:

> 7th January [December 25th OS], 1917
>
> Dear Scale,
> No response has thus far been received from London in
> respect of your oilfields proposal.
> Although matters here have not proceeded entirely to plan,
> our objective has clearly been achieved. Reaction to the demise
> of "Dark Forces" has been well received, although a few awkward
> questions have already been asked about wider involvement.
> Rayner is attending to loose ends and will no doubt brief
> you on your return.
> Yours,
> Stephen Alley, Capt.

The first line of the letter seems to refer to events in Romania. "Dark
Forces" was Rasputin's code name, and the rest of the letter obviously

concerns his murder. Although the message did not admit British involvement, it notes that the reaction to Rasputin's death on the part of Russians who were working with the BSIS was positive. The problem from Alley's point of view was that other Russians were asking "awkward questions" about British involvement in the crime. This might refer to the fact that on November 19, 1916, three days after Rasputin's murder, Nicholas II confronted Buchanan with the rumors that "English officers" had been involved in the assassination. Sir George protested that the stories stemmed from the fact that Rayner was Yusupov's friend, but there was "not a word of truth" to them.

Oleg Shishkin concluded that Sir Samuel Hoare fired the fatal shot. That was almost certainly not true. The description of the event that Hoare sent to his superiors in London was riddled with errors. Moreover, he and his wife were entertaining guests at the time that Rasputin was being murdered. Andrew Cook and Richard Cullen think that Rayner was the architect of the conspiracy; they also think that Rayner was at Yusupov's palace that night and that he fired the fatal shot.

Cook engaged Professor Derrick Pounder, the senior Home Office pathologist and head of Forensic Medicine at the University of Dundee, to review the autopsy and the ballistic evidence of Rasputin's murder. After analyzing photographs of the corpse, Pounder expressed the opinion that the shot to Rasputin's forehead came from "a large, lead, non-jacketed bullet" fired by a .455 English Webley revolver. This gun was unique to the BSIS. Cook believes that this proves that Rayner was at Yusupov's home that night and used that gun to deliver the third (and fatal) shot to Rasputin's forehead.

It is not likely that a Webley was used on Rasputin. Pounder was shown an unreliable autopsy report alleging that Kosorotov concluded that the assassins used three guns of three different calibers. Pounder was also presented with grainy black-and-white photographs that allegedly would permit a modern commentator to estimate the dimensions of the gunshot wounds. Neither Dr. Kosorotov nor Dr. Zharov claimed to be able to determine the type, number, or caliber of the weapons. Nor is Pounder's belief that an unjacketed bullet caused the wound tenable. An unjacketed bullet explodes on impact, and such a shell would have torn Rasputin's head apart. That did not happen.

But Rayner clearly did play a role in Yusupov's life just before and after the murder. Yusupov wrote that he was met on December 19, 1916, "by my friend, Oswald Rayner, an English officer whom I had known since our Oxford days." A half-hour before his train was scheduled to leave for the Crimea, Yusupov entered the passenger car with several Russians "and Rayner." When his departure was blocked, Yusupov returned to Alexander Michaelovich's residence. "I was tired out by the events of the day, and as soon as I reached my room I lay down. I asked Prince Fedor and Rayner to stay with me a while." When Nicholas Michaelovich arrived to see Yusupov, Rayner and Fedor left the room, but they rejoined him as soon as the (unwelcome) visitor left.

The Yusupov-Rayner relationship reached a yet higher level a year later, when the anti-Bolshevik government in Ukraine was falling to the Reds. The British dispatched the *Marlborough* to the Crimea to bring Nicholas II's mother, Maria Fedorovna, and others to safety. Yusupov and his family also boarded the battleship on April 7, 1919. And who should be with Felix but Oswald Rayner? The former BSIS agent probably helped Yusupov write *The End of Rasputin* in 1927. At least Rayner's name appears on the title page as the translator of the English edition, and in type that is almost as large as the letters used to render Yusupov's name.

Andrew Cook notes a "rich seam of oral history" in the families of Rayner, Alley, and Scale suggesting that they played a role in killing Rasputin. William Compton, the British chauffeur who drove Rayner to the Yusupovs' home a half-dozen times on the eve of the murder, always maintained that Rasputin's real assassin had been a British lawyer. (Rayner was a barrister.) Allegedly Rayner had a ring that was set with one of the bullets that killed Rasputin. Prince Felix Yusupov, incidentally, had a similar ring.

The Oxfordshire newspaper that published Rayner's obituary in 1961 made a startling claim: he had been "in the palace when Rasputin was killed." But Rayner's nephew recalled that his uncle never spoke about Rasputin; the obituary just cited was written by a distant relative. As for Muriel Scale's insistence that her father was involved in the murder, her other claims make us question her reliability. For example, she asserted that Rayner "was attached to the Tsar" and "part of his household"; he "lived in the palace," although on the night of the murder he was "away with the Tsar somewhere." In this instance, information from the family might not prove very much.

MI6 promised to publish its files on Rasputin's murder, but it has delayed doing so, presumably for good reasons. The controversy placed a chill on relations between Moscow and London, with President Vladimir Putin displaying outrage at the very thought that a foreign power had the right to murder a Russian citizen. As more evidence comes to light, we will probably find that King George V's government was involved in Rasputin's assassination in some way.

It is not likely, however, that the British initiated or controlled the operation. Had they done so, they might have used Prince Yusupov and the tsar's cousin, Dmitry Pavlovich—but not the mercurial Vladimir Purishkevich, who as universally regarded as unstable. Stanislaw Lazovert and Sergei Sukhotin posed different problems: their low social status almost guaranteed that they would confess under pressure. Had the British needed poison or a doctor on the scene, they almost certainly would have supplied them.

Rayner's six visits to Yusupov's palace suggest that the British were advising the prince in some way. (Their discussions might have also involved the possibility that the prince would, if necessary, seek asylum in Great Britain.) Although Rayner and Yusupov were friends, these calls could not have been social in nature. Rasputin's imminent demise was a political problem, and it would have demanded guidance from the highest BSIS officials. Rayner hovered about Yusupov after the murder—that must have been significant. But it is not likely that Rayner's superiors would have permitted him to be at Yusupov's home that tumultuous night or that a BSIS agent would have fired any of the shots. Why would he have done that? The locals were able to do their own killing. And that is exactly what they did.

Epilogue

Rasputin's death began a sad downward spiral for his family. Maria and Varvara moved into a smaller apartment in Petrograd and occasionally visited Tsarskoye Selo. Maria recalled that Nicholas II "was very emotional and tender with us," and he told the girls that "I will try to replace your father." The next time they visited they found that the tsar had already left for Stavka, but Alexandra received them. They were astonished to see angry crowds in the area of Alexander Palace. "I can still see her in her white nurse's costume," Maria wrote, "preoccupied and confident, reassuring us in spite of her own anxiety with that sad smile hiding her tears." She urged the girls to pray and to realize that Our Friend, although in the other world, "is nearer than ever to us."

Alexandra asked Alexander Protopopov to give the family 100,000 rubles, but the government was in such bad shape by early 1917 that this was impossible. Maria and Varvara were arrested when the tsarist regime fell in March, but they were soon released. They fled to Pokrovskoye only to learn just how vulnerable their mother was now that the Provisional Government controlled Russia. Shortly before the girls returned home, soldiers had broken into the house and pushed Rasputin's widow aside to steal valuable objects.

Rasputin should have left a fortune when he died, given that hundreds of thousands of rubles had passed through his hands. Since Rasputin left no will, his estate was placed in probate and the court had a full inventory made of his property. These records show that he had 5,092 rubles and 66 kopecks in the Tyumen State Bank. Of this sum, 2,192 rubles and 59 kopecks were in cash; the balance was in bonds. Another 3,800 rubles that was supposedly in Rasputin's apartment in the capital disappeared as hordes of people stampeded through it after his death.

Court records describe the family home as a "two-story wood house made of round logs trimmed with boards painted a green color and covered by a tin roof." It stood on the standard 105-square-foot lot with a barn, stable, bathhouse, and storage buildings, and was valued at 10,000 rubles. An additional 8,415 rubles in the Rasputin family's personal possessions included a fur coat (valued at 500 rubles); a gold watch (700 rubles); the Offenbach piano (900 rubles); the gramophone "in good working order" with fifty records (100 rubles); two dining tables; thirty-two chairs; two buffets; a pine china hutch; a sofa; three clocks; a large mirror; two samovars; a silver tea service; china; and various household items. Beside this, Rasputin owned eight horses (the youngest being a stud worth 1,000 rubles) as well as two cows, a bull, and eight sheep listed at 980 rubles. These animals raised the total value of his estate to 23,507 rubles and 66 kopecks. (A bishop at this time received an annual salary of 18,000 rubles.) Rasputin clearly squandered the fortune that passed through his hands in the capital. He died in the middle of the middle class, and his economic strength at the end of his life was where it was at the beginning of his career: in Siberia.

The law specified that a widow had to place her husband's estate in probate within six months of his death; it took Praskovaya eight months to do it. The court took advantage of this to levy "fines" and "fees" that reduced the 5,092 rubles and 66 kopecks in the Tyumen State Bank to 76 rubles and 40 kopecks; the penalties totaled 98.5 percent! Not that it mattered, really. By the time the ruling was announced on December 5, 1917, the Bolsheviks were in power and Russia stood at the brink of civil war, famine, and runaway inflation. The people who plundered Praskovaya's inheritance did not enjoy it for long. As for Praskovaya, her situation continued to deteriorate.

With Dmitry in the army, Maria and Varvara looked after their mother as best they could. In the autumn of 1917, Maria married Boris Soloviev, a young officer. But Soloviev seemed more interested in raising money through schemes to rescue the Romanovs, now imprisoned in nearby Tobolsk, than in caring for his new family. No rescue was even attempted. When the Bolsheviks increased their power in this area, Maria and Boris fled to Vladivostok, leaving Praskovaya and Varvara alone.

By now Dmitry was back, caring for his mother, but he could not pacify the new Soviet government. Since Rasputin symbolized the imperial regime, his family could not escape official condemnation. Vengeance was in the air: although the Rasputins lost their cash, the family's house and possessions made them members of the "propertied class." In November 1919 officials broke into their house and confiscated the family's piano and gramophone; eight months later they came back for the furniture, mirrors, and dishes.

The family grew increasingly desperate. In June 1920 the communists expelled Praskovaya, Dmitry, and his wife, Feoktista, from their home, forcing them into an abandoned village building. Dmitry built a small house on the outskirts of Pokrovskoye. The three tried to live quietly, but they could not overcome the notoriety of the Rasputin name. The fact that Dmitry had ten long-horned cattle made him a kulak (a prosperous peasant). The officials stripped the Rasputins of their property in 1930. They could keep only the clothes and household utensils that Dmitry could fit into the small wagon that carried his family away, into exile.

The trio was sent to the inhospitable northern Siberian city of Salekhard. Dmitry, described in records as a "skilled migrant," was forced into agricultural work, while Feoktista got a job at a local fishery. Disaster struck in 1933. Tuberculosis swept the city, claiming Dmitry's wife and their small daughter in September. Weakened by illness, Dmitry succumbed to dysentery three months later at the age of thirty-eight. Praskovaya was alone again, reliant on Soviet charity until her death in 1936.

Varvara made peace with the Communist regime and worked for the justice administration in Pokrovskoye as a stenographer. Aaron Simanovich arranged for his old boss's daughter to leave for Germany in 1923. When officials in Moscow searched Varvara at the train station, they found a large manuscript on the imperial family's life at Yekaterinburg. Varvara was arrested, and disappeared into a Soviet prison; apparently she died mysteriously of poison in 1924 or 1925.

Maria was the only member of her family to escape Russia. From Vladivostok she and her husband went to Europe. When Soloviev died in 1926, he was working on the assembly line of a French automobile factory. This left Maria to care for her daughters, Tatiana and Maria, as best she could. She sang and danced in cabarets, relying on her infamous name to attract crowds. She later developed a big cat act in the circus and made her way to the United States, where she continued to publish books and articles minimizing her father's faults and emphasizing his religious character. Maria sued Felix Yusupov and Grand Duke Dmitry Pavlovich for her father's murder, but the French court declared that it had no jurisdiction over a crime committed in Russia. Maria died in Los Angeles in 1977, describing her father's murder as the "Watergate of Russia."

Grand Duke Dmitry Pavlovich never spoke or wrote about his role in Rasputin's murder, and he was appalled at the way Felix Yusupov reveled over his role in the deed. Dmitry died of tuberculosis in Switzerland in 1941 at the age of fifty. Felix and Irina Yusupov settled in Paris. In 1934 they sued MGM for libel over the film *Rasputin and the Empress*, in which the peasant (played by Lionel Barrymore) seduced a character clearly modeled on Irina. Since the Yusupovs were awarded substantial damages, future motion pictures began bearing the disclaimer that "any similarity to any person living or dead is purely coincidental." Yusupov died in Paris in 1967. Vladimir Purishkevich succumbed to typhus in 1920 while fighting on the White side during the Civil War. Sergei Sukhotin married Leo Tolstoy's granddaughter Sophia in 1921, but they soon divorced. Yusupov brought Sukhotin to Paris for treatment in 1926 when he fell ill, but he died shortly after his arrival. Dr. Stanislaw Lazovert escaped Russia after the revolution and died in France.

Many of Rasputin's associates were arrested after Lenin seized power. The Bolsheviks executed Protopopov, Alexis Khvostov, and Stephen Beletsky in 1918, and Prince Andronikov and Dr. Peter Badmaev the following year. Iliodor returned to Russia and supported the efforts of the Communist regime to organize a church that agreed with Marxist social objectives. But Iliodor was difficult even as an ally, and he was deported in 1922. He spent his last days in New York City, preaching in a Russian Baptist church and working as a janitor in the Metropolitan Life Insurance Building. He died at Bellevue Hospital in 1952.

Anna Vyrubova spent five months in the Peter and Paul Fortress, once reserved for the tsar's enemies. Authorities hoped to indict her for criminal behavior, but she maneuvered through the interrogations by feigning childish innocence and was finally released after being deemed incapable of intrigue. Maxim Gorky befriended her and encouraged Anna to write her memoirs, while Zinaida Gippius, one of Russia's most gifted artists, spoke of Vyrubova as a worthy companion to such poets as Alexander Blok and Valery Bryusov. In December 1920 she went to Finland. Anna became a Russian Orthodox nun, although she continued to live in her own apartment due to poor health. Visitors noted the large portrait of Nicholas and Alexandra hanging in her living room; just to the left was a smaller picture of Rasputin. Anna died in Helsinki on July 20, 1964, four days before what would have been her eightieth birthday.

"What did they hope to achieve?" Nicholas II's sister, Olga, moaned as she recalled Rasputin's murder. "Did they really believe that the killing of Rasputin would mend our fortunes at the front, and bring to an end the appalling transport chaos and all the resultant shortages?" The assassination, she said, "was the greatest disservice to the one man they had sworn to serve," the tsar. Samuel Hoare agreed, saying that Rasputin's murder was one of those enormous crimes that tries to change the course of history and in the process "blurs the well-defined rules of ethics." Hoare initially supposed that the situation would improve with Rasputin gone, only to learn that the tsar's "rickety machine of government" could not take such a "sudden shock." "Startling events" were dangerous, in such a situation, even if the perpetrators were well intentioned, and it was better for conservatives to strengthen authority when a regime was in crisis than to weaken it.

Today Rasputin's former apartment has a small display telling visitors that he once lived there. The basement of Moika Palace across the city features a carefully re-created evocation of the murder scene, complete with waxwork figures of Yusupov and Rasputin. Rasputin's presence can still be felt in Pokrovskoye. Soviet authorities were embarrassed to see French tourists visiting Rasputin's house and photographing it. Lenin's heirs leveled the house in February 1980—the response was predictable. A museum to his memory stands nearby in a

Rasputin's house during demolition. In the late 1970s, French tourists developed an interest in visiting Pokrovskoye and photographing Rasputin's boarded-up house. Soviet authorities responded by demolishing the building in February 1980. Boris Yeltsin, as the first secretary of Sverdlovsk Oblast, was responsible for carrying out these orders from Moscow.

nearly identical dwelling that is crowded with artifacts, documents, and photographs of the village's most famous son.

A wood cross now marks the site of the grave Rasputin temporarily occupied in the park at Tsarskoye Selo. He spent ten weeks buried in the foundation of Anna Vyrubova's small church. On March 6, 1917, just four days after Nicholas II abdicated, a group of drunken soldiers uncovered what a newspaper described as his "desolate and forbidding" frozen grave. "Here lies Grishka Rasputin, shame of the House of Romanov and the Orthodox Church" was scrawled on the nearby wall of the church that was under construction, next to obscene drawings of the empress. The men drank and danced—they spat and relieved themselves at the site while axes and picks tore into the top of the zinc coffin. The icon resting on Rasputin's chest had been signed by the empress, her four daughters, and Anna Vyrubova; an American collector eventually bought it, although its whereabouts are unknown today. "The face was totally black," a reporter recalled. "Lumps of frozen earth were imbedded in the dark long beard and hair; a black hole from a bullet wound [was visible] on the forehead." Soldiers supposedly stripped Rasputin and "took measurements" of his penis with a brick.

The coffin was so heavy "that a whole platoon lifted it with difficulty." It was taken to the Tsarskoye Selo town hall, and the body was put on public display. The head "rested on a lacy silk pillow," a newspaper reported. "His arms were folded on his chest; the left side of his head was battered and disfigured. His body had turned black." The crowd fought over pieces of the coffin. "It was for good luck, like rope from a hanging," someone commented. After the coffin was loaded onto a truck, it disappeared into the night.

The Provisional Government obviously did not know what to do with the peasant's remains. Fearing that a public grave would attract demonstrations and desecration, Rasputin was secretly buried at an unknown spot at Konyushennaya Square in Petrograd. Then the order came to move the body to a remote, undisclosed location outside the capital. "We do not know who gave this order," the historian Alexander Bokhanov writes. "But one thing is certain: Kerensky very much wanted to be done with the matter of Rasputin's body."

It was surely no coincidence that the truck carrying Rasputin on that snowy winter broke down and that the soldiers posted to the detail cremated their cargo. This sort of maneuver would often be repeated in Russia: "The authorities" would make their wishes known to underlings, though without written instructions. If anything "went wrong," the higher-ups would disavow the "local enthusiasts" and blame everything on them—ignoring the fact that they were just following orders.

In this case a burial detachment loaded Rasputin's body onto a truck and left Petrograd on the night of March 10. The officer in charge was told to head to a place far beyond the city, in the direction of the Vyborg Highway. It was winter, and the weather was terrible. When the truck broke down, the soldiers sprang into action, gathering wood and dousing the body with gasoline (a considerable quantity just happened to be on the truck), setting it ablaze. The commander reported that "Rasputin's body was destroyed on the morning of March 11, between 7 and 9 o'clock, near the main road from Lesnoe to Peskarevka, at a forest in the total absence of anyone but us, the humble participants in this event." Rasputin was no longer a problem for the Provisional Government. Rasputin? Who was he?

Journalists swarmed to the site as soon as news got out—they were anxious to interview anyone who knew anything about the grim event. Newspaper accounts expressed a mixture of contempt, satisfaction, and joy. The *Petrograd Leaflet* reported that "Rasputin's body, wrapped in muslin, could be seen by the light of the moon and the reflection of the fire. The body had been embalmed; traces of color were visible on the face. The arms were arranged in the figure of a cross. The fire quickly enveloped the body, and continued for about two hours." The amateurs who attempted this cremation apparently did not know that such a slapdash effort would not reduce a corpse to ashes. When the "skeleton did not give in to the destruction" of the flames, a reporter noted that the soldiers "threw the remains into [a local stream]." Another journalist wrote that the spring rains came and washed this "trash" of the "previous regime" from the "face of the Russian land."

Rasputin's career began in the sunshine—it was cheerful and bright, for at the outset he was well intentioned and optimistic. Rasputin's life ended tragically, in the darkness of night. Rasputin was intelligent, magnetic, and capable of doing much good. He was also greedy. Craving power, he realized that the way for him to get it would be by exploiting the fears and weaknesses of those who held life's advantages—the bishop of Kazan, the Montenegrin sisters, Nicholas and Alexandra. Working through the empress, Rasputin got people in his favor elevated to leadership positions in the Church; he then began meddling in state affairs. Rasputin ended in a position in which it was up to him to decide if and when a prime minister would leave office and who would take his place. This was against the natural order of things, and so, by definition, it could not last. Given that the tsar could not part with his despised favorite, the story could end in only one way: Rasputin had to die. His passing was widely celebrated—which is not to deny that Rasputin had admirers then and now. But those who know the full story and its consequences might conclude that the world would have been a better place if Rasputin had never been born.

Notes

1. The Outsider

4 *village children could attend classes* Smirnov, chap. 1, discusses the early history of Pokrovskoye and Rasputin's family.

5 *"time of Catherine the Great"* Markov, 20.

5 *threatened to destroy the town* TFGATO, F. 156, op. 1, khr. 877, list 10.

5 *"better souls" of the village* GATO, F. I-205, op. 1, d. 1, l. 1–19.

6 *last favorite of the last tsar* GATO, F. I-205, op. 1, d. 1, l. 1–19.

6 *"mental illness in their families"* Shchegolev, *Padenie*, vol. 4: 147; Smitten, 10: 119; Rasputin, *My Father*, 45.

7 *penchant for "strong vodka"* Spiridovich, *Raspoutine*, 9, 10; Rasputin, *My Father*, 27, 29; Iliodor, 115; Smitten, 10: 119; de Jonge, 33.

7 *best farmland in the Russian Empire* Tooke, vol. 1: 62, 65.

7 *comfortable, if not wealthy* Spiridovich, *Raspoutine*, 9–10; Smirnov, 12.

7 *"some momentous event," she noted* Rasputin and Barham, 17.

7 *pestilence and death* Samuel Hazard Cross, ed., *Russian Primary Chronicle* (Cambridge, MA: Medieval Academy, 1953), pp. 136, 144–145, 173–174, 181, 184–185, 202–205.

7 *Church of Our Lady* GATO, F. I-205, op. 1, d. 1, l. 1–19; Smirnov, 10; Chernyshov, 112.

8 *godfather to her two children* Okhrana Report of September 9, 1915, in Vulliamy, *Red Archives*, 40–41; Smirnov, 11, argues unconvincingly that Feodosiya Rasputin was Gregory's sister. Anna Nicholaevna Rasputin, who was living with Gregory at the time of his death, claimed to be his niece. This would make her father, Nicholas, Gregory's brother. I have not been able to verify this claim. See her deposition to the police, December 18, 1916, published in *Byloe* 23, no. 1 (July 1917).

8 *long, drawn out, and slurred* Maria Rasputin and Barham, *Rasputin*; Rasputina, chap. 1; Kotsiubinskii, 13–26.

9 *"I had to carry on"* Smirnov, 46–48.

9 *"learn to understand God"* Dzhanumovaia, 101, 103, 108.

9 *"St. Nicholas the Miracle-Worker!"* Wallace, *Russia*, vol. 1: 91–92.

9 *in their household were illiterate* Fuhrmann, *Rasputin*, 3; Smitten, 10: 119–120.

10 *"an outsider," he recalled* "Life of an Experienced Pilgrim," manuscript in GARF, F. 612, op. 1, d. 31, l. 2.

10 *"weaknesses of others"* Bokhanov, *Rasputin*, 46.

10 *Gregory recovered, but Dmitry died* Rasputin and Barham, *Rasputin*, 13–14.

10 *everyone had this ability* Rasputin and Barham, *Rasputin*, 13–16.

10 *"place apart in the village"* Rasputin, *My Father*, 43–44; see also Fülöp-Miller, 14–15.

11 *offered was often rebellion* "Life of an Experienced Pilgrim," GARF, F. 612, op. 1, d. 31, l. 2.

11 *reputation of a village rake* Smitten, 10: 119.

11 *"good life for a peasant"* "Life of an Experienced Pilgrim," GARF, F. 612, op. 1, d. 31, l. 2.

11 *"couldn't determine their color"* Bokhanov, *Rasputin*, 148–149.

11 *even alternately blue and brown* Radzinsky, 230; Vorres, 134–135.

12 *"Sniveler" and "Snotnose"* Smitten, 10: 119–120.

12 *"kiss upon her willing lips"* Rasputin, *My Father*, 45; Rasputin and Barham, *Rasputin*, 58–60.

13 *"sell them to buy drink"* Anfisa Motorina, villager interviewed on *The Real Rasputin*, London, BBC, Time Watch Program, 1994.

13 *"nothing to do with it"* "Life of an Experienced Pilgrim," GARF, F. 612, op. 1, d. 31, l. 2.

13 *willingly went to the authorities* Smitten, 10: 119–120.

13 *"odd little bump"* Radzinsky, caption to illustration, p. 111.

13 *"sorta strange and stupid"* Smitten, 10: 119–120.

14 *"forty nights each spring"* "Life of an Experienced Pilgrim," GARF, F. 612, op. 1, d. 31, l. 2.

14 *"turned to drink"* GARF, F. 1467, op. 1, d. 479, l. 1.

2. Seeker and Teacher

15 *"for our many blessings"* Rasputin, "Life of an Experienced Pilgrim," GARF, F. 612, op. 1, d. 31, l. 12.

16 *the search for salvation* Radzinsky, 138–139.

17 *"cross and follow me"* Vyrubova, 164; Telitsyn, 28–29.

17 *"I worked hard"* Rasputin, "Life of an Experienced Pilgrim," GARF, F. 612, op. 1, d. 31, l. 7.

17 *"singing and waving his arms"* Smitten, 10: 121; Telitsyn, 27.

17 *experiences with everyone he met* Rasputin, *My Father*, 44–45.

17 *"made grimaces" throughout the Liturgy* TFGATO, F. 156, op. 28, khr. 1962-II, l. 11–12.

18 *he returned to Pokrovskoye* TFGATO, F. 156, op. 28, khr. 1962-II, l. 11–12.

18 *"It's hard being illiterate!"* Smirnov, 32.

19 *sectarian group, the Khlysty* Smitten, 10: 120; TFGATO, F. 156, op. 28, d. 1962-II, l. 4.

20 *the "dark courage" to sin* See "Khlysty"; Munro; Wallace, *Russia*, vol. 2: 46–47. Radzinsky, 46–52, offers a brilliant discussion of the Khlysty.

20 *"cleanse the people of their sins"* Rasputin, *My Father*, 26–27; Spiridovich, *Raspoutine*, 18–19; Radzinsky, 37–38.

21 *became a "pilgrim out of laziness"* Smirnov, 11–13; Bokhanov, *Rasputin*, 150; Spiridovich, *Raspoutine*, 15–17.

21 *"I took in life furiously"* Rasputin, "Life of an Experienced Pilgrim," GARF, F. 612, op. 1, d. 31, l. 11.

21 *God's purpose for his life* GARF, F. 612, op. 1, d. 31, l. 2ff.

22 *"save your soul in the world"* Rasputin, *My Father*, 47; Kilcoyne, 17–18.

22 *convinced that he was a man of God* Rasputin, *Real Rasputin*, 10–11; Rasputin, *My Father*, 46.

22 *celebrating the Holy Trinity* Smitten, 10: 121.

23 *"purpose of life was to mumble prayers"* Rasputin, *Real Rasputin*, 12–13.

25 *him for guidance and comfort* Fuhrmann, *Rasputin*, 9–10.

25 *"Long Hair," or "Fella"*   Kotsiubinskii, 22–23.

25 *"and that's the truth!"*   Telitsyn, 76–77.

25 *Nothing sexual occurred*   Smitten, 10: 120.

25 *"has dawned for your daughters"*   Spiridovich, *Raspoutine*, 38–39; Radziwill, *Rasputin*, 46.

26 *precognition and mystical gifts*   Kotsiubinskii, 22–23.

27 *ready to meet Bishop Sergei*   Spiridovich, *Raspoutine*, 38. See also Rasputin, *My Father*, 49; de Jonge, 73.

27 *its ties with the common people*   Radzinsky, 54–57.

27 *Saint Petersburg's Orthodox elite*   Smirnov, 18; Telitsyn, 46.

27 *sincerity of the pastor's words impressed Rasputin*   Rasputin and Barham, 105.

27 *to persevere in his calling*   Rasputin, *My Father*, 49.

28 *"emitted a disagreeable odor"*   Iliodor, 15, 30.

29 *"he made a strong impression"*   Iliodor, 163; Bokhanov, *Rasputin*, 56.

29 *avenues for him to explore*   Iliodor, 163; on Feofan's prestige, see Rodzianko, 4.

29 *at the Saint Petersburg Academy*   Spiridovich, *Raspoutine*, 45–46.

29 *"we commonly use the word"*   Wallace, *Russia*, vol. 2: 8.

30 *called them the "Black Peril"*   Nostitz, 144; Yusupov, *Lost Splendor*, 55.

30 *"was penetrating and original"*   Spiridovich, *Raspoutine*, 51–52.

30 *not the case at Feofan's*   Radziwill, *Rasputin*, 34. See also Witte, *Vospominaniia*, vol. 3: 565, and Maevskii, 131.

3. Nicholas and Alexandra: Waiting for a Friend

32 *scene in Alexander's bedroom shook Nicholas*   Alexander, 59–60.

32 *"descends upon my head"*   Paléologue, vol. 1: 98, citing Job 3:25–26.

32 *and lacking in self-confidence*   Pares, *History of Russia*, 407.

32 *"the business of ruling"*   Alexander, 168–169.

32 *no flair for critical analysis*   Wortman, vol. 2: 311.

32 *ruled by instinct and emotion*   Witte, *Memoirs*, 125.

32 *"his conscience and to God"*   Mosolov, 10–11.

33 *"entrusted to my care"*   Pipes, 20.

33 *"or even a county"*   Trotsky, 49.

33 *government were nothing more than "senseless dreams"*   Warth, 20; Florinsky, *Russia*, vol. 2: 1147.

33 *quite critical of the government*   Gurko, *Features and Figures*, 8.

34 *1894 they were engaged*   Nicholas, *Journal Intime*, 52; Nicholas, *Secret Letters*, 65.

34 *"behind a coffin," people whispered*   Gilliard, 48.

34 *" too much on the defensive"*   Queen Marie of Romania, vol. 1: 331–132.

35 *"don't laugh at my faults"*   Fuhrmann, *Complete Wartime Correspondence*, AF to N: September 22, 1916.

35 *"mainstays of Holy Russia"*   Iliodor, 88. On Alexandra's religious views, see the excellent studies by Janet Ashton listed in the bibliography.

36 *invited the Frenchman to visit Russia*   Paléologue, vol. 1: 203–206.

36 *people in his company invisible*   Yusupov, *Lost Splendor*, 62; Coppens.

36 *were stunned and angry*   See Maylunas and Mironenko, "Letters of Grand Duchess Xenia Alexandrovna to King Christian IX of Denmark," August 19 and 20, 1902, and selections from the "Diary of Constantine Constantinovich," August 20 and 22, 1902.

36 *"will speak to you of God"*   Fuhrmann, *Complete Wartime Correspondence*, AF to N: June 16, 1915; see also April 8, 1916. For Philippe's career in Russia, see Fuhrmann, *Rasputin*, 19–20.

37 *"clearly visited by God's grace"* Entry of July 30, 1904, Nicholas II, *Dnevnik Imperatora Nikolaia Vtorogo*, 173.
37 *"joy of his parents"* Gilliard, 72.
37 *displayed ugly, dark bruises* Radziwill, *Nicholas II*, 181; Buxhoeveden, *Life and Tragedy*, 125.
37 *cries were unusually piercing* Tisdall, 243.
37 *"bleeding may prove fatal"* Voeikov, 182–183.
38 *for a lifetime of misery* Massie, 148–150.
38 *the ignorance of physicians* Alexander, 182–183.

4. The New Rasputin

39 *"Gregory, from Tobolsk province"* Nicholas II, *Dnevnik*, 220.
40 *had been seeking for so long* Radzinsky, 59; Spiridovich, *Raspoutine*, 51–52.
41 *turn the tables on them* Smitten, 12: 99. Spiridovich, *Raspoutine*, 93. Radzinsky, 90.
41 *with them on July 18, 1906* Rasputin's telegram is simply dated 1906; on this meeting see Feofan's testimony in Radzinsky, 83.
41 *unwell at this time and was restless* Maylunas and Mironenko, 284.
41 *the first time in 1906* Rasputin, *My Father*, 35–36.
41 *"an hour instead of five minutes"* Vinogradoff, 115–116.
42 *never again mentioned Rasputin to him* Vinogradoff, 115–116; Radzinsky, 88; Maylunas and Mironenko, 284.
42 *heard at Alexander palace* Naryshkina-Kurakina, 190.
42 *"We talked about Gregory"* Spiridovich, *Raspoutine*, 93.
42 *was dated December 22, 1906* For the petition, see Chernyshov, 114, who cites GARF, F. I-205, op. 1, d. 3, l. 88.
42 *"get him out of this habit"* Fuhrmann, *Complete Wartime Correspondence*, AF to N: January 7 and April 9, 1916.
43 *adopt the name "Novyi" or "Novykh"* Rasputin sometimes gave his name as *Novykh*, the genitive plural of *Novyi*. Siberian surnames are often rendered in the genitive plural because this makes them seem more "grand" and dignified. *Novykh* also has overtones of Old Church Slavonic, the archaic but elegant language of the Russian Orthodox Church. For the ways Rasputin used his new name, see TFGATO, F. 164, op. 1, d. 437, l. 5–6, also d. 439, l. 11 and 51.
43 *"crying out, "New! New!"* Iliodor, 111–112.
43 *identify the bearer as "Rasputin-Novyi"* Like all Russians, Rasputin carried an internal passport. His was issued by Pokrovskoe volost'; he was classified as an "official resident" of the capital beginning on October 5, 1909. TFGATO, F. 156, op. 28, khr. 1962-II, l. 2.
43 *on April 6, 1907, and June 19* Spiridovich, *Raspoutine*, 71–72.
43 *night and prayed for her son* Vorres, 138–139; Spiridovich, *Raspoutine*, 71–72.
43 *"children would have recovered!"* Buxhoeveden, *Before the Storm*, 116–119.
43 *"his insistence on her guilt"* Naryshkina-Kurakina, 195.
44 *strangeness garnered interest and respect* Report of the commission that investigated Rasputin for heresy in 1907 to 1908: TFGATO, F. 156, op. 28, khr. 1962-II, l. 11.
44 *"seemed to read one's inmost thoughts"* Dehn, 100–101.
44 *"What's this, little mother"* Evlogii, 217–118.
44 *"truth and discerns everything"* Smitten, 10: 122–123. For Uexkuell, see Evlogii, 217–218.
44 *"learn to understand God"* Shchegolev, *Padenie*, vol. 4: 241; Smitten, 10: 123; Spiridovich, *Raspoutine*, 78–90.

45 *"looked rather uncomfortable"* Vorres, 135.
45 *that they had long abandoned* Smitten, 10: 122.
45 *called them his "little ladies"* TFGATO, F. 156, op. 28, khr. 1962-II, l. 4.
45 *"free of my illness"* Radzinsky, 84.
45 *wise sayings and amazing character* Shchegolev, *Padenie*, vol. 3: 434; vol. 4: 500;
     Simanovich, 101; Paléologue, vol. 1: 142–43; Iliodor, 187; Spiridovich, *Les dernières
     années*, vol. 1: 290.
46 *who gathered around him* TFGATO, F. 156, op. 28, khr. 1962-II, l. 5–6.
46 *"only to bad people"* Radzinsky, 86.
46 *"extremely crafty and rather sly"* Maylunas and Mironenko, 418.
47 *union would be unhappy* Vyrubova, 29–32; Smitten, 12: 90–91; Shchegolev, *Padenie*,
     vol. 3: 233–234, 235.
47 *beat her—and was impotent* Vyrubova, 258–259; Rudnev, 395–396; Dehn, 97.
47 *locked him out of their house* Dehn, 97–98; Naryshkina-Kurakina, 187.
47 *little yellow house* Fülöp-Miller, 94–96, offers a splendid discussion of Anna Vyrubova
     and her house.
47 *"portico to power"* Shchegolev, *Padenie*, vol. 3: 234–235.
47 *"way that one treats a helpless child"* Dehn, 48.
48 *lacked a formal education* Shchegolev, *Padenie*, vol. 3: 237, 250.
48 *"truth about the Empress and Rasputin"* Dorr, 110.

5. The Church Strikes Back

49 *friendship with the imperial family* Smirnov, 37.
49 *wife of a high official* TFGATO, F. 156, op. 28, khr. 1962-II, l. 4; Radzinsky, 94.
49 *"sometimes they do"* Radzinsky, 86.
49 *pilot on the Tura River* GATO, F. I-239, op. 1, d. 90, l. 199. See also Bokhanov, *Rasputin*,
     44, 58, and Nelipa, 13.
49 *windows and a tin roof* Dehn, 110; Radzinsky, 95–96.
50 *"how rich people lived in the cities"* Radzinsky, 140, 149–150; Kotsiubinskii, 27–28.
50 *his new and exalted status* GATO, F. I-239, op. 1, d. 90, l. 199. See also Bokhanov,
     Rasputin, 44, 58.
50 *"perspicacious," and "wise"* See police reports dated January 4 and 7, 1910, in GATO,
     F. I-239, op. 1, d. 90, l. 199 and 199–200. Also Smirnov, 33–34.
50 *everything that Rasputin had bought* Smirnov, 31.
51 *"satanic pride and 'demonic charm'"* Police report of January 7, 1910: TFGATO, F.
     156, op. 28, khr. 1962-II, l. 11.
51 *"I got other shirts she sewed"* Kotsiubinskii, 27–28.
51 *"and other important figures"* TFGATO, F. 156, op. 28, khr. 1962-II, l. 11–12.
51 *"in every sort of way"* Smirnov, 37.
52 *into leaving him alone* See GARF, F. 612, op. 1, d. 13, l. 2; TFGATO, F. 156, op. 28,
     khr. 1962-II, l. 2; Smirnov, 31–32; and Bokhanov, *Rasputin*, 44. The icon was the image
     of Christ "Not Made by Human Hands," which according to tradition miraculously
     appeared on a veil at Edessa. It is also called "Christ on a Napkin."
52 *"advice on the spiritual life"* Report of the commission that investigated Rasputin
     for heresy in 1907: TFGATO, F. 156, op. 28, khr. 1962-II, l. 11. See also Bokhanov,
     Rasputin, 44, 159, 301.
52 *decrease his influence with Alexandra* See, for example, Radzinsky, 97, and Nelipa, 32.
53 *"spreading false, Khlyst-like doctrines"* TFGATO, F. 156, op. 28, khr. 1962-II, l. 4, 10.
53 *Rasputin, a basso profundo, sang well* TFGATO, F. 156, op. 28, khr. 1962-II, l. 4, 11–12.
54 *something improper was taking place* TFGATO, F. 156, op. 28, khr. 1962-II, l. 5–6.

54 *anything more about her* TFGATO, F. 156, op. 28, khr. 1962-II, l. 5, 12–13.
54 *"it represents the Khlyst heresy"* TFGATO, F. 156, op. 28, khr. 1962-II, l. 5, 12.
54 *"entire family does the same"* TFGATO, F. 156, op. 28, khr. 1962-II, l. 11.
55 *"love each other and do good"* TFGATO, F. 156, op. 28, khr. 1962-II, l. 11. See also Bokhanov, *Rasputin*, 44, 159, 301.
55 *"missionary against the sectarians"* TFGATO, F. 156, op. 28, khr. 1962-II, l. 13.
55 *"sacrifices to the parish church"* See Bokhanov, *Rasputin*, 44, or the issue of the *Tobolsk Diocese News* on file in the Rasputin Museum at Pokrovskoye. For the parish meeting of May 9, 1907, see Smirnov, 31–32.
55 *"to church is only a formality"* TFGATO, F. 156, khr. 2314, d. 29, l. 2, 4, 5–6, 8, and others.
56 *"sing and read in a crude"* V. D. Bonch-Bruevich as quoted in Smirnov, 43.
56 *lives would aid his own search* V. D. Bonch-Bruevich as quoted in Smirnov, 43.
56 *"sincere friendship and never quarreled"* Simanovich, 30.
56 *"and this is his"* Radzinsky, 200, 270.
56 *"charming, sensible woman"* Dehn, 110.

6. The Romanovs' Holy Fool

57 *open and closely observed* Voeikov, 30.
58 *check into Rasputin's background* Shchegolev, *Padenie*, vol. 3: 11–12; Rodzianko, 2; Kurlov, 178; Spiridovich, "Nachalo Rasputina," 4–5.
58 *no need for the police to worry* Kurlov, 178–180.
58 *told his daughter* Von Bock, 45.
59 *would not see Rasputin again* Kurlov, 178–180; Spiridovich, *Les Dernières Années*, vol. 1: 297–299, and "Nachalo Rasputina," 9; Shchegolev, *Padenie*, vol. 3: 11–12.
59 *the capital was destroyed* Spiridovich, *Les dernières années*, vol. 1: 208–209; and *Raspoutine*, 91–92; see also Shchegolev, *Padenie*, vol. 3: 12.
60 *hurled her fork into the floor* Spiridovich, *Raspoutine*, 73–74, and *Les dernières années*, vol. 1: 295.
60 *see him do anything improper* Spiridovich, *Raspoutine*, 96–104; Vyrubova, 162–163.
60 *with "rustic faith and fervor"* Vyrubova, 162–163.
60 *dismissed the incident as a misunderstanding* Spiridovich, *Raspoutine*, 96–104; Vyrubova, 162–163.
61 *"can do nothing at all about it"* Gurko, *Tsar i tsaritsa*, 90.
61 *before he destroyed the throne* Iliodor, 186–187, 216–220; Evlogii, 220; Spiridovich, *Raspoutine*, 69, 104, 124–125; Kilcoyne, 133–134.
61 *danger to the Romanov dynasty* Iliodor, 186–187, 216–220; Evlogii, 220; Spiridovich, *Raspoutine*, 69, 104, 124–125; Kilcoyne, 133–134.
61 *Alexandra dismissed her* Fuhrmann, *Rasputin*, 62–63; Vyrubova, 64–65.
62 *life free of scandal* Rodzianko, 27–28; Pol'skii, 14.
62 *would go to discredit Rasputin* Fuhrmann, *Rasputin*, 62; Spiridovich, *Raspoutine*, 125–126; Iliodor, 116–120; Gurko, *Tsar i tsaritsa*, 43, 44, 70; Oldenburg, vol. 3: 81.
63 *"the least illusion about him"* Vorres, 135.
63 *Alexandra looked on uncomfortably* Vorres, 135.
63 *"vestry—but not tipsy"* Fuhrmann, *Complete Wartime Correspondence*, AF to N: November 5, 1916.
64 *was a man of "pure faith"* Rodzianko, 11; Oldenburg, vol. 3: 83.
64 *shut out all contrary opinions* Dehn, 94.
64 *"with all the fringe benefits!"* Shavel'skii, vol. 1: 67; see also Vorres, 132, and Aronson, 74.
65 *"Jewish society for His followers"* Dehn, 104.

7. The Captain's Mysterious Report

67 *"every accent except Russian"* Fuhrmann, *Rasputin*, 56–60; Patrick J, Rollins, "Iliodor," MERSH, vol. 14: 146–149.

68 *"Orthodox Tsar and autocrat!"* Radzinsky, 132.

68 *Russia under Catherine the Great* Rollins, 147.

69 *"new one from right to left"* Iliodor, 57, 97, 103.

69 *return to his flock at Tsaritsyn* Iliodor, 57, 59, 97, 103.

69 *unruly bishop under control* Shchegolev, *Padenie*, vol. 7: 324; Fuhrmann, *Rasputin*, 59 and 232, note 11; Oldenburg, vol. 3: 199; Curtiss, 254, 336.

69 *a "worthy, pious man"* TFGATO, F. 164, op. 1, khr. 437, l. 220–221.

70 *"such a scoundrel?" they grumbled* Iliodor, 106; Spiridovich, *Raspoutine*, 105–117; emennikov, *Za kulisami*, 13, 21–22; Evlogii, 198.

71 *"and thought it was a miracle"* Iliodor, 116–21.

71 *let Iliodor remain with his followers* Fuhrmann, *Rasputin*, 57–58.

71 *"One of your relatives"* Spiridovich, *Raspoutine*, 135.

72 "It is even said" Fuhrmann, *Rasputin*, 233.

72 *were truly angry with him* Ibid., 64–65.

72 *perhaps on several occasions* Rasputin and Barham, *Rasputin*, 162–168; Lukomskii, 27.

72 *"surrounded by a bevy"* Rasputin and Barham, *Rasputin*, 162–168.

73 *"many services to the Crown"* Ibid.

73 *which arranged their trips* Graham, 99–100.

74 *large, scrawled G for "Grigory"* Concerning the authorship of *Moi mysli i razmyshleniia*, see Spiridovich, *Raspoutine*, 139–140, and *Les dernières années*, vol. 2: 55–59. It was reprinted in Semennikov, *Za kulisami*, 142–160, and is available in a good English translation in Rasputin, *My Father*, 121–157. See also Dzhanumovaia, 106. Citations in this chapter are from Semennikov.

74 *did the actual writing* Radzinsky, 163–164.

8. Black Boars Become Bishops

77 *bishops supported his promotion* Witte, *Vospominaniia*, vol. 3: 552–553.

77 *never even met Rasputin* The letter to Paul Milyukov was dated November 28, 1912. See GARF, F. 612, op. 1, d. 16. See also Fuhrmann, *Rasputin*, 75–76, for Sabler's background and career at the Holy Synod.

78 *"spirit of the living God"* Maevskii, 115–16. On Varnava, see Sofronov, 249–252.

78 *"satyr or the god Pan"* Smitten, 12: 100.

78 *"modest face and polite bows"* Maevskii, 115–116; Sofronov, 249–252.

79 *"very many good qualities"* Shavel'skii, vol. 1: 369–70; Maevskii, 115; Shchegolev, *Padenie*, vol. 4: 153.

79 *imperial couple to support Varnava* Smitten, 12: 100; Shchegolev, *Padenie*, vol. 1: 385; Iliodor, 206–207; "V tserkovnykh krugakh," 204–211.

79 *a voice among church leaders* "V tserkovnykh krugakh," 204–211.

79 *make Varnava a vicar bishop* "V tserkovnykh krugakh," 211–212; Smitten, 2: 104; Maevskii, 117–119; Nikon, vol. 4: 55–56.

79 *"be responsible for consecrating rascals!"* Smitten, 12: 100; Shchegolev, *Padenie*, vol. 1: 385; Iliodor, 206–207; "V tserkovnykh krugakh," 204–211.

80 *agreed to Varnava's promotion* "V tserkovnykh krugakh," 211–212; Smitten, 2: 104; Maevskii, 117–119; Nikon, vol. 4: 55–56.

80 *"takes part in their rituals"* "V tserkovnykh krugakh," 211–212; Smitten, 2: 104; Maevskii, 117–119; Nikon, vol. 4: 55–56.

80 *on the imperial yacht Standart* Radzinsky, 210–212.

80 *it also pleased Nicholas and Alexandra* Alexis's report is in GARF, F. 612, op. 1, d. 13; see also Smitten, 2: 105.

81 *again Nicholas had his way* Smitten, 2: 105.

81 *future investigations of Rasputin* Smirnov, 42.

81 *"get to take it easy"* Shchegolev, *Padenie*, vol. 1: 385, vol. 4: 153; Smitten, 12: 100; Radzinsky, 388.

82 *next item on its agenda* Maevskii, 119–120.

82 *yielded to this intimidation* Gurko, *Tsar i tsaritsa*, 97.

83 *for the tsar and his favorite* Iliodor, 53.

83 *nothing more than an adventurer* Spiridovich, "Nachalo Rasputina," 9; Tisdall, 243; Zhevakov, vol. 1: 270; Spiridovich, *Raspoutine*, 107, 130, 154.

83 *Hermogen's harebrained schemes* Spiridovich, *Raspoutine*, 157–158; Iliodor, 106, 130, 158–159, 167, 215, 227–228; Rasputin, *Real Rasputin*, 63, and Rasputin, *My Father*, 20, 66–67.

84 *undermined the prestige of the throne* See de Jonge, 202–203, for a good account of the strange "trial."

84 *"an anathema against you"* Fuhrmann, *Russia*, 236, n. 5, reviews the sources that permit us to construct this account.

85 *"More guards. Yes"* Vonliarliarskii, 204; Iliodor, 237–238, 244–245, 249–250; Curtiss, 371–372; Kokovtsov, *Out of My Past*, 293.

85 *"rule the state, not the Tsar"* For the police report, see TFGATO, F. 164, op. 1, khr. 439, l. 71.

85 *like marriage and the sacraments* This report is dated January 28, 1914, and is in TFGATO, F. 164, op. 1, khr. 439, l. 23–26.

85 *"Paganism is a fine religion"* Iliodor, 256, 259–260, 270; Oldenburg, vol. 3: 206.

9. "You Are Our All"

88 *"his own motives and thoughts"* Fuhrmann, *Rasputin*, 71.

88 *"conduct him to the railway station"* Ibid., 72–74.

88 *no one took him seriously* Shul'gin, 260–263; Witte, *Vospominaniia*, vol. 3: 567; Salisbury, 658–659; Simanovich, 81–83.

89 *"Forgive me!"* Spiridovich, *Les dernières années*, vol. 2: 188.

89 *"not there with the others"* Petra H. Kleinpenning, ed., *Correspondence of the Empress Alexandra of Russia with Ernst Ludwig and Eleonore, Grand Duke and Duchess of Hesse, 1878–1916*, 351–352. I thank Griffith Henninger II for bringing this letter to my attention.

89 *"no longer count on divine protection"* Yusupov, *Lost Splendor*, 146.

89 *"of poor Stolypin's death"* Fuhrmann, *Complete Wartime Correspondence*, N to AF: October 28, 1916; see also Spiridovich, *Les dernières années*, vol. 2: 188.

90 *a solid and experienced official* Kokovtsov, *Iz moego proshlego*, vol. 2: 265, 493; Shchegolev, *Padenie*, vol. 1: 3–5.

90 *"but he lacks something"* Kokovtsov, *Iz moego proshlego*, vol. 2: 265, 493; Shchegolev, *Padenie*, vol. 1: 3–5.

90 *"So long!"* Kokovtsov, *Iz moego proshlego*, 2: 265, 493; Shchegolev, *Padenie*, 1: 3–5.

91 *"a smile on their lips"* Kokovtsov, *Iz moego proshlego*, vol. 2: 265–266, 493; Shchegolev, *Padenie*, 1: 5.

91 *supported by people in "high places"* Shulgin, 219; de Basily, 62–63; Oldenburg, vol. 3: 80–81.

91 *"become embittered and restless"* Nekliudov, 67; see also Katkov, 336–337.

91 *"uses the Church as a cover"* Rodzianko, 31–34; Kulikowski, 80; Shulgin, 230–231; Pares, *Fall of the Russian Monarchy*, 146–147.

92 *sold for enormous sums* Mosolov, 177; Kokovtsov, *Iz moego proshlego*, vol. 2: 290–291; Curtiss, 374–75; Rodzianko, 31.

92 *"fattest man in Russia"* Rodzianko, 47.

92 *"comply with her wishes"* Ibid., 53.

93 *be expelled from the capital* Ibid., 33–35.

93 *subject not be raised again* Kilcoyne, 159–163; Kokovtsov, *Iz moego proshlego*, vol. 2: 294; Spiridovich, *Les dernières années*, vol. 2: 196–200.

93 *"Saints are always calumniated!"* Botkin, 123.

93 *she told Anna Vyrubova* Vyrubova, 162.

93 *"everything that concerned it"* Oldenburg, vol. 3: 111; Evlogii, 196–198; Kokovtsov, *Iz moego proshlego*, vol. 2: 317.

94 *"heretic or the righteous man?"* GARF, F. 612, op. 1, d. 15 and 16. The communications are dated November 24 and 28, 1912.

94 *was behind their publication* See Fuhrmann, *Rasputin*, 82, 87; Oldenburg, vol. 3: 112; Kokovtsov, *Iz moego proshlego*, vol. 2: 291–300; and Milyukov, 234.

95 *"I am Your child"* GARF, F. 612, op. 1, d. 42, l. 5. In referring to Rasputin, Alexandra uses *vy*, the formal version of the Russian pronoun *you*, and she capitalizes it. Her letter is signed "A." Olga's letter is dated December 12, 1909, Tatyana's letter is dated March 25, 1909, and Maria's letter is simply dated 1909.

95 *when they were finally retrieved* Kokovtsov and Maklakov would have said that Bokhanov, *Rasputin*, 176–177, and Nelipa, 69, are wrong in thinking that the letters were fabricated.

95 *prophecy was fulfilled* Smitten, 10: 131–132; Kokovtsov, *Iz moego proshlego*, vol. 2: 293; Gurko, *Features and Figures*, 518–519.

95 *dumped at the next station* Kokovtsov, *Iz moego proshlego*, vol. 2: 294; Iliodor, 254–255; Rodzianko, 60–63.

95 *"everything will go well"* Voeikov, 68–69.

10. "God Has Heard Your Prayers!"

97 *jumping into a boat* Alexander Spiridovich writes that Alexis injured himself while playing in the bathtub (*Les dernières années*, vol. 2: 272). But Nicholas II's letter to his mother (dated October 20, 1912, see Nicholas II, *Secret Letters*, 271–276) and the official bulletin that the ministry of the Imperial Court issued on October 21, 1912 (see Maylunas and Mironenko, 359), indicate that Spiridovich was wrong.

97 *imperial hunting preserve at Spala* Nicholas, *Secret Letters*, 271–276; Spiridovich, *Les dernières années*, vol. 2: 272–285; Gilliard, 28; Vyrubova, 90.

97 *by the time they reached Spala* Vyrubova, 90–92.

98 *let the doctor examine the swelling* Spiridovich, *Les dernières années*, vol. 2: 281.

98 *"Lord, have mercy upon me!"* Ibid., vol. 2: 289; Nicholas II, *Secret Letters*, 276; Vyrubova, 92; Buxhoeveden, *Before the Storm*, 131; Gilliard, 29.

98 *nothing she could do* Vyrubova, 93; Buxhoeveden, *Before the Storm*, 132.

98 *"composure in all circumstances"* Nicholas, *Secret Letters*, 276.

98 *after he was gone* Buxhoeveden, *Before the Storm*, 131–132; Vyrubova, 92–93.

98 *dinners for the Polish nobles* Vyrubova, 93; Gilliard, 29–31.

99 *game that dominated her life* Ibid., 28–30.

99 *son's stomach was hemorrhaging* Ibid., 31; Spiridovich, *Les dernières années*, vol. 2: 280–282.

99 *"came in crowds and wept"* Nicholas II, *Secret Letters*, 275.

99 *announcing the tsarevich's death* Spiridovich, *Dernières années*, vol. 2: 283; Vyrubova, 93–94.

99 *Pokrovskoye on her behalf* Vyrubova, 94.
99 *"arrived early the next morning"* Vyrubova, 94.
100 *"he has reassured me completely"* Paléologue, vol. 1: 148.
100 *"bother him too much"* Vyrubova, 94.
100 *two cables into one text* Compare Spiridovich, *Raspoutine*, 187, and *Les dernières années*, vol. 2: 290, with Trewin, 24.
101 *revive his atrophied muscles* Mosolov, 150–151; Vyrubova, 95; Nicholas II, *Secret Letters*, 277–278; Trewin, 24–25; Paléologue, vol. 1: 148–149; Gilliard, 70; Damer, 7.
101 *less than one in a hundred* Spiridovich, *Les dernières années*, vol. 2: 288.
101 *operation to relieve the pressure* Ibid.
102 *"from a medical point of view"* Mosolov, 150–151; Vorres, 143.
102 *common and unavoidable* *EB* 9th ed. (1885), vol. 18: 375.
102 *prayed, the bleeding stopped* Lukhomskii, 28.
102 *"how he managed it"* Mosolov, 148.
102 *"briefest time the bleeding stopped"* Shakhovskii, 119.
102 *"relief to the Heir" on several occasions* Fabritskii, 134–135.
102 *"healing magnetism" of Rasputin* Vecchi, 55.
103 *Rasputin was a miracle worker* Shchegolev, *Padenie*, vol. 7: 304 and vol. 1: 115; Semennikov, *Za kulisami*, iv, ix–x, xxxiii–xxxiv; Mel'gunov, *Legenda*, 229; Smitten, 1: 108.
103 *early years at court* Smitten, 12: 100; Semennikov, *Za kulisami*, 17; Salisbury, 208, 658; Kurlov, 187–188.
103 *the secret of Rasputin's success* Trewin, 22.
103 *"adrenalin and similar drugs"* Katkov, 203.
103 *viewing it as "Satanic"* Rasputin, *My Father*, 35.
103 *with Gerasim Papandato* Radzinsky, 280; concerning the letter, see Markov, 20; Shchegolev, *Padenie*, vol. 4: 502.
103 *just as Rasputin had predicted* Shchegolev, *Padenie*, vol. 4: 354; Lukhomskii, 28; Simanovich, 18.
104 *"conscious of the man's sincerity"* Vorres, 138.
104 *Rasputin's miracles* Gilliard, 55.
104 *"to be attributed to him"* Buxhoeveden, *Life*, 142.
104 *and his cousin Alexander Michaelovich* Dehn, 100; Tisdall, 250; Alexander, 184.
105 *occasionally they treated people* Poliakoff, 274–275.
105 *and the bleeding abruptly ceased* Buxhoeveden, *Before the Storm*, 116–119; de Basily, 78.
105 *"a person lives, he sins"* Rasputin, *My Father*, 30.

11. Spiritual Crisis

107 *"glorious banner of our Fatherland"* "300th Anniversary of the Romanov Dynasty, 1913," www.angelfire.com/pa/ImperialRussian/royalty/russia/1913.html.
108 *proudly exited the cathedral* Rodzianko, 75–77.
108 *than loyalty or goodwill* Buchanan, 35–36; Vyrubova, 98–101; Spiridovich, *Les dernières années*, vol. 2: 315–316.
108 *"anything approaching enthusiasm"* Kokovtsov, *Iz moego proshlego*, vol. 2: 360–361.
109 *she concluded helplessly* Maylunas and Mironenko, 377–378.
109 *"their hearts are ours"* Concerning the trip, also see Oldenburg, vol. 3: 127; Shavel'skii, vol. 1: 61; Narishkina-Kurakina, 205–206.
109 *No. 70 Nicholaevsky Street* Fuhrmann, *Rasputin*, 240; Molchanov in Radzinsky, 180, 204–205.
109 *to come to Tsarskoye Selo* Dehn, 103.

110 *"acquaintances who asked for his help"* Radzinsky, 180, 204–205.

110 *Rasputin got his money* Bokhanov, *Rasputin*, 271.

110 *became steadily more complicated* Radzinsky, 250.

110 *was worth the price* Spiridovich, "Nachalo Rasputina," 8, and *Raspoutine*, 128.

110 *"write horrors about me"* de Schelking, 118.

110 *"I'll ring the bell"* Smirnov, 59–60, citing *Russian Morning* (*Utro Rossii*), July 3, 1914.

110 *"despair of all Russia"* Rodzianko, 97–98, 101–102; Curtiss, 375–376. The newspaper was *Vechernee Vremya* (*Evening Times*).

111 *immediately in the future* Voeikov, 30.

111 *"and began to fall asleep"* Maylunas and Mironenko, 379–380.

111 *her husband's "help and counselor"* Fuhrmann, *Complete Wartime Correspondence*, AF to N: November 6, 1915. See Barbara Evans Clements, *Russian Masculinities in History and Culture* (London: Palgrave, 2002), 85, and Healey, 23–25.

112 *"especially the meaning of life"* Radzinsky, 280.

112 *"Papandato (nicknamed the 'Musician')"* Radzinsky, 280; on the 1913 experience, see Markov, 20, and Shchegolev, *Padenie*, vol. 4: 502.

113 *"the only way we'll succeed"* Smirnov, 60, citing *Russian Morning* (*Utro Rossii*), July 3, 1914.

114 *"more real estate?!"* Smirnov, 32–36; Fuhrmann, *Rasputin*, 102, 108–11.

114 *"Now we understand everything"* *St. Petersburg Gazette*, October 13, 1913, as cited in Semennikov, *Politika*, 227.

114 *"It's good for foreigners"* *Novoe Vremya* (*New Times*), in Semennikov, *Politika*, 227–228.

114 *"killing the very soul from the outset"* Ibid.

115 *"therefore a fact of life"* Witte's interview appeared in *Foseevskaya gazeta*, cited in Smirnov, 60.

115 *"helm of our highest politics"* Curtiss, 375–376.

115 *"This troubles me"* Nicholas II, *Secret Letters*, 278–279; Simanovich, 153–154; Shchegolev, *Padenie*, vol. 6: 370.

12. The Woman with the Missing Nose

118 *being exiled from Saint Petersburg* Ibid., 282–283.

118 *from her own private chancery* Bokhanov, *Rasputin*, 269.

118 *"a powerful force, really good"* Smirnov, 60.

119 *"they are threatening war"* See Rasputin's telegrams in Tret'iakova, vol. 4: 384.

119 *July 13, on the Gregorian calendar* There has been confusion over the date of Khioniya Guseva's attack due to the fact that two different calendars were in use in different parts of Europe at this time. The archduke was killed on June 28, according to the Gregorian calendar. Russian sources tell us that Rasputin was stabbed on June 29, which would seem to be the next day. But this date was according to the Julian calendar, which would be July 12 on the Gregorian calendar. So Rasputin was attacked thirteen days after the tragedy of June 28 in Sarajevo. See TFGATO: F. 164, op. 1, d. 437, l. 5–6; also the police report in F. 164, op. 1, d. 439, l. 13, and Spiridovich, *Raspoutine*, 201–203.

119 *from striking another blow* For the police report with Rasputin's statement, see TFGATO: F. 164, op. 1, d. 437, l. 5–6 and d. 439, l. 13.

120 *to hear his last confession* Smirnov, 61.

120 *"hope for God's goodness. Alexandra"* Bokhanov, *Rasputin*, 296.

120 *be a matter of top priority* Spiridovich, *Raspoutine*, 202.

120 *"They sent for a doctor"* Tret'iakova, vol. 4: 383.

252 NOTES

120 *"I'll pull through!"* The hospital's "Admissions and Record Form" is in TFGATO: F. 164, op. 1, khr. 437, l. 25.
120 *"I'll be in bed three weeks"* Tret'iakova, vol. 4: 383–395.
120 *fell a few hours later* The information about Rasputin's temperature and condition is from the newspaper clippings in GARF for July 1914: see F. 612, op. 1, d. 31, l. 30.
120 *"the stench was terrible"* Tret'iakova, vol. 4: 383–395.
121 *"must we cross in life?"* Spiridovich, *Les dernières années*, vol. 2: 470, and *Raspoutine*, 203; Amalrik, 184.
121 *as did various female friends* TFGATO: F. 164, op. 1, d. 437, l. 5–6.
122 *"can't say more than this"* Rasputin's statement to the police is in TFGATO: F. 164, op. 1, d. 437, l. 5–6.
122 *with a matching bonnet* Under newspaper clippings for July 1914 in GARF: see *Den'* in F. 612, op. 1, d. 31, l. 46 (see also l. 41).
122 *refused these requests* GARF: F. 612, op. 1, d. 31, l. 30.
122 *found in most of the stories* GARF: F. 612, op. 1, d. 31, l. 1–59.
123 *"intelligent, newspaper reading public"* For these newspapers, see GARF: F. 612, op. 1, d. 31, l. 3, 30, 35, 41, 42, 45, 50, 55, and Bokhanov, *Rasputin*, 296.
123 *"failed me and I fell down"* GARF: F. 612, op. 1, d. 31, l. 30.
123 *these stories at face value* See Radzinsky, 287, 341–342; Nelipa, 45–48.
123 *"irregularly shaped hole in its place"* TFGATO: F. 164, op. 1, khr. 436, l. 14–15.
123 *circle of followers at Tsaritsyn* See the police report in TFGATO: F. 164, op. 1, khr. 439, l. 23–26.
124 *"has to be fed with something"* TFGATO: F. 164, op. 1, khr. 439, l. 55.
124 *young person with a hopeful future* TFGATO: F. 164, op. 1, khr. 439, l. 14.
125 *a clear view of Rasputin's house* On the knife, see TFGATO: F. 164, op. 1, khr. 436, l. 113; also TFGATO: F. 164, op. 1, khr. 439, l. 30–31.
125 *described Guseva as quite religious* GARF: F. 612, op. 1, d. 31, l. 50.
126 *good or bad, with the peasant* Smirnov, 68.
126 *did not want her brought to trial* Bokhanov, *Rasputin*, 296.
126 *"clinic until she is well"* TFGATO: F. 164, op. 1, khr. 439, l. 104, 116, and 118.
126 *authorities denied the request* TFGATO: F. 164, op. 1, khr. 439, l. 104, 116, and 118. Concerning Guseva's petition, see the report to the court dated December 16, 1914, in TFGATO: F. 164, op. 1, khr. 437, l. l. 246.
127 *"particularly acute fashion"* TFGATO: F. 164, op. 1, khr. 439, l. 125. The report was dated February 24, 1915.
127 *into the pages of history* TFGATO: F. 164, op. 1, khr. 439, l. 126, 128–131, 133; Radziwill, *Rasputin*, 123; Shchegolev, *Padenie*, vol. 3: 233, 245; vol. 6: 219, 224–226; and vol. 7: 331.
127 *"reason to start yelling again"* Tret'iakova, vol. 4: 384.
127 *"how can they help you?"* Ibid.
129 *"he is not here now"* Semennikov, *Dnevnik*, 15–16.
129 *on trial for treason* Vyrubova, 105.
129 *"no matter for a court"* Radzinsky, 294, 296.
129 *"upon you and the Tsarevich"* A. F. Kerensky, *Rossiia na istoricheskom povorote* (Moscow: 1993), 116–117; Smirnov, 69.
129 *"the end of everything"* Vyrubova, 105.
130 *"God Save the Tsar"* Rodzianko, 108–109; Paléologue, vol. 1: 50–52.

13. Disaster Lurks in Moscow

131 *"He was very depressed"* Radzinsky, 297, quoting Molchanov.
132 *"would certainly win the War"* Vyrubova, 172–175.
132 *alert him to potential threats* Shchegolev, *Padenie*, vol. 3: 248.

133 *or the "lovesick creature"* Vyrubova, 346–347; Spiridovich, *Raspoutine*, 89–90; Fuhrmann, *Complete Wartime Correspondence*, AF to N: October 6, 1915.

133 *with the aid of a "stout stick"* Vyrubova, 118–121.

133 *to avoid appearing gullible* Ibid.; Shchegolev, *Padenie*, vol. 3: 65.

133 *"says God will help"* Fuhrmann, *Complete Wartime Correspondence*, AF to N: April 15, 1915, and May 7, 1915.

134 *director rejected their application* Shelley, *Speckled Domes*, 67.

134 *Pokrovskoye to cook and clean* Fuhrmann, *Rasputin*, 117–118.

134 *detectives surrounding Rasputin grew* Fülöp-Muller, 181.

135 *"just as he had received it"* The English visitor was Shelley, *Speckled Domes*, 55. See also Dzhanumovaia, 108–110.

135 *"What a man!"* Korovin, 1–2.

136 *revolutionary (revolyutsioner) was "lyutsoner"* GARF, F. 612, op. 1, d. l. 1–3 and 42. Concerning Rasputin's peculiar spellings, see GARF, F. 612, op. 1, d. 3, l. l. 1 and d. 42, l. l. 1 and 10.

136 *"really did need it"* Mosolov, 153; Anonymous, *Fall*, 51–52; Sliuzberg, vol. 3: 348; Simanovich, 28.

136 *"To his own house"* GARF, F. 612, op. 1, d. 10, l. 1–3.

136 *matter was beyond his jurisdiction* Mosolov, 153.

137 *acting on behalf of a friend* Shchegolev, *Padenie*, vol. 4: 323–324, 356–357; Vasil'ev, 133.

137 *sound to the silver screen* Ranee utro, July 2, 1914, in GARF, F. 612, op. 1, d. 37, list 50.

137 *monthly rent on his apartment* Bokhanov, *Rasputin*, 269.

137 *total of just 5,000 rubles* Spiridovich, *Les dernières années*, vol. 2: 419–421; Katkov, 68–69; Vulliamy, 51–52; Fuhrmann, *Rasputin*, 123.

138 *500 rubles worth of flowers* Shchegolev, *Padenie*, vol. 5: 239; Spiridovich, *Les dernières années*, vol. 2: 419–421; Katkov, 68; Pares, *Fall*, 387.

138 *the entire "affair" was fabricated* The revisionists include Nelipa, 89–92; Platonov, 202–204; and Bokhanov, *Rasputin*, 233–234.

139 *"the Old Girl"* Fuhrmann, *Rasputin*, 120.

139 *"snarling and vowing vengeance"* Report of Colonel Alexander Martynov, Chief of the Moscow Okhrana, June 5, 1915, in GARF as cited in Platonov, 204–205.

139 *the interior and police director* Paléologue, diary entry for April 11/24, 1915, vol. 1: 334–335.

139 *to keep the matter confidential* Shchegolev, *Padenie*, vol. 5: 101.

139 *or slandering the empress* Beletsky in Shchegolev, *Padenie*, vol. 4: 151–152.

139 *although he provided no details* Vasil'ev, 152.

139 *to discredit the Siberian holy man* See Nelipa, 89–91; Bokhanov, *Rasputin*, 232; Platonov, 202–206.

140 *the Yar that fateful evening* Platonov, 202; Bokhanov, *Rasputin*, 233; Nelipa, 90–91.

140 *it was a clumsy forgery* Nelipa, 89–90; Bokhanov, *Rasputin*, 233–234; Platonov, 204.

140 *man who was planning a wild evening* Platonov, 210–212; Nelipa, 90.

140 *restaurants after Guseva's attack* Nelipa, 90.

140 *Petrograd throughout the war* The Okhrana notes Rasputin's presence at the Great Northern Hotel (February 21, 1915); Hotel Astoria (December 1 and 17, 1915); Dondon's Restaurant (December 8, 1915 and January 29, 1916); Hotel Rossiia (December 8, 1915); Villa Rode (December 14 and 15, 1915); Massalsky's Gypsy Chorus (December 14, 1915); and Hotel Europe (January 13, 1916). Also see Vecchi, 68–71, for Rasputin at the Hotel Astoria.

140 *before the worst excesses occurred* Paléologue, diary entry of April 2/15, 1915, vol. 1: 331–332.

140 *evening was* yerunda *("bunkum")* Shelley, *Blue Steppes*, 89–90.

140 *That is simply preposterous* Shelley, *Speckled Domes*, 35–37, 58, 60–67, and *Blue Steppes*, 81–89.
141 *the captain confirmed Rasputin's misbehavior* Nelipa, 90–91; Bokhanov, *Rasputin*, 245; Platonov, 205; Paléologue, vol. 1: 334–335; and Tereshchuk, 389.
141 *"Friends of his Sovereign"* Fuhrmann, *Complete Wartime Correspondence*, AF to N: June 22, 1915.
141 *"Reign of Rasputin" was about to begin* Shchegolev, *Padenie*, vol. 4: 150–151 and vol. 5: 101–106; Pares, *Fall*, 225; Fuhrmann, *Complete Wartime Correspondence*, AF to N: June 22 and September 15, 1915.

14. The Tsar Takes Charge and Loses Control

144 *inspecting troops and visiting hospitals* Fuhrmann, *Complete Wartime Correspondence*, AF to N: September 19, 1914.
144 *beginning of the conflict* Gilliard, 148–149; Marie, *Education*, 194–195.
145 *just before Easter Sunday* On Myasoedov, see Katkov, 119–132. The quote is from Hoare, 54.
145 *working for Russia's defeat* Vecchi, 55, 57, 62–63.
145 *"Lord's anointed for the Germans"* Shelley, *Speckled Domes*, 50–51.
145 *obviously a German front* Shishkin, *Rasputin, Istoriia prestupleniia*, 184–185, 211–212.
146 *information for his German handlers* Shishkin, *Rasputin, Istoriia prestupleniia*, 184–185, 211–212, 216.
147 *if we failed to protect Rasputin* Fuhrmann, *Complete Wartime Correspondence*, AF to N: June 12, 16, and 25, 1915.
148 *at the head of his army* The seven surviving telegrams from Rasputin on this subject are dated August 15–23, 1915; see Tret'iakova, vol. 4: 383–395.
149 *not permit them to resign* Fuhrmann, *Rasputin*, 132–133.
149 *"I absolutely believe it"* Fuhrmann, *Complete Wartime Correspondence*, AF to N: August 22, 1915. Rasputin's telegram of that date is in Tret'iakova, vol. 4: 389.
150 *Rasputin to his bedside* Fuhrmann, *Complete Wartime Correspondence*, AF to N: September 19, 1914.
150 *suffering that he witnessed* Gilliard, 149.
150 *"even attempt to explain the cure"* Vyrubova, 169–170.
150 *returned to Stavka alone* Gilliard, 155–156; Nicholas's diary for December 5–6, 1915, in Maylunas and Mironenko, 444.
151 *"thanks to [Rasputin's] intervention"* Gilliard, 156.
151 *"not to be cut off from behind"* Fuhrmann, *Complete Wartime Correspondence*, AF to N: November 7 and 8, 1915.
151 *"write it to you at once"* Fuhrmann, *Complete Wartime Correspondence*, AF to N: November 15, 1915.
151 *"flour, butter, and sugar"* Fuhrmann, *Complete Wartime Correspondence*, AF to N: October 10, 1915.
152 *police at his disposal* Shchegolev, *Padenie*, vol. 4: 62–63.
152 *"he's in the wrong spot!"* Ibid., vol. 4: 77–78; vol. 2: 67, 439.
152 *most lethal battles in history* Fuhrmann, *Complete Wartime Correspondence*, N to AF: March 9, 1916.
152 *sustained 1.4 million casualties* "Brusilov Offensive," Wikipedia, http://en.Wikipidia.org/wiki/Brusilov, accessed on October 27, 2011.
152 *"His blessing for your decision"* Fuhrmann, *Complete Wartime Correspondence*, AF to N: September 23, 1916.

15. Rasputin Conquers the Russian State

156 *"sweetheart, show your mind"* Fuhrmann, *Complete Wartime Correspondence*, AF to N: March 17, April 4, May 4, and June 14, 1915.

156 *idea would "be Russia's ruin"* Fuhrmann, *Complete Wartime Correspondence*, AF to N: June 14, 17, 25, August 22, and September 7, 1915.

156 *and was ready to lead* Fuhrmann, *Complete Wartime Correspondence*, AF to N: June 10, 16, and August 22, 1915.

156 *"can dominate [and] bridle her"* Narishkin-Kurakin, 203–204.

156 *"when He speaks so seriously"* Fuhrmann, *Complete Wartime Correspondence*, AF to N: June 10, 11, 15, and 17, 1915.

156 *"received it from your father"* Smirnov, 25, 32, 36. The foreign observer is Vecchi, 63. See Rasputin's telegram dated November 25, 1916, in Maylunas and Mironenko, 482.

156 *"ready to understand anything"* Fuhrmann, *Complete Wartime Correspondence*, AF to N: December 5, 1916.

157 *"it wld. be nice"* Fuhrmann, *Complete Wartime Correspondence*, AF to N: January 11, 1916; August 23 and June 14, 1915.

158 *uniform and attend social functions* Fuhrmann, *Rasputin*, 140–147.

158 *soon became an influential figure* Smitten, 12: 98; Mel'gunov, *Legenda*, 407–409; Shchegolev, *Padenie*, vol. 4: 152, 241.

158 *"years of service to him"* Smitten, 12: 96.

159 *"sure of herself, not prudent enough"* Fuhrmann, *Complete Wartime Correspondence*, AF to N: November 3, 1915. See also Smitten, 12: 91, and Shavel'skii, vol. 1: 193–194.

160 *that it would "be good"* Fuhrmann, *Complete Wartime Correspondence*, AF to N: September 11 and 16, 1915.

160 *"eyes had been opened" about "Father Gregory"* Fuhrmann, *Complete Wartime Correspondence*, AF to N: September 17, 1915.

160 *"attacks upon Our Friend"* Fuhrmann, *Complete Wartime Correspondence*, AF to N: September 18, 1915.

160 *"good man and a close ally"* Radzinsky, 390–391.

161 *"shoved it into his pocket"* Radzinsky, 393, citing Beletsky's testimony to the Investigatory Commission in 1917.

162 *"very dry and hard"* Fuhrmann, *Complete Wartime Correspondence*, AF to N: November 10, 11, and 13, 1915.

162 *his wishes finally carried the day* S. V. Kulikov, "Naznachenie Borisa Shtiurmera," reviews the factors that might have made Nicholas hopeful that Sturmer would be a good choice to lead his government.

163 *the tsar to act at once* Fuhrmann, *Complete Wartime Correspondence*, AF to N: January 8 and 9, 1916.

163 *"that doesn't matter. He'll do!"* Shchegolev, *Padenie*, vol. 1: 44; vol. 5: 338–339; Gurko, *Features*, 188; Paléologue, vol. 2: 166.

163 *"they'll toss the old guy out!"* Shchegolev, *Padenie*, vol. 1: 67; vol. 2: 46–51, 78; vol. 4: 396; vol. 5: 162–163; "Aleksandro-nevskaia lavra," 208.

163 *ignored the request* Paléologue, vol. 2: 186–188; Rodzianko, 176–177.

164 *between the prince and the peasant* Beletsky's testimony in Shchegolev, *Padenie*, vol. 3: 169; vol. 4: 241–242; Radzinsky, 404.

165 *"go to save the motherland!"* Shchegolev, *Padenie*, vol. 1: 39; vol. 6: 80.

165 *changed his mind and would not go* Smitten, 2: 105; Shchegolev, *Padenie*, vol. 4: 174–176, 437–439, 448; vol. 6: 80; Radzinsky, 401–402.

165 *he did not commit* Shchegolev, *Padenie*, vol. 1: 43–44, 368, 378; vol. 4: 363–364, 371–374; Simanovich, 93.

166 *annual salary of 18,000 rubles* Witte, *Memoirs*, 441; Shchegolev, *Padenie*, vol. 2: 42; vol. 4: 417–426.

166 *"behave like the Mafia"* Fuhrmann, *Rasputin*, 249, n. 26.

16. The Church at the Feet of a "Low Hound"

167 *number of graves grew daily* Massie, 314–315.

168 *"best representatives of his class"* Lockhart, 129.

168 *"& cant get calm."* Fuhrmann, *Complete Wartime Correspondence*, N to AF: June 15 and 16, 1915.

168 *"put an end to all this"* Curtiss, 387–389.

168 *introduced into Russia by the Germans* Fuhrmann, *Rasputin*, 134–139.

169 *"give Samarin the short order"* Fuhrmann, *Complete Wartime Correspondence*, AF to N, August 29, 1915.

169 *correct that impression* Shavel'skii, vol. 1: 371–372; the tsar's telegram is in Tret'iakova, vol. 4: 388. "Last of its kind" in de Jonge, 273.

170 *"through thunder and lightning"* Fuhrmann, *Complete Wartime Correspondence*, AF to N: September 9 and 10, 1915. For Rasputin's telegram, see Tret'iakova, vol. 4: 391–393.

170 *jealous streak in Nicholas's character* Shchegolev, *Padenie*, vol. 4: 168.

170 *"ober-procurator much longer"* Okhrana Notes, August 5, 1915.

170 *leader of the Holy Synod* Naumov, vol. 2: 306–307, 339.

170 *"Anna Vyrubova, and Rasputin"* Spiridovich, *Velikaia voina*, vol. 1: 247. See also D'iakin in Anan'ich, 615; D'iakin, 625; Rodzianko, 158; Shavel'skii, vol. 1: 373 note; see also Lockhart, 25.

171 *shared critical documents with Rasputin* Shchegolev, *Padenie*, vol. 1: 25, 26; vol. 4: 166, 222–226, 355; vol. 7: 341, 383; Smitten, 2: 104; "Aleksandro-nevskaia lavra," 201. On Skvortsov, see Shchegolev, *Padenie*, vol. 4: 169; vol. 7: 418.

171 *"touched me very much"* Fuhrmann, *Complete Wartime Correspondence*, AF to N: October 6 and 8, 1915; Shchegolev, *Padenie*, vol. 4: 164–165, 168.

171 *on September 26, 1915* Fuhrmann, *Rasputin*, 154.

172 *when he was a young man* Rasputin, *My Father*, 47.

172 *member of Rasputin's circle* Smitten, 2: 105–106, 114; Shchegolev, *Padenie*, vol. 4: 194, and vol. 7: 396; Zhevakov, vol. 1: 125; Shavel'skii, vol. 1: 376; Cunningham, 206–208.

172 *Russian Orthodox Church at that time* Fuhrmann, *Complete Wartime Correspondence*, AF to N: January 7, 1915; Shchegolev, *Padenie*, vol. 7: 396; see also Vyrubova, 192–193.

173 *"your very looks betray you"* Rodzianko, 172–173. See also Shchegolev, *Padenie*, vol. 7: Naumov's interrogation of April 17, 1916.

173 *"marvelous metropolitan in the future"* Fuhrmann, *Complete Wartime Correspondence*, AF to N: September 21, 1916; Shavel'skii, vol. 1: 67.

173 *they greatly amused him* "Aleksandro-nevskaia Lavra," 201, 204–205.

174 *"such a peaceful, harmonious atmosphere"* Concerning Isidor: Shchegolev, *Padenie*, vol. 4: 199; vol. 7: 348–349; Smitten, 2: 110; for Isidor's ties to Rasputin, see Shavel'skii, vol. 1: 67, and Fuhrmann, *Rasputin*, 246–247.

174 *had received from the bishop* Healey, 26, 276. On Palladi and Rasputin, see Shavel'skii, vol. 2: 59–60, 149. I thank Dan Healey for sharing information with me about Palladi, for example I. Sh.[pitsberg], "Delo episkopa Palladiia," *Revoliutsiia i tserkov'*, issue 3–5 (1919): 39–44.

174 *exiled to remote monasteries* Paléologue, vol. 2: 173–174.

174 *before a church commission* Fuhrmann, *Rasputin*, 157–158.

175   *a certain icon to the front*   Fuhrmann, *Complete Wartime Correspondence*, AF to N: October 10, 1915; Shavel'skii, 2: 70–71; Zhevakov, 1: 88–95; de Jonge, 145.

175   *backed away from the appointment*   Fuhrmann, *Complete Wartime Correspondence*, AF to N: November 6, 1915; Beletsky in Shchegolev, *Padenie*, vol. 4: 222–225; Zhevakov, vol. 1: 103–105, 134–128.

175   *be removed from his post*   Zhevakov, vol. 1: 162–163, 190–191.

175   *lead the Holy Synod*   Shavel'skii, vol. 1: 386–387, 391; Zhevakov, vol. 1: 105, 139–141, 164–165; Fuhrmann, *Complete Wartime Correspondence*, AF to N: November 10, 1915, and June 25, 1916.

175   *cooperation with their benefactors*   Fuhrmann, *Rasputin*, 160–161.

176   *"everything concerning our Church"*   Fuhrmann, *Complete Wartime Correspondence*, AF to N: June 25, 1916. On Raev, see Fuhrmann, *Rasputin*, 160–161.

176   *"is a real God's send"*   Fuhrmann, *Complete Wartime Correspondence*, AF to N: September 6, 1916.

176   *"defend the Church" against its own leaders*   Curtiss, 401–403.

176   *Many Russians were depressed*   Paléologue, vol. 2: 222–223.

176   *reeked of "carbon monoxide"*   Zhevakov, vol. 1: 162–163, 190–191.

176   *"a sort of nasty joy"*   Shul'gin, 281.

17. "Our Friend's Ideas about Men Are Sometimes Queer"

177   *agreed, and it was done*   Shchegolev, *Padenie*, vol. 2: 50; "Aleksandro-nevskaia lavra" 77(4) (1936): 207.

177   *"history of civilized nations"*   Florinsky, 64, 86–90.

178   *improving their legal rights*   Zaslavskii, 19–23.

179   *six months during the war*   Semennikov, *Za kulisami*, iv, ix–x, xxxiii–xxxiv; Mel'gunov, *Legenda*, 229; Smitten, 1: 108; Shchegolev, *Padenie*, vol. 1: 115.

180   *to be left alone*   Fuhrmann, *Russia*, 250.

180   *"Our Friend's wisdom & guidance"*   Fuhrmann, *Complete Wartime Correspondence*, AF to N: September 7, 1916.

180   *Protopopov as minister of the interior*   Shchegolev, *Padenie*, vol. 1: 65–71; vol. 4: 14.

180   *"also into the administration"*   Fuhrmann, *Complete Wartime Correspondence*, N to AF: September 9, 1916.

180   *"& shut their mouths"*   Ibid.

180   *"It shall be done," her husband cabled tersely*   Fuhrmann, *Complete Wartime Correspondence*, N to AF: September 10, 1916.

180   *"wise act in naming him"*   Fuhrmann, *Complete Wartime Correspondence*, AF to N: September 14, 1916.

181   *that permitted him to function*   Zaslavskii, 37–38, 49–54, 56–57; Shchegolev, *Padenie*, vol. 4: 6, 56–57, 75; vol. 7: 364.

181   *fired Sturmer on November 9, 1916*   Fuhrmann, *Complete Wartime Correspondence*, N to AF: November 8, 1916.

181   *"did not ask his advice"*   Fuhrmann, *Complete Wartime Correspondence*, AF to N: November 1, 1915.

181   *the empress and Rasputin*   Ulam, 272; Florinsky, 111.

181   *this would infuriate Alexandra*   Pares, *Fall*, 393–394.

181   *"free to choose accordingly"*   Fuhrmann, *Complete Wartime Correspondence*, N to AF: November 10, 1916; Pares, *Fall*, 393–394.

182   *"a serious, personal quarrel"*   Fuhrmann, *Complete Wartime Correspondence*, N to AF: December 4, 1916; Massie, 363.

182   *"Let reason come to you," Rasputin implored*   Telegram dated November 20, 1916, in Bokhanov, *Rasputin*, 346.

182 *"kept you where you are"* Fuhrmann, *Complete Wartime Correspondence*, AF to N: December 16, 1916.

183 *after forty-seven days in office* Paléologue, vol. 3: 107–108; Mosolov, 168–173; Shchegolev, *Padenie*, vol. 4: 15–16, 30.

18. Shadows Come at Twilight

185 *"a man, like all the others?"* Rasputin, *My Father*, 88; Rasputin and Barham, *Rasputin*, 203–211.

186 *drinking and eating, singing and dancing* Okhrana Notes: *Krasnyi Arkhiv* for December 1, 8, 14, 15, 17, 1915; January 13 and 15, 1915; and January 29, 1915.

186 *"being connected with Rasputin"* Vecchi, 68–71.

186 *"totally overcome with drink"* Vulliamy, 30, 43–45, 46, 48.

187 *"stomping" about his apartment* Ibid., 30, 44, 46.

187 *"far too much these days"* Okhrana Notes: *Krasnyi Arkhiv* for April 27, 1915.

187 *talk that way about the imperial Family* Shchegolev, *Padenie*, vol. 1: 251; vol. 2: 70–71; de Jonge, 271–272.

187 *asked her to return the next day* Okhrana Notes: *Krasnyi Arkhiv* for October 22, November 3 and 6, December 3, 1915; January 29, 1916; Shchegolev, *Padenie*, vol. 7: 151–152.

188 *until a servant intervened* Vulliamy, 25–28, 30, 43–48; Shchegolev, *Padenie*, vol. 7: 151–152; Dzhanumovaia, 101.

188 *"young-looking body—and that's all"* Radzinsky, 265, 266.

188 *"He seldom appears on the street alone"* Ibid., chap. 7.

189 *"Little fool!"* Ibid., 236–237.

190 *"attracting the attention of passers-by"* Ibid., 184.

190 *with other women in silence* Okhrana Notes: *Krasnyi Arkhiv* for June 24, July 7, 9, 11, 13, 20, and July 20, 1915.

190 *injuring his son's hip* Vulliamy, 40–41; Fuhrmann, *Rasputin*, 127.

190 *"same relationship to women"* Shchegolev, *Padenie*, vol. 4: 324–325.

190 *would ever see her son again* Fuhrmann, *Complete Wartime Correspondence*, AF to N: August 28, 1915; Dehn, 111.

191 *"when he was away"* Fuhrmann, *Complete Wartime Correspondence*, AF to N: September 1, 1915.

191 *would survive life at the front* Radzinsky, 379.

191 *"they were always beaten"* Knox, *With the Russian Army*, 350, as cited in Vulliamy, 86.

191 *"winter awaits us soon"* Fuhrmann, *Complete Wartime Correspondence*, AF to N: September 11, 1915, quotation slightly revised.

192 *the infamous Gregory Rasputin* Telitsyn, 21–22; Platonov, 16; for Shishkina's memoirs, see Smirnov, 18–20.

193 *"all the revolutionary propaganda combined"* Vecchi, 63; Gurko, *Features*, 10 and 569; Paléologue, vol. 2: 265; D'iakin, 246; see also Fuhrmann, *Complete Wartime Correspondence*, AF to N: January 7, 1916.

193 *there was no retraction* The article in *Sibirskaia torgovaia gazeta* was dated September 4, 1915; see Kulikowski, 56, 134, 141. Rasputin's telegram (dated September 2, 1915) is in Tret'iakova, vol. 4: 388.

194 *Iliodor's former power base* Fuhrmann, *Rasputin*, 192; Bokhanov, *Rasputin*, 346–347; Hoare, 113, 140, 158.

194 *"They'll kill Papa and Mama also"* Paléologue, vol. 2: 240, quotation slightly revised; Dehn, 108; Blok, 6.

194 *threatening names as "The Avenger"* Police report dated September 25, 1914, in TFGATO, F. 164, op. 1, d. 439, l. 55–56.

194 *"The die has been cast"* Anonymous letter in Okhrana Notes: *Krasnyi Arkhiv* for September 19, 1915; Radzinsky, 384.

194 *"end's coming soon?" he asked* Teffi, 290; the follower was Vera Zhukovskaya as quoted by Radzinsky, 472.

195 *"you to bless me, not I you"* Fuhrmann, *Rasputin*, 193; Fuhrmann, *Complete Wartime Correspondence*, AF to N: January 7, 1916.

19. The Assassin

198 *killed her lover in a duel* See Gretchen Haskin, "His Brother's Keeper," *Atlantis*, 2, nos. 3 and 4, 2000.

198 *fabulous collection of diamonds* For the Yusupov family history, see Felix Yusupov's autobiography, *Lost Splendor.*

200 *the man who threatened Russia* de Jonge, 308; Yusupov, *Lost Splendor*, 183–185.

200 *between Alexandra and Rasputin* Yusupov, *Lost Splendor*, 56–68.

200 *make him the "Savior of Russia"* Bokhanov, *Rasputin*, 353–354.

200 *high degree of respect for him* Kotsiubinskii, 225; Figes, 189; Nelipa, 102–106; Cockfield, 179, does not agree with this theory.

201 *masterminded the murder* See Cockfield, 174–178.

201 *to take Rasputin's place* Yusupov, *Rasputin*, 118–121, and *Lost Splendor*, 60–66; also Mel'gunov, *Legenda*, 369; Spiridovich, *Raspoutine*, 200.

202 *"a good constitutional monarch"* Bokhanov, *Rasputin*, 359.

202 *Alexandra and her peasant "friend" were destroying Russia* The letter from Dmitry Pavlovich to Yusupov dated April 23, 1917, appears in "K istorii poslednikh dnei tsarskogo rezhima (1916–1917 gg.)," *Krasnyi Arkhiv* 14 (1926): 247–249.

202 *"hanged as a political criminal"* Letter of Dmitry Pavlovich to Felix Yusupov, dated February 17, 1920; Dr. Will Lee owns this and other important documents, and I thank him for sharing them with me. See also Pares, *Fall*, 402.

203 *"open his eyes to the terrible reality!"* Kalpashchnikoff, 179–184.

203 *some "uncontrollable emotion"* Eddy, 161–163; Paléologue, vol. 3: 153.

203 *agreed to join Yusupov's conspiracy* Purishkevich, *Murder of Rasputin*, 11–13.

203 *dignity of his aristocratic colleagues* Cook, 295n; Bokhanov, *Rasputin*, 395, 409; also see the unsigned article on "Sergei Sukhotin" in *La Russie Ilustree* 14 (April 2, 1932): 15.

203 *included the Saint George Cross* I thank Dr. Will Lee for sharing the letters of "Stanislas de Lazovert" dated August 4 and 5, 1918. The information is from the Public Record Office in Kew, England, F.O. 371 3338. See also Kalpashchnikoff, 179–184.

204 *promise to return, and soon* Yusupov, *Rasputin*, 75–80, 103–105; the quotations are slightly revised according to the Russian text in Tret'iakova, vol. 4: 103–214.

204 *found Rasputin to be sexually attractive* Bokhanov, *Rasputin*, 357; Rasputin and Barham, 213–218.

205 *"drove me away like a dog!" Ella cried* Yusupov, *Rasputin*, 53–55, 126.

205 *erased Yusupov's lingering doubts* Bokhanov, *Rasputin*, 349–350; Vulliamy, 101, 104–113.

205 *moved toward their final preparations* Yusupov, *Rasputin*, 121–123; Purishkevich, *Murder of Rasputin*, 17–23.

205 *Nicholas II and his family* Yusupov, *Rasputin*, 121, 122; Mel'gunov, *Legenda*, 367.

20. Murder at the Palace

207 *Madeira throughout the day* Fuhrmann, *Complete Wartime Correspondence*, AF to N: December 16, 1916; Simanovich, 161; Shchegolev, *Padenie*, vol. 4: 505; de Jonge, 319–320.

207 *"the hour of our death"*   GARF, F. 612, op. 1, d. 34, l. 50.

208 *dismissed it from their thoughts*   Spiridovich, *Raspoutine*, 375.

208 *"hidden from mortal eyes"*   Yusupov, *Rasputin*, 131–135, 137, revised in light of the Russian text in Tret'iakova, vol. 4: 39–102 and 103–214; see also Solov'ev, 21.

208 *their grand encounter with destiny*   Purishkevich, *Murder of Rasputin*, 22, and Yusupov, *Rasputin*, 131–135, 137.

209 *whatever the night would bring*   Rasputin and Barham, *Rasputin*, 12–13.

211 *returned to the prince's study*   Yusupov, *Konets Rasputina*, 174–178; Purishkevich, *Murder of Rasputin*, 85–87.

211 *in a low, guttural voice*   Yusupov, *Rasputin*, 156.

211 *middle of Rasputin's forehead*   Yusupov, *Rasputin*, 143–160; Purishkevich, *Dnevnik*, 69–79, 91–95.

212 *staircase that led to the cellar*   Purishkevich, *Dnevnik*, 79–83; Yusupov, *Rasputin*, 157–159; Spiridovich, *Raspoutine*, 383.

213 *carried away to his bedroom*   The Russian term for Yusupov's weapon was *rezinovaia palka*, a stick or staff covered in Indian rubber. See Purishkevich, *Dnevnik*, 79–83; Yusupov, *Rasputin*, 157–159, 162–163, and *Konets Rasputina*, 183–184.

213 *"sleeping as in a dead sleep"*   Purishkevich, *Murder of Rasputin*, 84–94; Yusupov, *Rasputin*, 159–163;. Purishkevich writes, "No one noticed us when we returned." This would suggest that at least one other person was with him; yet he seems to have been alone when he returned to his famous train that was scheduled to leave for the front the following day with books, food, clothing, medicine, and supplies for the Russian troops.

21. The Aftermath

215 *had vanished*   Rasputin, *My Father*, 13; Vyrubova, 179–180; Hoare, 152; Pereverzev, "Ubiistvo Rasputina," contains police reports of the investigation.

215 *"with me and my party!"*   Yusupov, *Rasputin*, 165; Purishkevich, *Murder of Rasputin*, 93, 94, 96; Vyrubova, 180–81; "K istorii ubiistva Grigoriia Rasputina," *KA*, vol. 4 (1923): 424–426.

216 *and the police left*   Yusupov, *Rasputin*, 173; Pereverzev, "Ubiistvo Rasputina," 66–68.

216 *"let him write it to me"*   Vyrubova, 180. See Voeikov, 14–16, for Yusupov's letter to Alexandra, dated December 17, 1916.

216 *statement from Yusupov into his diary*   Yusupov, *Rasputin*, 184–85. See Nelipa, 124–127, for her understanding of this meeting. See also Nicholas Michaelovich's Diary in *KA*, "Podrobnosti ubiistva Rasputina," vol. 49 (1931): 98–100.

216 *placed under house arrest*   Yusupov, *Rasputin*, 180–182.

216 *"anguished and horrified"*   Fuhrmann, *Complete Wartime Correspondence*, N to AF: December 18, 1916.

217 *"in the center of Petrograd"*   Katkov, 426; Hoare, 137–144; Hanbury-Williams, 145–146; Mel'gunov, *Legenda*, 372.

217 *river's icy embrace*   "Kak nashli trup Rasputin," *Birzh. ved.*, December 20, 1916, in GARF, F. 612, op. 1, d. 39, l. 52; see also "Ubiistvo Rasputina," *Byloe* 1, no. 23 (July 1917); Spiridovich, *Raspoutine*, 398; "K istorii ubiistva Grigoriia Rasputina," *KA* 4 (1923): 424–426; Pereverzev, "Ubiistvo Rasputina," 68–81.

218 *awaiting the autopsy*   *Den* (Petrograd), 350 (December 20, 1916), 2.

218 *"[that's why] they killed him"*   See Fuhrmann, *Rasputin*, 209 with references, also Hoare's report (dated January 1, 1917/N.S.) in *Fourth Seal*, 113, 146.

219 *photographs associated with it have survived*   Andrew Cook, 70–72, reproduces "the autopsy," as does Cullen, 150–152. Cook claims that the autopsy is in the Museum of Political History in Saint Petersburg.

219 *Kosorotov's original interview* Nelipa, 7, 372–378.

219 *scene continued for four hours* Hoare, 153–154; Zharov et al., in Cullen, appendix 2, 214–226.

220 *"on my experienced eyes"* For an excellent account of the interview, the autopsy, and its background, see Shishkin, *Rasputin, Istoriia prestupleniia*, 50, 54–55.

221 *as to the guns used* Prosecutor Zadavsky, quoting Prosecutor Serada; see Nelipa, 381.

221 *weapons or their calibers* Zharov et al. in Cullen, appendix 2, 214–226.

222 *for burial the next morning* Shchegolev, *Padenie*, vol. 4: 106, 198–199, 480, 502–503, 505; Dorr, 116; Simanovich, 169; A. V. Romanov, 189.

222 *any say in the matter* Shchegolev, *Padenie*, vol. 4: 480; Semennikov (ed.), *Dnevik A. V. Romanov*, 188; Shavel'skii, vol. 2: 251.

222 *time years later* Rasputin, *My Father*, 17, and *Real Rasputin*, 149.

223 *"at the home of Yusupov"* Dehn, 122–124; Rasputin, *My Father*, 17, and *Real Rasputin*, 149; Shchegolev, *Padenie*, vol. 4: 107, 480; 3: 62; Voeikov, 178–182; Vyrubova, 182–183; Nicholas II, *Journal Intime*, 73.

223 *"assassins of Stolypin were hanged"* Vyrubova, 82; de Jonge, 335.

223 *in death, Rasputin destroyed it* Marie, *Education*, 260, 267, 282; Shchegolev, *Padenie*, vol. 4: 232.

224 *"your crown in six months"* Paléologue, vol. 3: 191; Simanovich, 171–172.

22. Who *Really* Killed Rasputin?

225 *man who had the power to resist death* See Nelipa, 389.

226 *"lethal poisoning affected Rasputin"* Zharov's Review in Cullen, appendix 2.

226 *present when Rasputin was murdered* See Stopford, *Russian Diary*, 83, and appendixes 2 and 3.

226 *was Rasputin's missing member* Rasputin and Barham, *Rasputin*, 213–218. For Thespé, see Serge Obolensky, *One Man in His Time* (1958), 229–230.

226 *its intelligence mission in Petrograd* Hoare, 28–34.

227 *as a communications censor* Yusupov, *Rasputin*, 180; Cook, 81–87, 89–92, 148–150.

227 *help their nation achieve victory* Cook, 163–164.

227 *Scale's daughter insisted* Rayner and Harding-Newman.

227 *late October to mid-November 1916* Cook, 164, 227.

227 *"anxious on my behalf"* Yusupov, *Rasputin*, 180.

227 *were behind the deed* Nicholas Michaelovich to Frederic Masson, February 7 (O.S.), 1917; I thank Dr. Will Lee for sharing this information with me from his private files.

227 *British complicity in the murder* See Nelipa, 124–127, 202.

228 *"Yours, Stephen Alley, Capt."* Cook, 228.

229 *"not a word of truth" to them* Buchanan, vol. 2: 51; Hoare, 156–157.

229 *fired the fatal shot* Cook, 148–150; Cullen, ix, 195–200; see also Nelipa, 197.

229 *.455 English Webley revolver* Cook, 214, 223–224.

230 *as the (unwelcome) visitor left* See Yusupov, *Rasputin*, chap. 17.

230 *used to render Yusupov's name* Cook, 165, 236–237.

230 *Yusupov, incidentally, had a similar ring* Cook, 165, 231.

230 *"away with the Tsar somewhere"* Rayner and Harding-Newman; this program cited Rayner's obituary, which appeared in the *Duneaton Observer*, March 25, 1961. See also Cook, 163–164.

Epilogue

233 *"nearer than ever to us"* Maria Rasputin, "Moi otets," 10; *Real Rasputin*, 150–51, 157–162; *My Father*, 114.

233 *this was impossible* Shchegolev, *Padenie*, vol. 4: 10, 483–484.

233 *steal valuable objects*   Bokhanov, *Rasputin*, 45.

234 *through it after his death*   TFGATO, F. 154, op. 24, khr. 58, l. 1–29; also see the many valuable newspaper articles in GARF, F. 612, op. 1, d. 43.

234 *estate to 23,507 rubles and 66 kopecks*   TFGATO, F. 154, op. 24, khr. 58, l. 9 and 29.

235 *leaving Praskovaya and Varvara alone*   Bokhanov, *Rasputin*, 25–26; Rasputin, *Real Rasputin*, 182–183; Massie, 464–467; Simanovich, 201–204.

235 *the furniture, mirrors, and dishes*   Bokhanov, *Rasputin*, 45.

235 *charity until her death in 1936*   Concerning Dmitry Rasputin: Smirnov, 90; on Praskovaya's fate: Nelipa, 565–566.

235 *died mysteriously of poison in 1924 or 1925*   Rasputin, *My Father*, 89; GATO, F. 198, op. 1, d. 67; Simanovich, 205.

236 *"Watergate of Russia"*   Her obituary is in *Newsweek*, October 10, 1977. See also King, 232–233.

236 *"living or dead is purely coincidental"*   King, 240–241.

237 *Alexander Blok and Valery Bryusov*   See Rudnev, 393, 394, and Gippius, 169.

237 *"sworn to serve," the tsar*   Vorres, 142.

237 *in crisis than to weaken it*   Vorres, 142; Hoare, 135–136, 159–160.

238 *his penis with a brick*   Bokhanov, *Rasputin*, 27; Shklovskii, 225; Long, 31.

239 *disappeared into the night*   Bokhanov, *Rasputin*, 29.

239 *"the matter of Rasputin's body"*   Ibid., 29–33.

239 *"humble participants in this event"*   Ibid., 32–33.

240 *"face of the Russian land"*   Ibid. On the cremation, see *Ogonek* 52 (1926), 3–4, and 1 (1927), 11–12; also *Solntse Rossii* 369 (1917): 11.

Bibliography

Archives

GARF: Gosudarstvennyi Arkhiv Rossiiskoi Federatsii. Fond (section) 612, opis' 1, is the record group devoted to Rasputin; dela [folders] 1 to 51. "List," "listy" (page, pages), refers to the page numbers of the individual folders. The correspondence between Nicholas II and the Empress Alexandra is in Fond 640, opis' 1. See Fuhrmann, *Complete Wartime Correspondence*, 8–10, for details.

GATO: Gosudarstvennyi Arkhiv Tiumenskoi Oblasti. Fond I-177, opis' 1, and Fond I-239, opis' 1, are the record groups devoted to Rasputin.

TFGATO: Tobol'skii Filial'nyi Gosudarstvennyi Arkhiv Tiumenskoi Oblasti. Fond 156, opis' 28, and Fond 164, opis' 1, are the record groups devoted to Rasputin.

Published Sources

AF to N: letter or telegram from the Empress Alexandra Fedorovna to her husband, the Emperor Nicholas II. See Joseph T. Fuhrmann (ed.), *Complete Wartime Correspondence*, listed below.

"Aleksandro-nevskaia lavra nakanune sverzhennia samoderzhaviia." *Krasnyi Arkhiv* 77 (1936): 200–211.

Fuhrmann, Joseph T., ed. *The Complete Wartime Correspondence of Tsar Nicholas II and the Empress Alexandra, April 1914–March 1917*. Westport, CT: Greenwood, 1999. AF to N are letters and telegrams from Alexandra Fedorovna to Nicholas II; N to AF are letters and telegrams from Nicholas II to Alexandra Fedorovna.

Hynes, A. L., trans. Commentary by C. E. Vulliamy. *Letters of the Tsar to the Tsaritsa, 1914–1917*. London: The Bodley Head, 1929.

——, trans. Commentary by C. E. Vulliamy. *Letters of the Tsaritsa to the Tsar, 1914–1916*. London: Duckworth, 1923.

Kleinpenning, Petra H., ed. *The Correspondence of the Empress Alexandra of Russia with Ernst Ludwig and Eleonore, Grand Duke and Duchess of Hesse, 1878–1916*. Norderstedt, Germany: Books on Demand, 2010.

Kulikov, S. V., ed. "'Uspokoeniia nichego ozhidat',' pis'ma kniazia M. M. Andronikova Nikolaiu II, Aleksandre Fedorovnai, A. A. Vyrubovoi i V. N. Voeikovu" ("'Tranquility Is Never to Be Expected': The Letters of Prince M. M. Andronikov to Nicholas II, Alexandra Fedorovna, A. A. Vyrubova and V. N. Voeikov"), *Istochnik (The Source)* 1 (1999): 24–44.

Maylunas, Andrei, and Sergei Mironenko. *A Lifelong Passion: Nicholas and Alexandra, Their Own Story*. Translated by Darya Galy. New York: Doubleday, 1997.

Nicholas II (Romanov). *Dnevnik Imperatora Nikolaia Vtorogo*. Berlin: Slovo, 1923.
————. *Journal Intime de Nicholas II*. Translated by A. Pierre. Paris: Payot, 1925.
————. *The Secret Letters of the Last Tsar, Being the Confidential Correspondence between Nicholas II and His Mother, Dowager Empress Maria Fedorovna*. Edited by Edward J. Bing. New York: Longmans, Green, 1938. The tsar's early diary is in *Krasnyi Arkhiv* 4, 6, 9 (1931), its contents from December 16, 1916, to June 30, 1918, are in *Krasnyi Arkhiv* 1–3 (1927) and 2 (1928).
N to AF: letter or telegram from the Emperor Nicholas II to his wife, the Empress Alexandra Fedorovna. See Joseph T. Fuhrmann (ed.), *Complete Wartime Correspondence*, listed above.
Rasputin, Grigori. "Life of an Experienced Pilgrim." In Iliodor, *The Mad Monk of Russia, Iliodor: Life, Memoirs, and Confessions of Sergei Michailovich Trufanoff (Iliodor)*, pp. 154–164. New York: Century, 1918. Reprinted in V. Tret'iakova, *Grigory Rasputin*, vol. 4, pp. 351–364.
————. "Moi mysli i razmyshleniia. Kratkoe opisanie puteshestviia po sviatym mestam i vyzvannye im razmyshleniia po religioznym voprosam." First published in V. P. Semennikov, *Za kulisami tsarizma*, pp. 142–160. Also see Maria Rasputin, *My Father*, as "My Thoughts and Meditations," and V. Tret'iakova, *Grigory Rasputin*, vol. 4, pp. 365–382.
————. "Velikie dni torzhestva v Kieve! Poseshchenie vysochaishei semi! Angel'skii privet!" Reprinted as Appendix XIV to V. P. Obninsk, *Poslednyi samoderzhets. Ocherk zhizni i tsarstvovaniia imperatora Rossii Nikolaia II*. Berlin, n.d.
Sergeev, A. A., trans. and ed., *Perepiska Nikolaia i Aleksandry Romanovykh*, vols. 3, 4, 5 covering 1914–1917 (Moscow, Petrograd, and Leningrad, 1923, 1926, 1927).
Shchegolev, P. E., ed. *Padenie tsarskogo rezhima: Stenografisheskie otchety doprosov i pokazanii, dannikh v 1917 g. v Chrezvychainoi Sledsvennoi Komissii Vremennogo Pravitel'stva*. 7 vols. Moscow and Leningrad: 1924–1927.
Smitten, B. N. "Poslednyi vremenshchik poslednago tsaria. (Materialy Chrezvychainoi Sledstvennoi Komissii Vremennogo Pravitelstva o Rasputine i razlozhenii samoderzhaviia)." Edited by A. L. Sidorov and published in four parts in *Voprosy istorii* 10 (1964): 117–135; 12 (1964): 90–103; 1 (1965): 98–110; 2 (1965): 103–21.
Stremoukhov, P. P. "Moia bor'ba s episkopom Germogenom i Iliodorom." *Arkhiv Russkoi Revoliutsii* 16 (1925): 5–48.
Tooke, William. *View of the Russian Empire during the Reign of Catherine the Second* (London, 2nd ed., 1800), vol. 1.
Tret'iakova, V., ed. *Grigory Rasputin: Sbornik istoricheskikh materialov* in four volumes. Moscow: Terra, 1997. Contains Rasputin's telegrams: "Kopii telegram i pisem G. E. Rasputina tsarskoi sem'e," vol. 4: pp. 383–395.
Vinogradoff, Igor. "Nicholas II, Stolypin, and Rasputin: Letter of 16 October 1906." *Oxford Slavonic Papers* 12 (1965): 115–116.
Vulliamy, C. E., ed. *Red Archives: Russian State Papers and Other Documents relating to the Years 1915–1918*. Translated by A. L. Hynes. London: Geoffrey Bles, 1929. Contains "Letters [of the Yusupov family] relating to the Last Days of the Tsarist Regime," 98–130, and "Rasputin as Known to the Secret Police (Okhrana)," 21–56.

Memoirs

Alexander (Alexander Michaelovich Romanov). *Once a Grand Duke*. Garden City, NY: Garden City, 1932.
Beletsky, S. P. *Grigory Rasputin (iz zapisok)*. In *Ubit' Rasputina*, O. A. Shishkin, pp. 217–342. See V. Tret'iakova, vol. 1, pp. 127–222, and V. S. Brachev, "S. P. Beletskii i ego 'Zapiski,'" in *Ubit' Rasputina*, O. A. Shishkin, pp. 349–374.

———. "Vospominaniia." *Arkhiv Russkoi Revoliutsii* 12 (1923): 5–75; reprint of "Grigory Rasputin: iz vospominanii." *Byloe* 20 (1922): 194–222, and 21 (1921): 237–269.

Bogdanovich, (Madame) A. V. *Journal de la générala A. V. Bogdanovich.* Translated by M. Lefebvre. Paris: Payot, 1926.

Botkin, Gleb. *The Real Romanovs.* New York: Revell, 1931.

Buchanan, Sir George. *My Mission to Russia, and Other Diplomatic Memories.* Boston: Little, Brown, 1923.

Bulgakov, Sergei. *Aftobiograficheskii zametki.* Paris: YMCA Press, 1946.

Buxhoeveden, Sophie. *Before the Storm.* London: Macmillan, 1938.

Cantacuzène, Princess. *Revolutionary Days, Recollections of Romanoffs and Bolsheviki, 1914–1917.* New York: Scribner's, 1926.

Coppens, Philip. "The Master: Philippe de Lyon." http://www.philipcoppens.com/philippe-delyon.html.

de Basily, Nicholas. *Memoirs.* Stanford, CA: Stanford University Press, 1973.

de Schelking, Eugene. *Recollections of a Russian Diplomat.* New York: Macmillan, 1918.

Damer, Aleksandr. "Rasputin vo dvorets, Vospominaniia pridvornago skorokhoda." *Illiustrirovannaia Rossiia* 16 (April 16, 1932): 7–8.

Dehn, Lili. *The Real Tsaritsa.* Boston: Little, Brown, 1932.

Dorr, Rheta Childe. *Inside the Russian Revolution.* New York: Macmillan, 1917.

Dzhanumovaia, Elena F. "Moi vstrechi s Grigoriem Rasputinym." *Russkoe proshloe* 4 (1923): 97–116.

Evlogii, Georg'evskii. *Put' moei zhizni, vospominaniia mitropolita Evlogiia.* Paris: YMCA, 1947.

Fabritskii, S. S. *Iz proshlago: Vospominaniia fligel'-ad'iutanta gosudaria imperatora Nikoliaia II-go.* Berlin, 1926.

Francis, David R. *Russia from the American Embassy.* New York: Scribner's, 1921.

Gilliard, Pierre. *Thirteen Years at the Russian Court.* Translated by F. Appleby Holt. New York: Doran, 1921.

Gippius, Zinaida. *Zhiviia litsa, Blok, Briusov, Vyrubova, Rozanov, Sologub, o mnogikh.* 2 vols. Prague, 1925.

Graham, Stephen. *With the Russian Pilgrims to Jerusalem.* London: Macmillan, 1914.

Hoare, Sir Samuel. *The Fourth Seal: The End of a Russian Chapter.* London: Heinemann, 1930.

Kalpaschikoff, Andrew. *A Prisoner of Trotsky's.* Garden City, NY: Doubleday, Page, 1920.

Kerensky, Alexander. *Road to the Tragedy,* published in the same volume with Captain Paul Bulygin, *The Murder of the Romanovs: The Authentic Account.* Translated by Gleb Kerensky. New York: McBride, 1935.

Kokovtsov, Count Vladimir Nikolaevich. *Iz Moego Proshlago.* Paris: Council on Foreign Relations, 1933.

———. *Out of My Past: The Memoirs of Count Kokovtsov.* Edited by H. H. Fisher. Translated by Laura Matveev. Stanford: Oxford University Press, 1935. A useful abridgement of his two-volume *Iz Moego Proshlago.*

Korostovetz, Vladimir. *Seed and Harvest.* Translated by Dorothy Lumby. London: Faber and Faber, 1931.

Korovin, Konstantin. "Svyataya Rus', Vospominaniia." *Illiustrirovannaia Rossiia* (April 2, 1932).

Kurlov, P. G. *Konets russkogo tsarizma.* Moscow and Petrograd, 1923.

Lazovert, Stanislaus. An account of Rasputin's assassination in Charles F. Horne and Walter F. Austin, eds. *Source Records of the Great War,* in 7 vols. Alabama: National Alumni, 1923; vol. 5, pp. 86–88. This is obviously a bogus document.

——. Letters of "Stanislaus de Lazovert" dated August 4 and 5, 1918. Public Record Office, Kew, Great Britain, F.O. 371 3338.

Lockhart, Robert Bruce. *The Diaries of Sir Robert Bruce Lockhart*, Volume I: 1915–1938. Edited by Kenneth Young. London: Macmillan, 1973.

Lukhomskii, A. S. "Izvospominanii." *Arkhiv Russkoi Revoliutsii* 2 (1921): 14–44; 3 (1921): 247–270; 5 (1922): 101–190; 6 (1922): 81–160; appeared in English as *Memoirs of the Russian Revolution*. Translated by Mrs. Vitali. London: Unwin, 1922.

Marie, Grand Duchess of Russia (Maria Pavlovna Romanova). *Education of a Princess: A Memoir*. Translated under editorial supervision of Russell Lord. New York: Viking, 1931.

Marie, Queen of Romania. *The Story of My Life*. New York: Charles Scribner's Sons, 1934.

Mel'gunov, S. "Kak my priobretali zapiski Iliodora." *Na chuzoi storone* 2 (1923): 47–56.

Milyukov, Paul. *Political Memoirs, 1905–1917*. Translated by Carl Goldberg and edited by Arthur P. Mendel. Ann Arbor: Michigan, 1967.

Mosolov (Mossolov), A. A. *At the Court of the Last Tsar.* Edited by A. A. Pilenco. Translated by E. W. Dickes. London: Methuen, 1935.

Narishkin-Kurakin, Elizabeth. *Under Three Tsars.* Edited by René Fülöp-Miller. Translated by Julia E. Loesser. New York: Dutton, 1931.

Naumov, A. N. *Iz utselevshikh vospominanii, 1868–1917 gg.* 2 vols. New York, 1954, 1955.

Nekliudov (Nekludoff), Anatoli Vasilievich, *Diplomatic Reminiscences before and during the World War, 1911–1917*. Translated by Alexandra Paget. London: Murray, 1920.

Nikon (Rklitskii). *Zhizneopisanie blazheineishago Antoniia, mitropolita Kievskago i Galitskago*, 10 vols. New York: Russian Printing House, 1956–1963. A biography of Bishop Antony Krapovitskii, one of Rasputin's fiercest enemies. This massive work contains valuable information about Rasputin, only a portion of which is noted in the index.

Paléologue, Maurice. *An Ambassador's Memoirs*. 3 vols. Translated by F. A. Holt. New York: Hippocrene, 1925.

Purishkevich, V. M. *The Murder of Rasputin*. Edited by Michael E. Shaw. Translated by Bella Costello. Ann Arbor: Ardis, 1985.

Rasputin, Maria. "Moi otets, Grigory Rasputin." *Illiustrirovannaia Rossiia* 13 (March 26, 1932): 8–10.

——. *My Father*. London: Cassell, 1934.

——. *The Real Rasputin*. Translated by Arthur Chambers. London: Long, 1929.

Rasputin, Maria, and Patte Barham. *Rasputin: The Man behind the Myth*. Englewood Cliffs, NJ: Prentice-Hall, 1977.

Rasputina, Matrena. *Rasputin. Pochemu?* Moscow: Zakharov, 2000.

Rodzianko, M. V. *Reign of Rasputin: An Empire's Collapse*. Translated by Catherine Zvegintzoff. London: Philpot, 1927.

Shakhovskoi, Prince Vsevolod. *Sic Transit Gloria Mundi (Tak prokhodit mirskaia slava)*, 1893–1917. Paris: Privately published, 1952.

Shavel'skii, Georgy. *Vospominaniia poslednago protopresvitera russkoi armii i flota*. New York: Chekhov, 1954.

Shulgin, V. V. *The Years: Memoirs of a Member of the Russian Duma, 1906–1917*. Translated by Tanya Davis. New York: Hippocrene Books, 1984.

Simanovich, Aron. *Rasputin i evrei; vospominaniia lichnago sekretaria Grigoriia Rasputina*. Riga: n.d. Also in V. Tret'iakova, vol. 2: 351–478.

Sliuzberg, Genrikh Borisovich. *Dela minuvshikh dnei, zapiski russkago evreiia.* 3 vols. Paris: 1934.

Stopford, Albert. *Russian Diary of an Englishman*. London: Heinemann, 1919. Originally published as "Anonymous."

Teffi, N. A. (Nadezhda Aleksandrovna Buchinskaia) (Lokhvitskaia). *Vospominaniia*. Paris: Vozrozhdenie, 1931.

Tret'iakova, V., ed. *Grigory Rasputin: Sbornik istoricheskikh meterialov* in four volumes. Moscow: Terra, 1997.

Trewin, J. C. *House of Special Purpose: An Intimate Portrait of the Last Days of the Russian Imperial Family Compiled from the Papers of Their English Tutor, Charles Sydney Gibbes.* New York: Stein & Day, 1975.

"V tserkovnykh krugakh pered revoliutsii: Iz pisem arkhiepiskopa Antoniia volynskogo k mitropolitu kievskomu Flavianu." *Krasnyi Arkhiv* 31 (1928): 202–213.

Viroubova (Vyrubova), Anna. *Memories of the Russian Court.* New York: Macmillan, 1923.

Voeikov, V. N. *S tsarem i bez tsaria, vospominaniia poslednago dvortsovago komendanta gosudaria imperatora Nikolaia II-ogo.* Helsingfors, 1936.

Vonliarliarskii, V. *Moi vospominaniia,1852–1939 gg.* Berlin: n.d.

Vorres, Ian. *The Last Grand Duchess: Her Imperial Highness Grand Duchess Olga Alexandrovna.* New York: Scribner's, 1964.

Witte, S. Iu. *The Memoirs of Count Witte.* Translated and edited by Sidney Harcave. London: Sharpe, 1990.

———. *Vospominaniia*, 3 vols. Moscow: 1960.

Woytinskii, W. S. *Stormy Passage.* New York: Vanguard, 1961.

Yusupov, Felix. *Lost Splendor: The Amazing Memoirs of the Man Who Killed Rasputin.* Translated by Ann Green and Nicholas Katkoff. London: Cape, 1953.

———. *Konets Rasputina* (Vospominaniia), is in Tret'iakova, 103–214.

———. *Rasputin.* New York: Dial, 1927.

Zhevakov, Prince N. D. *Vospominaniia*, 2 vols. Munich: 1923.

Zhukovskaia, V. A. "Moi vospominaniia o Grigore Efimoviche Rasputine, 1914–1916 gg." in *Rossiiskii Arkhiv, Istoriia Otechestva v svidetel'stvakh i dokumentakh XVIII–XX vv.* Vols. 2–3, pp. 252–317. Edited by S. G. Blinov. Moscow: Studiia Trite Nikity Mikhalkova, 1992.

Books and Articles Dealing with Rasputin

Amalrik, Andrei. *Raspoutine.* Translated by Basil Karlinskii. Paris: Scud, 1982.

Bokhanov, A. N. *Rasputin, Anatomiia mifa.* Moscow: AST, 2000.

Chernyshov, A. V. "O vozraste Grigoriia Rasputina i drugikh biograficheskikh detaliakh." *Otechestvennye arkhivy* 1 (1991): 112–114.

Cook, Andrew. *To Kill Rasputin: The Life and Death of Grigori Rasputin.* London: Tempus, 2006.

Cullen, Richard. *Rasputin: The Role of Britain's Secret Service in His Torture and Murder.* London: Dialogue, 2010.

de Jonge, Alex. *The Life and Times of Grigorii Rasputin.* New York: Coward, McCann and Geoghegan, 1982.

Fuhrmann, Joseph T. *Rasputin: A Life.* New York: Praeger, 1990.

Fülöp-Miller, René. *Rasputin, the Holy Devil.* Translated by F. S. Flint and D. F. Tait. Garden City, NY: Garden City, 1928.

Hanbury-Williams, Sir John. *The Emperor Nicholas II as I Knew Him.* London: Humphreys, 1922.

Iliodor (Sergei Trufanov). *The Mad Monk of Russia, Iliodor: Life, Memoirs, and Confessions of Sergei Michailovich Trufanoff (Iliodor).* New York: Century, 1918.

Judas, Elizabeth. *Rasputin: Neither Devil nor Saint.* Los Angeles: Wetzel, 1942.

"K istorii poslednikh dnei tsarskogo rezhima (1916–1917 gg.)," *Krasnyi Arkhiv* 14 (1926): 247–249.

"K istorii ubiistva Grigoriia Rasputina." *KA*, 4 (1923): 424–26.

"Kak nashli trup Rasputin," *Birzh. ved.*, December 20, 1916, in GARF, F. 612, op. 1, d. 39, l. 52.

Kilcoyne, Martin. "The Political Influence of Rasputin." Unpublished PhD dissertation, University of Washington, April 1961. Interesting and overlooked.

King, Greg. *The Man Who Killed Rasputin: Prince Felix Youssoupov and the Murder That Helped Bring Down the Russian Empire.* Secaucus, NJ: Citadel, 1995.

Kotsiubinskii, A. P., and D. A. Kotsiubinskii. *Grigorii Rasputin: Tainyi i iavnyi.* Saint Petersburg: Limbus Press, 2003.

Kulikowski, Mark. "Rasputin and the Fall of the Romanovs." Unpublished PhD dissertation, SUNY Binghamton, 1982. Argues that Rasputin's influence has been greatly exaggerated.

Moynihan, Brian. *Rasputin: The Saint Who Sinned.* New York: Random House, 1997.

Nelipa, Margarita. *The Murder of Grigorii Rasputin, a Conspiracy That Brought Down the Russian Empire.* Ontario: Gilbert's Books, 2010.

Okhrana Notes, accessed on April 20, 2012, at the Alexander Palace Association website, http://www.alexanderpalace.org/palace/rasputinreport.html.

Pares, Sir Bernard. "Rasputin and the Empress: Authors of the Russian Collapse." *Foreign Affairs* 6 (1927): 140–154.

Pereverzev, P. N. "Ubiistvo Rasputina." *Illiustrirovannaia Rossiia* 21 (May 21, 1932): 6–11.

Platonov, Oleg. *Zhizn' za tsaria, Pravda o Grigorii Rasputina.* Saint Petersburg: Voskresenie, 1996. Platonov argues that the "image of Rasputin as the all-powerful favorite of the last tsar was created by the forces which were destroying Russia."

Radzinsky, Edvard. *Rasputin, zhizn' i smert'.* Moscow: Vagrius, 2000. Translated as *The Rasputin File* by Judson Rosengrant. New York: Talese, 2000.

Radziwill, Princess Catherine. *Rasputin and the Russian Revolution.* New York: Lane, 1918.

Roullier, Alain. *Raspoutine est innocent.* France: Europe Editions, 1998. His version of the autopsy is not reliable.

Rudnev, V. M. "The Truth Concerning the Russian Imperial Family: Statement by Vladimir Michailovitch Roudneff, Appointed by Minister of Justice Kerensky." In Anna Vyrubova, *Memories of the Russian Court*, pp. 383–399.

Shishkin, Oleg. *Rasputin, Istoriia prestupleniia.* Moscow: Eksmo Iauza, 2004.

———. *Ubit' Rasputina.* Moscow: Olma-Press, 2000.

Smirnov, V. L. *Neizvestnoe o Rasputine.* Tyumen: Slovo, 1999.

Smirnova, M., and V. L. Smirnov. *Rasputin, Post Scriptum.* Kurgan: Zaural'e, 2004.

Solov'ev, M. E. "Kak i kem byl ubit Rasputina?" *Voprosy istorii* 3 (1965): 211–217.

Spiridovich, Alexander. "Nachalo Rasputina." *Illiustrirovannaia Rossiia* 15 (April 9, 1932): 1–9. Adds valuable information to his fine books.

———. *Raspoutine, 1863–1916: D'après les documents russes et les archives privées de l'auteur.* Translated by M. Benouville. Paris: Payot, 1935.

Telitsyn, V. L. *Grigory Rasputin, zhizn' i smert "sviatogo greshnika".* Saint Petersburg: Neva, 2004.

"Ubiistvo Rasputina." *Byloe* 1, 23, (July 1917).

Wilson, Colin. *Rasputin and the Fall of the Romanovs.* New York: Farrar, Straus, 1964.

Other Secondary Studies Dealing with Subjects Related to Rasputin

Anan'ich, B. V., et al. *Krizis samoderzhaviia v rossii, 1895–1917* gg. Leningrad: 1984.

Aronson, Georgii. *Rossiia nakanune revoliutsii, istoricheskie etiudy: Monarkhisty, liberaly, masony, sotsialisti.* New York: 1962.

Ashton, Janet. "'God in All Things': The Religious Beliefs of Russia's Last Empress and Their Personal and Political Context." (Electronic) *British Library Journal*, article 6 (2006).

———. "The Reign of the Empress?—A Re-evaluation of the War-Time Political Role of Alexandra Fedorovna." *Atlantis* 4 (2) (January 2003): 51–68.

Berry, Thomas E. "Séances for the Tsar: Spiritualism in Tsarist Society and Literature." *Journal of Religion and Psychical Research*, published in nine installments from January 1984 to January 1986.

Betskii, K., and P. Pavlov. *Russkii Rokambol' (prikliucheniia I. F. Manasevicha-Manuilova).* Leningrad: 1925.

Blok, Aleksandr. "Poslednie dni starogo rezhima." *Arkhiv Russkoi Revoliutsii* 4 (1922): 5–54.

Bokhanov, Alexander, Manfred Knodt, Vladimir Oustimenko, Zinaida Peregudova, and Lyubov Tyutyunnik. *Romanovs: Love, Power and Tragedy*. Translated by Lyudmila Xenofontova. London: Leppi, 1993.

Buxhoeveden, Sophie. *Life and Tragedy of Alexandra Fedorovna, Empress of Russia*. London: Longmans, Green, 1928.

Cockfield, Jamie H. *White Crow: The Life and Times of the Grand Duke Nicholas Mikhailovich Romanov, 1859–1919*. Westport, CT: Praeger, 2002.

Conroy, Mary Schaeffer. *Peter Arkad'evich Stolypin: Practical Politics in Late Tsarist Russia*. Boulder, CO: Westview, 1976.

Cross, Samuel Hazard, ed. *Russian Primary Chronicle*. Cambridge, MA: Medieval Academy, 1953.

Cunningham, James W. *A Vanquished Hope: The Movement for Church Renewal in Russia, 1905–1906*. Crestwood, NY: St. Vladimir's, 1981.

Curtiss, John Shelton. *Church and State in Russia, The Last Years of the Empire, 1900–1917*. New York: Columbia, 1940. Excellent work.

D'iakin, V. S. *Russkaia burzhuaziia i tsarizm v gody pervoi mirovoi voiny (1914–1917)*. Leningrad: 1967.

EB: Encyclopaedia Britannica (New York, 11th ed., 1911).

Eddy, Eleanor Madeleine. "Last President of the Duma: A Political Biography of M. V. Rodzianko." Unpublished PhD dissertation, Kansas State University, 1975.

Erickson, Carolly. *Alexandra: The Last Tsarina*. New York: St. Martin's Griffin, 2001.

Ferro, Marc. *Nicholas II: The Last of the Tsars*. Translated by Brian Pearce. New York: Oxford, 1990.

Figes. Orlando. *A People's Tragedy*. New York: Viking, 1996.

Florinsky, Michael T. *End of the Russian Empire*. New Haven, CT: Yale, 1931.

Gurko, V. I. *Features and Figures of the Past: Government and Opinion in the Reign of Nicholas II*. Translated by Laura Matveev. Stanford, CA: Stanford, 1939; reprinted, 1970.

———. *Tsar i tsaritsa*. Paris: Vozrozhdenie, n.d.

Hall, Coryne. *Little Mother of Russia: A Biography of the Empress Marie Feodorovna (1847–1928)*. New York and London: Holmes & Meier, 1999.

Haskin, Gretchen. "His Brother's Keeper." 2 parts. *Atlantis*. Vol. 2: Numbers 3, 4 (2000).

Healey, Dan. *Homosexual Desire in Revolutionary Russia: The Regulation of Sexual and Gender Dissent*. Chicago and London: University of Chicago Press, 2001.

Katkov, George. *Russia 1917: The February Revolution*. New York: Harper & Row, 1967.

"Khlysty." In *Entsiklopedicheskii slovar'*, vol. 73 (1890), 402–409. Edited by F. A. Brokgauz and I. A. Efron, as reprinted in V. Tret'iakova, vol. 4, pp. 338–350.

King, Greg, and Janet Ashton. "'It Was Heavenly in the Forest': Hunting in Poland with the Two Last Tsars." *Royalty Digest Quarterly* 2 (2006): 39–51.

Kulikov, S. V. "Naznachenie Borisa Shtiurmera predsedatelem Soveta ministrov: Predystoriia i mekhanizm." *Istochnik* 1 (Saint Petersburg: Fakultet Istorii, Evropeiski Universitet, 2001): 387–428.

Lemke, Mikhail. *250 dnei v tsarskoi stavke (25 sent.–2 julia 1916)*. Petrograd, 1920.

Maevskii, V. I. *Na grani dvukh epokh: Tragediia imperatorskoi rossii*. Madrid: 1963.

Markov, S. V. *Pokinutaia tsarskaia sem'ia*. Vienna: Amalthea-Verlag, 1928.

Massie, Robert K. *Nicholas and Alexandra*. New York: Athenaeum, 1967.

Mel'gunov, S. *Legenda o separatnom mire: (kanun revoliutsii)*. Paris: Renaissance, 1957.

———. *Na putiakh k dvortsovomu perevorotu: Zagovory pered revoliutsiei 1917 goda*. Paris: La Source, 1931.

MERSH: Modern Encyclopedia of Russian and Soviet History. Gulf Breeze, FL, in progress, 1976–.

Munro, George. "Khlysty." *MERSH* 16: 152–153.

Oldenburg, S. S. *Last Tsar: Nicholas II, His Reign and His Russia*. 4 vols. Translated by Leonid I. Mihalap and Patrick J. Rollins. Gulf Breeze, FL: Academic International Press, 1975–1978.
Pares, Sir Bernard. *Fall of the Russian Monarchy: A Study of the Evidence*. New York: Knopf, 1939.
———. *History of Russia*. New York: Knopf, 1937.
Pipes, Richard. *The Russian Revolution*. New York: Knopf, 1990.
Poliakoff, Vladimir. *The Empress Marie of Russia and Her Times*. London: Thornton, 1926.
Pol'skii, Mikhail. *Novye mucheniki rossiiskie, pervoe sobranie materialov*. Jordainville, NY: 1949. Abridged in English, *New Martyrs of Russia*. Montreal: Brotherhood of St. Job of Pozhav, 1972.
Radziwill, Princess Catherine. *Nicholas II: The Last of the Tsars*. London: Cassell, 1931.
Rayner, Gordon, and Muriel Harding-Newman in "Time Watch: Rasputin: Marked for Murder," aired on BBC2 on October 1, 2004.
Rollins, Patrick J. "Iliodor." *MERSH* 14: 146–149.
Salisbury, Harrison E. *Black Night, White Snow: Russia's Revolutions, 1905–1917*. Garden City, NY: Doubleday, 1978.
Semennikov, V. P., ed. *Dnevnik b. velikogo kniazia Andreia Vladimirovich, 1915 g.* Leningrad and Moscow: 1925.
———. *Monarkhiia pered krusheniem, 1914–1917 gg., bumagi Nikolaia II-ogo i drugie dokumenty*. Moscow and Leningrad: 1927.
———. *Politika Romanovykh nakanune revoliutsii (ot Antanty k Germaniiu) po novym dokumentam*. Moscow and Leningrad: 1926.
———. *Za kulisami tsarizma; arkhiv tibetskogo vracha Badmaeva*. Leningrad: 1925.
Shelley, Gerard. *The Blue Steppes, Adventures among Russians*. London: John Hamilton, n.d.
———. *The Speckled Domes: Episodes of an Englishman's Life in Russia*. New York: Scribner's, 1925.
Sofronov, V. I. *Svetochi zemli sibirskoi*. Yekaterinburg: Ural'skii Rabochy Publishing House, 1998.
Spiridovich, Alexander. *Les dernières années de la cour de Tzarskoie-Selo*. 2 vols. Translated by M. Jeanson. Paris: Payot, 1928, 1929.
———. *Velikaia voina i fevral'skaia revoliutsiia 1914–1917 gg.* 3 vols. New York: Vseslavianskoe Izdatel'stvo, 1960.
Sh.[pitsberg], I. "Delo episkopa Palladiia." *Revoliutsiia i tserkov'*, nos. 3–5 (1919): 39–44.
Tereshchuk, A. *Grigoryi Rasputin: Poslednyi starets imperii*. Saint Petersburg: Vita Nova, 2006.
Thomson, Thomas John. "Boris Sturmer and the Imperial Russian Government, February 2–November 22, 1916." Unpublished PhD dissertation, Duke University, 1972.
Tisdall, E. E. P. *Dowager Empress*. London: Paul, 1957.
Trotsky, Leon. *History of the Russian Revolution*. New York: Simon and Schuster, 1932.
van der Kiste, John, and Coryne Hall. *Once a Grand Duchess: Xenia, Sister of Nicholas II*. London: Sutton, 2002.
Vasil'ev (Vassilyev), A. T. *The Ochrana: The Russian Secret Police*. Edited by René Fülöp-Miller. Philadelphia and London: Lippincott, 1930.
Vecchi, Joseph. *The Tavern Is My Drum: My Autobiography*. London: Odhams, 1948.
von Bock, Maria Petrovna. *Reminiscences of My Father, Peter A. Stolypin*. Edited and translated by Margaret Patoski. Metuchen, NJ: Scarecrow, 1970.
Wallace, Donald MacKenzie. *Russia*. London: Hutton, 1877.
Warth, Robert D. *Nicholas II: The Life and Reign of Russia's Last Monarch*. Westport, CT: Praeger, 1997.
Wortman, Richard S. *Scenarios of Power: Myth and Ceremony in Russian Monarchy from Peter the Great to the Abdication of Nicholas II*. New abridged one-volume paperback edition. Princeton, NJ: Princeton University Press, 2006.
Zaslavskii, D. *Poslednyi vremenshchik Protopopov*. Leningrad, n.d. Based upon the same author's "A. D. Protopopov," *Byloe* 23 (1924): 208–242.

Photo Credits

Pages 5, 28, 124, 192 (right), 217, 220, 238, *Neizvestnoe O Rasputine* by V. L. Smirnov; p. 16, Wikipedia; p. 18, State Archive of the Russian Federatation (GARF); pp. 63, 70, 113 (left), 132, Roger Violet/The Image Works; pp. 100, 149, Mansell Collection; p. 113 (right), Peter Kingsford Topfoto/The Image Works; p. 121, Mary Evans Picture Library; p. 128, TFGATO (The Tobolsk Affiliated State Archive of Tyumen Oblast); p. 164, Iberfoto; p. 199, Mary Evans/CharlotteZeepvat; p. 228, Andrew Cook

Index

Page numbers in *italics* indicate illustrations.